PRAISE FOR DAVID DEIDA

"Finding God Through Sex is the deepest, most alive, insightful book I have ever read on the wonders and subtleties of sexuality as a spiritual path. It inspires us to the knowing of total openness to who we are as the lover and the beloved ... until we disappear into love."

GABRIEL COUSENS, M.D. Author of *Spiritual Nutrition and the Rainbow Diet*

"David Deida's writings give both men and women rare insight into the profound and transformative realms of spiritual sexuality."

CHARLES MUIR Author of *The Art of Conscious Loving*

"The openness, the love! What lively new language David Deida finds for the unsayable!"

COLEMAN BARKS Author of *The Essential Rumi*

"In the area of sacred intimacy, David Deida is holding a lightening bolt. He sheds an astonishing light."

MARIANNE WILLIAMSON Author of *A Return to Love*

"David Deida's teachings on this central human concern, sexuality, emanate from a deeply trustworthy source. He has undergone his own rigorous training and practice, which manifests in precise, gentle, and thorough teachings. Many spiritual traditions, including Zen, have excluded or marginalized the sexual experience. David's work fills this gap, and gives us a mature approach for bringing the energetic, emotional, and physical experience of sex into our life and practice. And like Zen, the fruition of David's work is openness, compassion, and love."

GENPO ROSHI Author of *The Eye Never Sleeps*

"Finding God Through Sex is an enlightened, uninhibited sexual guide for anyone seeking to improve mind, body, and ᵢₙₜᵢₘₐₜₑ ᵣₑₗₐₜᵢₒₙₛₕᵢₚ. Dₐᵥᵢ𝑑

T0043627

FINDING
GOD
THROUGH
SEX

FINDING GOD THROUGH SEX

Awakening the One of Spirit
Through the Two of Flesh

DAVID DEIDA

Foreword by Ken Wilber

Important Caution
Please Read This

Although anyone may find the practices, disciplines, and understandings in this book to be useful, it is made available with the understanding that neither the author nor the publisher are engaged in presenting specific medical, psychological, emotional, sexual, or spiritual advice. Nor is anything in this book intended to be a diagnosis, prescription, recommendation, or cure for any specific kind of medical, psychological, emotional, sexual, or spiritual problem. Each person has unique needs and this book cannot take these individual differences into account. Each person should engage in a program of treatment, prevention, cure, or general health only in consultation with a licensed, qualified physician, therapist, or other competent professional. Any person suffering from venereal disease or any local illness of his or her sexual organs or prostate gland should consult a medical doctor and a qualified instructor of sexual yoga before practicing the sexual methods described in this book.

Sounds True, Inc., Boulder CO 80306

SOUNDS TRUE is a trademark of Sounds True, Inc.

Published 2005

ISBN 978-1-59179-273-4

Library of Congress Control Number: 2005924954

Previously published by Plexus, 2002 as *Finding God Through Sex: A Spiritual Guide to Ecstatic Loving and Deep Passion for Men and Women*

TABLE OF CONTENTS

FOREWORD
by Ken Wilber

F inding God through sex? And why not? The only thing that is astonishing in that equation is that it ever should have seemed odd to begin with. For many of the world's great wisdom traditions, particularly in their mature phases, sexuality was deeply viewed as an exquisite expression of spirituality—and a path to further spiritual realization. After all, in the ecstatic embrace of sexual love, we are taken far beyond ourselves, released from the cramp of the separate self, delivered at least temporarily into timeless, spaceless, blissful union with the wondrous beloved: and what better definition of spiritual release is there than that? We all taste God, taste Goddess, taste pure Spirit in those moments of sexual rapture, and wise men and women have always used that rapture to reveal Spirit's innermost secrets.

David Deida is a such a wise one, who has worked with countless men and women to help them use the sexual encounter to further their own deep spiritual realization. In the following pages, he speaks directly to both the masculine and feminine principles in each of us, using precise examples and practices that move us through our gendered existence and into the vast expanse of radiant Spirit, which is itself neither male nor female but simply Free and Full.

If you are affiliated with a particular religion, that is fine; if not, that's fine, too. I have it on good authority that Spirit does not belong to any particular church, but resides in the deepest part of your very own heart every time you love. This is a book about releasing that love into such painful bliss that you will be undone in the very embrace of the Divine itself, insanely radiant to infinity, even here and now.

David's language is a model of evocative spirituality; it teases us out of our contracted ways and into the infinite expanse of pure awareness, beyond the minor joys and major terrors that define the loveless self. Let the language seep into your being, let the richness of your heart unfold in the gentle invitations, follow that current of spiritual bliss that will lead you to your own original face, swoon into that radiant light that is your own true nature. The secrets to all of this are given in the following pages, so let the passionate adventure in sexual spirituality begin ...

You can read and practice the following with a partner, or you can experiment on your own, following Woody Allen's advice: "Don't knock masturbation; it's sex with somebody I love." But in any event the discoveries awaiting you are the most miraculous in existence. The very current of sexuality is plugged straight into God, and once you find that current, you will never be the same. And you will have David Deida to thank.

KEN WILBER
Boulder, Colorado

A Note to the Reader

Our deepest nature, our true spirit, is full of love and boundless freedom. When we lose touch with our fullness, we begin to yearn for that which seems missing. The feminine in each of us longs for deeper love and tries to find it in intimate relationship, family, or friends. The masculine in each of us struggles for greater freedom and tries to achieve it through financial, creative, or political challenges.

Yet, our life often feels dissatisfying because we are searching for a joy that can only emerge by being who we are, fully and deeply. The feminine grows spiritually by learning to live *as* love rather than by hoping for it. The masculine grows spiritually by learning to live *as* freedom rather than by struggling for it.

These two sexual paths, though distinct, actually lead to one spiritual bliss. Nowhere is this more obvious than in the embrace of lovers, where the play of sexual differences leads to a unity of blissful oneness, the "Oh, God!" beyond even pleasure. Therefore, each chapter in this book begins with an explicitly sexual vignette to illustrate how the one of spirit can know itself through the two of flesh.

Because more women than men identify with the feminine path, certain sections of this book are entitled "For Her." These sections are devoted to the feminine in all of us, as well as to the more feminine-playing partner in a heterosexual or homosexual relationship. The sections entitled "For Him" are devoted to the masculine in all of us, as well as to the more masculine-playing partner in any couple.

By understanding these distinct paths of growth, their differences are revealed as passionate gifts that can be awakened fully while finding God through sex.

PART I
SURRENDER

D eep in our hearts, we are all searching for ways to give and receive love, forever and for real. To open as love, to live as this freedom, is our deepest calling. Each of us must find our own unique way of living true to our deep being. But whatever way we find, we will discover that love is the only way to live that is not less than God, less than truth, less than our deepest need and divine potential.

The cultivation of utter freedom—which is to live as the flow of love—can be practiced during sex. Learning to have sex as an expression of your deepest being is like learning to play golf, tennis, or the violin. You have good days and bad days. Sometimes lovemaking is perfection itself, with genitals, heart, and mind all aligned. Other times sex is scattered, anxious, or wrought with conflict. Even so, there is no such thing as failure; every moment is a learning, every closure an opportunity to learn how to open in love.

Love can be practiced. To practice love is to be and express your deepest heart, whatever your religious persuasion or chosen spiritual method. If you don't practice love during sex, your thrusts and hugs become reduced to mere animal hunger or personal psycho-emotional need. For some, sex is a relatively dependable way to buck and snarl in pleasure, release stress in a spasm of orgasm, and get to sleep. For others, sex is a hope for their partner's affection, a ritual of security and familiar coziness.

Unencumbered from such habits, sex is fresh, alive, and open-ended. Sex is an art form, a prayer, a way of contemplating and communing with infinite love, naked, unafraid, raw, and totally open. Sex is a means for expressing this mystery of love through the music of your body.

Learning to have sex this way is not a matter of touchy-feely namby-pamby, but is as concrete as learning to play the piano. At first, actually making music seems almost impossible. Your fingers just won't move like you want them to. So your piano teacher gives you musical scales to practice, exercises to perform over and over. You practice and struggle and make mistakes and learn.

Soon, you find yourself effortlessly performing pieces that you previously couldn't have imagined playing. At some point, if you relax enough and become a transparent vehicle through which the creative spirit can move, actual *music* begins to come through the notes you are playing.

A profound depth of meaning and recognition, perhaps even something sacred and fundamentally ineffable, begins to flow through your fingers, through the piano keys, to the listener's heart. One day, you find that you are transmitting an unspeakable depth of feeling from your heart to your listener's heart through the way you play the piano. The genius of your deep being, the flow of divine love, is beginning to express itself, however simple your technique.

A monkey can be taught to play the piano. A robot can be programmed to tap out a simple ditty from its digital memory. A heartful musician, however, doesn't simply make sounds, but evokes a depth of meaning and feeling quite beyond the mechanics of hitting the proper keys. The *spirit* of the music is revealed through the medium of his or her performance. A deeper meaning that is inexpressible through words is somehow transmitted through the musical performance—however simple—bringing tears of recognition, smiles of joy, and openness of heart to the listener.

And so it can be while lovemaking. Except that the piano you are playing—your lover—is also playing you.

If you have never experienced profound sexual love, my words here may seem like gibberish to you, nonsensical utterances pointing to nothing. However, most people have at least momentarily been graced—perhaps even jolted or awakened—by an openness beyond their sense of limited self in which a sublime oneness of being suddenly became obvious or apparent. These unbidden moments of grace may occur while having sex—or while meditating, praying, simply sitting alone, or even while driving a car, feeding a baby, or taking a walk. This book is a guide to consciously cultivating and transmitting this awakened disposition of openness and oneness during sex.

Why practice this disposition of openness during sex? Because, for most people, no matter how enlightened they are in other areas of their lives, their sexual and emotional life remains troublesome. For most people, sex is one of the most pleasurable and frustrating parts of their lives. It is a hidden corner where they keep their embarrassing secrets and forbidden dreams. In general, a person's sexual life is among the least illumined aspects of their being; even men and women who are physically healthy, financially successful, and spiritually aware often have complicated and troublesome sex lives.

As you grow sexually, you are able to embrace your complications and secrets—they exist for virtually everyone—and make music *through* them. Emotional ups and downs as well as sexual kinks and twists are no obstacles, but provide a unique instrument through which the almighty music of love is played. The condition of your instrument—the history of your emotional and sexual pain, desire, and resistance—becomes irrelevant as your heart and your lover's heart swoon in the depth transmitted through your loving. A banged-up fiddle in the hands of a truly inspired musician evokes more heart than a Stradivarius in the hands of a pretender.

The discord of our sexual life derives not so much from our personal history or the condition of our "fiddle" but, to a larger extent, from our lack of inspired practice and depth. As teenagers, we are handed our genital instruments without any real instruction—without any outstanding examples, even, of the sublime art of a superior lover—and we struggle to bleat out our sexual music as best we can. Usually, the development of our sexual depth and skill stops at an early age—as did our parents'—and we end up playing the same simple song over and over again until we are too old to bother.

How do we continue growing in our capacity to transmit open-hearted wonder through the music of our sexual artistry? The single most important skill to learn is the practice of love, openness, or surrender—which are just different words for oneness, unobstructed feeling, or free being, the source of all true inspiration. You can practice various techniques of breath control and pelvic rumpus until your skin peels off, but you won't enjoy a single moment of authentic sexual ecstasy unless you are willing to let go of your boundaries and open beyond your resistance into the awe of love. A heart-guarded musician is no musician at all, and doubly so for a lover. How do you practice opening fully *as* love in the midst of sex?

I

SURRENDER
EVERYTHING

*I was lying on top of her naked body. She wanted to have sex.
In fact, she initiated it. But she wasn't really into it. Her body
seemed lifeless. Her eyes looked like a doll's eyes that were stuck
open, shallow, unseeing. I felt like I was having sex with a woman
who was protecting herself behind plastic skin; her flesh remained
uninhabited.*

    *I was frustrated. I wanted to feel her. I wanted to feel her open
to me. I wanted our hearts to open so that our sexing was stripped
of pretense, raw love sloshing into love, unprotected and trusting.
I wanted to let go completely into love. But she was closed, and I
was starting to close off too.*

    *I don't know what triggered it, but suddenly she relaxed. She
remembered love somehow, and all of her resistance evaporated.
She looked into my eyes without hiding, and I felt her depth.
She was no longer protecting herself behind her skin, but was
fully embodied as love. Her breasts seemed to soften and allow
me closer to her heart. Her vagina drew me in deeply, in spite of
my resistance to her previous closure. Her openness now seemed
endless, and it was I who felt like the limit to our loving.*

    *We continued practicing to open. Over time, her beauty, love,
and surrender drew me past my fear into her, and through her into*

the depths of love itself. Our breaths and bodies merged. I let go of
everything into her, and she opened so wide we both disappeared in
love, like a vortex of water opening into the ocean itself.

The word "surrender" is often interpreted as giving up, as weakness, as admitting defeat. Although this is one way to use the word, we will use it in a different way. Surrendering means letting go of your resistance to the total openness of who you are. It means giving up the tension of the little vortex you believe yourself to be and realizing the deep power of the ocean you truly are. It means to open with no boundaries, emotional or physical, so you ease wide beyond any limiting sense of self you might have.

Surrender means to love without limits. It means to relax your guard so your lover can feel your core—authentic, unhidden, and undefended. Your muscles relax. Your breath becomes soft and full. Your body and heart willingly open to your lover. If you are hurt, you are hurt, but in any case you practice to remain open and full, like the ocean. Surrender is the doorway to the deepest possible sex.

FOR HIM

Nothing turns your woman on more than your real presence. She wants to feel you *with* her. Not distracted or divided inside, half of you wanting to watch a basketball game on TV and the other half hurrying to have an orgasm. She wants to feel your consciousness free and clear, feeling into her through your whole body, not just through your penis, hands, and eyes.

Your woman is as sensitive to your presence—or its lack—as you are to the beauty of her radiance. She allows herself to surrender completely only when she feels you completely present. She actually feels the force of your strong, whole-bodied presence as if it were penetrating and opening her body.

She can feel your mind: is it an agitated puddle or a deep ocean? She can feel your breath: is it shallow and tense or full with pleasure and power? She can feel your body: is it uptight and needing a quick ejaculation, or is it relaxed, alive, and ready to meld with her body? When your mind, breath, and body are fully present, then you can really be *with* her, and her heart will be ready to open in trust with your heart.

Practice feeling into your woman with your heart just as you might feel into her with your penis: gently, deeply, unrelentingly loving. As your love enters her heart, your woman can practice surrendering to your penetration, to the tangible intensity of your masculine love. Over time, she will learn to trust and open herself more and more to the force of your unwavering and loving presence.

FOR HER

As much as you want your man's conscious presence, he wants your energetic openness. Your sexual responsiveness—your moans, writhes, and orgasms—attract him out of his dry world of fear into the bright colors of heart-surrender. If he is a man with a masculine essence,* his life is more or less bereft of feminine glory; you are his chosen source of feminine energy, which is the force of life itself. He wants to bathe in the warm sea of your undulations, taste the sweet grapes of your lips and nipples, feel the earthquakes of your uninhibited pleasure.

Faking it doesn't count. Your body must be truly full of pleasure if you want your man's full presence. His consciousness and your energy

---

*A man or woman with a more "masculine essence" is a shorthand way of saying that this person identifies more often with their inner masculine gifts than their inner feminine gifts.

magnetize each other. He wants to see the bright light in your eyes. He wants to feel your supple body quivering, heaving, and opening in ways his masculine chunk can only dream. He wants to be awed by your emotional surrender and deep trust.

Of course, you need to feel his complete presence before you will open your heart and body without guard. It's a step-by-step process of learning. He learns to be more present, you learn to be more open. Your openness draws him into you more deeply, and you feel him more fully inside of your heart. He relaxes his fears and enters you with more love, and you relax your fears and receive him more fully. Eventually, you both surrender so completely that there is no guarding or holding back at all. Sex has become unbounded love.

But until then, your man's love is probably trapped inside his head. He knows you love him. You know he loves you. But his body is unable to fully show it. First, practice attracting him from his head into his body with your body. The feminine beauty of your body—its capacity to flow with uninhibited and heart-connected pleasure—is irresistibly attractive to your man. Once he is in his body, attract him into his heart with your heart. The openness of your heart—fully expressed through your moans, words, and tears— resonates his heart into openness.

It may take some time for his heart and body to open as fully as yours, but, ultimately, he is making love with you to *make love*. In the meantime, continue attracting him into surrender by astounding him with the depth of your surrender. Swallow him into your heart through your vagina. Allow your limbs to splay pleasure like light radiating from the sun. Soften your belly and chest to receive your man's body into yours. Say your love in gasps of pleasure. Through your body, breath, and emotion, show him how deeply you trust him. If he is a good man, he will rise to the occasion and learn to meet the fullness of your trust with the depth of his presence.

2

SURRENDER THROUGH,
NOT TO

Earlier in the day she said something that hurt me, and now we were in bed. In addition to feeling hurt, I was now angry at her. A part of me wanted to force myself onto her and feel her weakness. I wanted to prove, mostly to myself, that I was stronger than her, able to do whatever I wanted.

She, of course, could feel my hostile demeanor. She lay with her arms crossed, her body rigid, and her face emotionless. I was being quite the jerk, and she didn't want to have anything to do with me.

My hurt continued to fester beneath my armor of anger. Grinding my jaw, I looked at her through tense eyes. She was closed to me, emotionally and physically, and I couldn't blame her.

But then, surprisingly, her body softened. She turned and looked me in the eyes. It was as if she was no longer stopping at my anger, but was feeling through it into my aching heart. She stopped resenting my anger and began to embrace my hurt. Her eyes were moist and receptive, her breath full and strong. She touched me and pulled me closer to her.

She was loving me. Moving with me. Breathing with me. Her love was actively saturating through my anger, as the heat of a hot bath might envelope, permeate, and relax a tight muscle. I could feel her love reach the need in my heart. My anger started melting.

Her love magnetized mine. My hurt came to the fore and
a few tears rolled down my cheeks. Her openness, her strength,
and her willingness to feel my hurt pulled me through my anger.
Before, I wanted to punish her for hurting me. Now, I only
wanted to love.

I held her body against mine, loving her, and she received me
without limits. The last residue of my anger was humbled by the
strength of her love. She opened herself fully to my heart and
gave love to the place that had been hurt by her words earlier.
Her choice to open and give love, rather than to close and defend,
converted my heart from animosity to open trust.

Practice surrendering not to your own fears, nor to the demands of an other, but directly to love. Do your best to feel through your own resistance as well as your lover's. Behind all resistive emotion is the motive of love. The desire to give and receive love underlies every emotional action and reaction, including hurt and anger, in yourself and in your partner.

Whatever the emotion—anger, fear, closure—feel through it, breathe through it, relax through it, into the love that lies behind it. And then, actively, surrender to that love. Open *as* that love. Magnify love by loving.

True sexual and spiritual surrender is not about adapting yourself to what will appease your partner. Nor is it about surrendering to your own momentary emotional needs. True surrender is about relaxing through these secondary needs, both yours and your partner's, and magnifying the primary desire to give and receive unbounded love.

FOR HIM

A woman's heart and genitals are usually deeply connected. When a woman's heart is truly open to a man, so are her genitals, and when she opens herself sexually to a man, she also opens herself emotionally. For most women, emotional openness, sexual openness, and spiritual openness are all part of the same single gesture of trust, relaxation, and love. In fact, for many women, their deepest sexual experiences *are* their deepest spiritual experiences.

This is why "sport" sex, or sex with random strangers just for fun, isn't such a big attraction for most women. Most women open emotionally during good sex—they don't want to open themselves up to just anyone. On the other hand, it's also why a woman tends to fall in love with whoever she has deep sex with: her heart opens along with her vagina and she feels love for the last man with whom she had great sex.

As a woman learns to surrender sexually, she learns to open through her emotions and feel the underlying love, yours and hers. No matter what you are feeling on the surface, deep down you want to give and receive unbounded love, and so does she. She can feel your deep heart beneath your anger and shame. She can feel her own deep heart beneath her hurt or resistance. As your mutual practice of surrender grows, you both become capable of surrendering as and magnifying love even in the midst of boredom, pain, and surface emotions. To help her do this, remember that her vagina and her heart are directly connected: treat her vagina as you would her heart, and vice versa.

FOR HER

If your lover is like most men, his heart and genitals are not connected. He learned sex while masturbating as a teenager alone in his room without any emotion at all. For him, love is something that happens in his heart. Sex is something that happens with his penis. Most men find it very easy to enjoy one without the other, which is reflected in the popularity of girlie magazines and prostitution.

Be patient with your man. For some men, it may take *years* of practice to achieve the deep connection between their heart and genitals that is very natural for you with no effort at all. Before he learns to connect the two, his energy will tend to go to one place or the other. When his heart is full, his genitals may wilt. When his penis is throbbing, he may forget his heart. Some men actually prefer having sex with women whom they don't love. That way, they can concentrate on having great sex without also feeling obliged to love. This sounds very strange to most women, for whom love and sex are one motion.

When you feel that he is sexing without loving you, don't close down. Whereas for you sex grows from love, for him sex grows from physical attraction and stimulation—it takes effort and practice for him to learn to keep his heart open during sex. To you it may feel like he is closing down emotionally. If you were to ask him, he might say he was just enjoying sex. Instead of assuming that he is rejecting you or closing down to you emotionally, assume that he is getting lost in the physical sensations of sex.

Help him learn to feel his heart in the midst of sex. This is probably much easier for you than for him. With practice, he can learn to surrender into love every bit as deeply as you. Give him your example of physical ecstasy *combined* with emotional openness, again and again. Give him a chance to practice connecting his heart and genitals without also having to deal with your hurt at his emotional closure—he probably isn't too aware that he's emotionally disconnecting from you in the first place.

3

SURRENDER ONLY
INTO LOVE

*As we were making love I began to gently suck her nipples. I cupped
her breasts in my hands and kissed them all over. I returned to her
nipples, biting them just hard enough to drive her crazy.*

*She began to squirm and buck beneath me. Her eyes were
closed. Her face squinshed up. She was squealing, pushing herself
against me, pulling my head against her breasts, grinding her
clitoris against my pubic bone, breathing short and fast.*

*Her responsiveness was sexy but also seemed shallow, as if
she was lost in sensation. No longer in relationship with me, she
seemed ensconced in the stimulation of her own nerve endings.
She was gone in her own pleasure. She was absent to my love.*

*I slowed down for a moment and stopped exciting her breasts.
I pressed my belly and chest against her and increased the fullness
of my breath, feeling into her with my breath as if I were breathing
through her body into her deep heart. Soon, she reconnected with
me, and we began to breathe together. When she opened her eyes, we
looked deeply into each other's core. Through our breath and gaze
we drew our feeling more deeply into our loving. When our hearts
grew most full in their connection, I began again to kiss her breasts.*

*I slowly increased the intensity of kissing and nipping, but
this time she was with me, not shut within the closed doors of her*

indulgence. As I caressed her breasts and grazed her nipples, her
back arched; the sound coming from her mouth was not a squeal
of superficial pleasure but a moan of deep and ravishing love. Her
eyes and heart and belly and breath stayed melded with mine. Her
intensity of sensation was now a passage through which we could
both surrender more deeply into the openness of love.

N ever surrender to something less than love. Even physical pleasure, in itself, is not worth surrendering to. Instead, surrender through it, be opened by it, into love ever more deep. There certainly is nothing wrong with physical pleasure. Don't avoid it. Allow utter bodily ecstasy to bloom your heart into waves of light. Meanwhile, surrender through the sensations of your bursting flowers and quivering ripples into love. No fleshy pleasure in itself equals love.

Sexual growth involves the practice of intensifying pleasure and desire while surrendering open, bit by bit, as unlimited love and freedom. But if you get lost in pleasure without also opening as heart-spaciousness, then you are limited by the pleasure. You are reduced to a moment of sensation, a one-pointed pig o'pleasure.

Always surrender to the largest love you can. Surrendering to less than this is, ultimately, pain. Only love can fulfill your deepest desire. All lesser emotions and sensations are substitutes for unbounded love. To surrender to them is like scratching an itch that only makes the itching worse. The only real cure is the total surrender to and as love, which is the freedom of open being.

For instance, you may feel accepted by your lover even though you are fat, or thin, or filled with guilt or self-loathing. But don't stop there, surrendering merely to the feeling of acceptance. Rather, freely feel through the sense of personal acceptance, into the most profound sense of open being of which you are capable. Relax *as* this love or openness. After all, there will be many moments when your lover, for one reason or another, does not accept you as you are. Neither acceptance nor rejection lasts for long.

Only love itself, the openness of being, is always true of your deepest heart. Love is always there, alive as your core. In any moment, you can remember to feel it, open as it, and give it. But this takes practice.

So practice surrendering into and as this deep love. Don't stop short of it and settle for a mediocre sense of emotional acceptance. Acceptance is fine, but practice feeling all the way into the fundamental flow of love that underlies even the desire to be accepted.

Your lover may lick your breasts or suck your genitals with such devotion that you feel adored, even worshipped. Don't surrender merely to this feeling of adoration; even an accidental bite can shatter your precious moment as genital god or goddess. To live free through the inevitable cycles of emotional inflation and deflation, learn to surrender as the openness of deep love even while feeling accepted or rejected.

Your lover may give you what you always wanted, but if you get lost in gratitude only, then you are like a child on his or her birthday, entranced by the shine of toys, aglow in the certitude of parental love forever. But parents die, and toys get old. Love itself, the open surrender of your heart as free feeling, is the only sanctuary untouched by time. Surrendering to anything less, as pleasurable or fulfilling as it may be for now, is chaining yourself to inevitable suffering.

FOR HIM

Your woman will tend to gravitate to your level of sexual depth. If your awareness becomes reduced to focusing on your woman's breasts, so will hers. If you want to feel like you are being a good "boy" by pleasing your woman, she will likewise want to feel like she is being a good "girl" by pleasing her man. Your reasons for having sex, moment by moment, will determine the depth of your sexing together. For the most part, it is the masculine partner who determines the *depth* of the sexual occasion while the feminine partner determines the fullness of *energy*.

If you want sex to go deeper, move your attention from the surfaces of sex to the depths of free feeling. When you notice your attention stopping at her breasts, relax your focus in two steps. First, widen your attention like a floodlight covering the entire scene. Feel everything, the smell of the air, the position of her feet, the rhythm of her breath.

Second, deepen your capacity to feel into your woman. Do your best to sense your lover's emotions and the flow of energy in her body. Try to feel her innermost secrets, the deepest chambers of her heart. Don't stop enjoying her breasts; simply deepen your awareness so you are also feeling much more. This is how you begin to cultivate sexual depth.

FOR HER

You can't make sex go any deeper than your lover is willing to go. For one thing, a man is turned off by a woman who doesn't trust his sexual capacity. For another, he won't even want to have sex if you don't seem to be enjoying yourself. Your man may limit the depth of your sexual experience together, but you are more likely to limit the sexual enjoyment: pleasure is the domain of the feminine.

Let's assume your man is fondling your breasts. You are really enjoying it. In fact, he is driving you crazy with the way he is sucking, licking, kissing, pinching, and caressing you. Let him worry about the depth of sex. Allow yourself to go wild with pleasure. Freely allow your body to churn with delight. Don't think about whether you should focus on this or that. Let go into the pleasure itself, but while doing so *remember love.*

Feel the tingles and ripples—and open your heart. Feel your man's care and sensitivity—and open your heart. Cry, scream, bray, and tremble—and open your heart. Let your man practice bringing the sexual occasion into deeper profundity while you practice allowing your body to receive pleasure, flow with pleasure, and demonstrate pleasure, all the while remembering to love. The openness of love invites the deepening of depth.

Depth without pleasure is too serious for great sex, and this is exactly what happens when your man tries to practice deepening sex by himself. He studies "how to do it." He really applies himself to solving all your sexual problems together and making something important happen. All the while, you feel his lack of flow and humor. On the other hand, pleasure without depth is too frivolous for great sex, and this is exactly what happens when you go wild in delight without also opening in love and receiving the force of your lover's deep presence.

Great sex is both blissful and profound, pleasurable and deep. Let your man practice bringing depth to your sexual play together. In the meantime, practice relaxing into your body's natural sexual bliss while opening your heart in love. Your man needs to be drawn beyond himself: *sexual ecstasy and emotional openness expressed through your writhing body are more attractive to your man than his own pleasure.*

4

SURRENDER
BEYOND EMOTIONS

In the midst of making love, she began to speak to me. "I love
you. I am yours forever. Nothing can break us apart."

In that moment, it was true. We were love, and we were forever.
Nothing could break us apart, since we were as one. But I could
also feel her emotional need. I could feel her desire for security
creeping in around the edges. Her confession was true enough, but
it was tinged by hope. And beneath the hope of forever, lurked the
fear of loss—in her and in me.

I wanted so badly to wallow in her confession of love. I
wanted to feel that she was mine. That she had given herself to
me for good. And, although this was true enough in the moment,
similar things had been spoken before, and forever didn't last.
As a confession of love in the moment, it was true and beautiful.
But as a hope, it was a lie. We did not own each other, and never
would. Our loving was as fragile as our personal fears were strong.
It would take only a hurtful moment of emotional collapse and
we would be broken apart. Maybe just for a few hours or days.
Maybe for good.

In that moment of our lovemaking I could feel both truths. The
truth that we had given ourselves to each other as love eternal.
And also the truth that we could leave each other in any moment,

due to emotional closure or meeting a better intimate partner, in the inevitable event of death, or simply because we were distracted by a fresh piece of ass or chocolate cake.

Surrendering to the truth of our love was blissful. Mixed in with that love, though, was the need to assure ourselves that it would last. True love was mixed with fear. Looking into her eyes and feeling into her body, I began to sense that we were drifting more toward the need for security. We were beginning to grasp on to the emotional need for feeling loved, rather than surrendering into the open gesture of being and giving love.

I practiced to recognize my own need for her, and, to the best of my ability, I felt through my neediness. Even though a part of me wanted to own her forever, I could recognize that this part of me was really formed by fear. Her adoration assuaged my fear and buoyed my self-sense. Her insecurity and neediness made me feel more secure in my ownership of her. This dynamic wasn't love, it was emotional bondage.

By recognizing and feeling through this neediness, even as we were both beginning to slide into it, I was able to rediscover, magnify, and surrender into the force of real love. Without saying a word, my authentic presence in love began to resonate her from sentimental need to deep-hearted devotion.

Her devotion was not to me as a separate person but to the love that we opened ourselves to through the practice of our relationship. Our attention shifted from the hope of our future together to the present depth of love that is always the truth of our very being, intuited in our deep heart.

Try to notice the moments when you surrender to something less than your deepest truth. Often, an emotion may be so pleasurable that you spend long periods of time wallowing in the comfort and false sense of security that the emotion gives you. Perhaps your lover's personal need to feel loved makes him or her do and say things that tie into your needs. Your lover knows your weaknesses. He or she senses your need to feel loved and knows just what to say or do to make you feel powerful, worshipped, or comforted by a love you have always wanted.

Your partner doesn't do this purposefully, usually. It is just an automatic emotional match: your partner's needs tie into your needs, and you hook each other. Suddenly, you are treated in a way that makes you feel invincible, certain of being loved. Or perhaps all at once you feel perfectly secure, even infantile, snuggled in the assured love of your partner—assured because your partner needs you as much as you need him or her.

Relationships based on the need to feel loved are always relationships based on fear; perhaps your need won't be fulfilled. Even in those moments when you do feel completely loved, another part of you fears the loss of this love. Recognize your moments of emotional need, feel them fully, and surrender open as the fullest giving of love.

Give love so completely that you are disappeared in the giving, existing as love, rather than sexing in the hope for love. You *are* love. This is your truth. All other sexual expressions are smaller than this truth, however pleasurable or emotionally satisfying they may be.

FOR HIM

Sexually speaking, a woman's weak link is her need to feel special. Her adolescent hormones started flowing in the midst of an emotional fantasy life filled with her version of princes and princesses, unicorns and damsels in distress, white knights and the hope for her father's love.

Then, in her young adulthood, sexual desire was probably mixed with her emotional need to feel loved by her intimate partner, even adored, exclusively, for her special qualities. As an adult, her desire for personal love—for romantic love—remains intertwined with her sexual desire. To grow beyond mediocre sex into the deepest blisses of love, she can learn to love larger than her personal relationship.

Your woman probably gets lost in emotional fantasies of a man who will rescue her from loneliness and make her feel special. She confuses romantic, personal love with love itself, which is eternal, boundlessly deep, and at the heart of every being.

Romantic love is very different from unqualified, unrestricted love. Love without boundaries won't make her feel special. In fact, it will dissolve her in utter radiance, bliss, and openness. The personal self and all its hopes are consumed in the hugeness of this love.

One of your woman's biggest blocks to spiritual growth is probably her attachment to personal affirmations of love: the way you care for her when she's sick; her imaginary faith in your spoken devotion to her; the security you provide. These are beautiful examples of personal love, not to be avoided. But the same could be said for a great handjob.

The point is this: Men often reduce infinite consciousness—their deepest bliss of being—to a few minutes of genital pleasure and a spasm of ejaculative release. Very few men know how to receive sensual pleasure and feel the infinite divine at the same time. Likewise, women often reduce divine love to personal care, emotional security, and affection. Very few women are able to enjoy a man's adoration (or rejection) and at the same time remain full in radiant, unbounded love.

A woman's capacity for sexual and spiritual bliss is based on her heart's capacity to remain open as unobstructed love—the love that is her very nature—even while enjoying or suffering her personal relationship with her man. You can help her in this growth by remaining aware of all the ways you actually try to hook her into depending on you emotionally. Practice liberating her heart from need rather than binding it.

Practice widening your woman's heart larger than the merely romantic: when you give her flowers and she melts into your embrace, penetrate her with your deepest love. Love her like the sun heats the earth, rather than according to her White Knight script. As awakening dissolves a dream, let the force of your love dispel the lingering remnants of her childish hope to be saved by a man. Help her grow toward surrendering as the bliss of love itself—with you and without you.

FOR HER

A man's weakest link sexually tends to be his need to release stress through sex: an addiction to ejaculation coupled with rituals of comfort. He will go through the same patterns over and over, setting the alarm clock, kissing you a certain way, touching you in the usual places, making the familiar grunts, lasting about the same amount of time, and ejaculating, followed by the customary ritual of post-ejaculative torpor: some cuddling, maybe some TV or a snack, often shutting down into deep sleep within minutes after his orgasm.

As a woman, you want to be *filled* by sex. You want to be filled by his penis, filled by his love, filled with energy and passion. But most men want to be *emptied* by sex. Your man probably treats you as a receptacle for his tension, his frustrations, his burdens, his semen. He wants you to absorb everything and leave him empty. For him, sexual pleasure involves being *relieved* of stress. For you, it involves being *fulfilled* by love.

It is easy for a woman to hook into a man's need for release and attempt to keep his love by hoping he depends on you for his comfort.

You end up tolerating his sexual rituals because you think he needs it. You suck out his stress and then watch him sleep in peace. But his true potential as a man is a far greater form of freedom.

Utter release—sheer boundless consciousness, free of fear and stress—is the quality of your man's true and deepest nature. He tries to approximate this openness by ejaculating while in your arms, just as he learned to empty himself of tension by masturbating as a teenager. While you were lying with teddy bears and ruffled pillows, dreaming of a hero who would love you forever, he was fantasizing about a woman's perfect body while beating his teenage meat. Mediocre lovers continue these fantasies into their adult partnerships.

With practice, your man learns to empty himself not simply of semen and tension, but of his entire sense of separate self. In sexual embrace with you, he confronts his fears—his needs for comfort and control—and yields himself like a skydiver jumping from an airplane. He learns to let go completely into love—*your* love. He practices letting go of himself and feeling into you every time you have sex. The more he can learn to let go of himself, the deeper he can enter your heart.

With practice, he realizes that the love he feels in *your* heart is also the nature of *his* heart. He realizes that the ease he seeks in your arms is actually available right now in the openness of deep being—with or without you. This could be scary for you if you hope to keep him dependent on you for comfort.

He learns that he can let go of his little rituals of consolation and breathe love in any moment. Ejaculating, drinking coffee while reading the newspaper, watching the same shows on TV every week from the same chair—they barely approach the depth of release and freedom afforded by a simple moment of complete surrender, letting go and opening as the depth of love directly.

If you want to maintain a mediocre relationship, then continue being the receptacle on which your man depends. Enjoy his cuddle after he has released his stress in your loving arms. But if you want to grow into a love not limited by familiar comfort, then trust total surrender, his and yours.

Without criticizing his habits, offer him love beyond personal de-stressing by not hiding your feelings of disappointment. How does your heart feel when he ejaculates in five minutes and goes to sleep? Are you truly fulfilled by his evening ritual of food, TV, smooch, and snooze? Show him your suffering, *but not in words at first.* Words will only engage debate. Rather, offer him an unarguable demonstration: the hurt in your body and heart.

Let the anguish show on your face. Let the pain water your eyes. You love him. He loves you. Show him how his mediocrity hurts you, if it does.

You may be quite happy with your relationship and sex life. However, if your sexual relationship is pretty good but not heart-rendingly blissful, then it may be time to invite your man into a new depth of intimacy. Let him feel your heart, unguarded and wide. If love is gushing out toward him, drown him in your love. If his superficial sexing denies your deepest desires for love, show him your pain through your facial expression, your wailing and tears, through your entire body.

If he needs your words to understand why you are suffering, then express your need rather than his lack. Instead of saying, "I hate when you go to sleep right after sex," try saying, "I need to feel you with me emotionally even after sex." Rather than, "Don't just come home, plop down, and expect me to jerk you off," try saying, "Even if you are tense from work, I need to feel the strength of your deep presence before I can open to you and trust you sexually."

Your raw expression and honesty will help your intimacy to grow. You'll still have the cozy comforts whenever you want them, but you won't be limiting yourself to their repeated ritual.

5

MAKE LOVE TO
OBLITERATE YOUR
PARTNER IN LOVE

She is enjoying our sexing. She is happy, smiling, moaning. She has one, two, three orgasms, each a little deeper. But something is missing: she is still there.

Her character remains. Her personality endures. But I want both of us gone in love. I want love to magnify beyond the sharing of two friends. I want our sexing to be an utter disappearance in the fullness of love, beyond the satisfactory enjoyment of two people rubbing bodies and sharing emotions. And, to invite this gasp of sudden vanishment, I need her openness. I need her to open so wide that I am drawn beyond my personality's effort and desire. Then, she and I will be vanished in the bright chasm of love.

I know she wants this as much as I do. I know that her deepest sexual need is to be obliterated in the force of love. To be smithereened in love. And so I stop at nothing.

I remain sensitive to her. I breathe with her, and then breathe us through any membrane of separation, until the one of our loving breathes wide as God. I move with her, and then move us through a dance of perfect synchrony until no effort remains to remember us.

The way I move my hips with her, breathe my belly against hers, and look into her eyes are all aligned with my desire to annihilate our tension of separate self in a super-saturation of loving.

She wants this, and so she participates fully, sometimes leading, sometimes following, always loosing her hold on all edges. And thus we dissolve—smiling, moaning, weeping—in the open bliss of heartrending sexual embrace. She has willingly surrendered, I have willingly surrendered, without hold, into love.

Your motive for sex determines its outcome. Don't stop at physical pleasure, so that you are spent in the grunt of neural upheaval. Don't stop at emotional sharing, so that you are known only in the coo of each other's smooch and tear. Don't settle for sensual and emotional completion. Go through every shudder and word to the point of no return. Go so far that your partner is disappeared in the intensity of love your sexing generates. Obliterate your partner in love.

Your partner's disappearance is your invitation to follow. Why hold back? Give yourself to love itself, without a shred of you remaining. Die completely into the loving. When you return, when your sense of self is recollected, you will be refreshed through and through, washed awake by the innocence lying wide on the other side of surrender.

FOR HIM

To obliterate your woman in love sexually, penetrate her in three ways simultaneously: physically, emotionally, and spiritually.

Penetrate her *physically* by entering her body with yours, when she is ready to receive you. Practice many styles of penetrative thrust, deep and shallow, fast and slow, filling her with the warmth and force of your body, remaining sensitive to her responses moment by moment. You have achieved the fullness of physical penetration when you move in perfect synchrony with her, like two dancers woven together in effortless grace and sensual magic. It is as if her body has become your body.

Penetrate her *emotionally* by entering her heart with yours. First, practice feeling your own emotions while having sex. Many men are so overwhelmed by the physical pleasure of sex that they aren't even aware they have emotions! Soften the area around your heart. Soften your belly as well as your chest. As the front of your body relaxes, feel as if you are melting into your woman, body to body.

Then, when it feels like your body occupies the same space as hers, practice feeling your woman's feelings. Actually try to sense her emotions, as well as the flow of energy in her body. It helps to breathe with her while you are feeling into her, inhaling while she inhales, exhaling while she exhales. With practice, your heart will completely coincide with hers, and you will be able to feel her sadness, the depth of her love, and her fear, as well as the ripples of need, thrill, and joy moving through her body. Eventually, her feelings become your feelings. Your hearts feel as one.

Spiritual penetration involves pervading her body with your consciousness. This is very difficult to describe in words but is an unmistakable and tangible experience. Your consciousness is who you are most fundamentally. It is the depth of your being, the openness of your awareness, the nature of your feeling, attention, and perception. Consciousness comes through your very soul; it is deeper and wider than your soul. It is the self or cognizant space of everything, of the entire universe, inside and out. With practice, you can develop your capacity to penetrate your woman with the force of consciousness itself.

Strictly speaking, consciousness itself isn't a force; it is the nature of existence. All forces arise in it. Nevertheless, as a lover, you can infuse your actions with consciousness or perform them mechanically. For instance, your breath can be either full or bereft of consciousness, and your woman can easily feel the difference. In fact, with practice, you can bring your woman to orgasm through the force of consciousness alone, transmitted through your breath and intention, with no physical penetration whatsoever.

You cannot sexually transmit consciousness if you are distracted. Your awareness must be fully attuned to you and your lover in the present moment. At first, focus and concentrate your awareness. Practice being present by not being somewhere else. Rather than thinking about your schedule tomorrow, focus your awareness on your body and your woman's body, on your breath and your woman's breath.

When you focus awareness in this way you are *pointing* consciousness. When you pay attention to your breath, for instance, you are not paying attention to the feel of the bedsheets or the fragrance of your lover's neck. Bringing your awareness to a point in this way is a good first step.

The next step is to allow the point to relax as a *field* of consciousness that includes everything. When you enter your woman with focused attention and pointed consciousness, it is like entering her with a normal penis: it gets the job done. But when you pervade your woman with the entire field of consciousness, it is like ravishing her with the force of the universe from the depth of your soul.

It is important to understand that consciousness is already pervading your woman, as well as everything else. You need not struggle to do anything. Simply feel *as* the consciousness that is already the very nature of yourself, your woman, the bed, and even the walls. Relax your "point" of attention so you rest as this open "field" of consciousness. This may sound abstract before you actually practice it, but your woman's response will be immediate.

While making love with your woman, practice pervading her with your consciousness step by step. First, carefully penetrate her physically, with your "flesh-penis." Then, lovingly penetrate her emotionally, with your "heart-penis." Then, practice gathering your awareness into the present moment, so that you are exquisitely attuned to every nuance of your body and her body, your breath and her breath. When you are able to stay totally present and aware of both you and your partner while also entering her with your body and heart, you are ready to practice penetrating her with consciousness.

Feel forward into her with your whole body. In other words, feel into the space in front of you, which includes her body. Then feel into the space behind you, as if you were sensing the walls, objects, and air that are behind your back. Feel to your left and right, up and down. Feel outward in all directions, until everything is within your relaxed sphere of awareness. Do not focus on any particular thing. Allow your awareness to remain open, loose, full, and spacious, like an ocean of clarity pervading the room.

Then feel beyond the room. Feel the whole house and the entire city. Listen to the farthest sound your can hear. Sense the millions of people all around the world. Do not concentrate on anything, but allow your open feeling-consciousness to include everything, effortlessly.

Continue feeling outward, beyond the entire earth, to include the moon, sun, and stars. Actually relax the "point" of your consciousness so much that without paying particular attention to anything, you feel *as* the entire universe, appearing in the ocean of open consciousness, made of its "water."

Remain sensitive, clear, and attentive to what is happening all around you, but not too focused on any one thing. It is something like being a football or basketball player. A good athlete has sensors feeling out in all directions so he can respond to players on his left and right, to his front and back; he can sense the location of his many teammates and opponents as they move across the field or on the far side of the court, still keeping the goal in mind and not dropping the ball.

In the same way, practice to remain totally present with your lover—exquisitely present to her every emotional shift and energetic flow—while simultaneously feeling outward without limits, relaxing attention as the depth of being while feeling outward in all directions so that your awareness coincides with the entire field of open consciousness. This takes practice, as does any art or skill.

When you are able to remain present with your woman while also relaxing as your deep being spread wide as the space around you, then you are ready to "fuck" your woman with the force of consciousness. (Throughout this book, we will unfold the word "fuck" far beyond its profane street use to help reveal how our deepest spiritual desires are often enfolded even in our most vulgar sexual expressions.)

Just as you felt outward to infinity with your awareness, now *breathe* to infinity. Combine your breath with your feeling. Breathe your woman, as if your breath were actually pumping her lungs. Breathe the space behind you, as if your breath circulated through the walls, objects, and air behind your back. Inhale and exhale through the entire sphere of awareness, left and right, up and down, forward and back. When your breathing and feeling coincide with your deep being spread wide as the entire field of open consciousness, penetrate your woman with it.

Feel as if the entire field of being has been gathered together through your breath, and breathe through your woman, like a huge thunderbolt of consciousness inhaling and exhaling through her every cell. In addition to entering her with your flesh and heart, penetrate her with the force of consciousness itself, guided by your breath and love. Rest as open being itself, coincident with the entire field of consciousness, full of its depth and power, obliterating your woman by impregnating and blooming her with this force, pervading her body, heart, and spirit.

You will know you are doing this when your woman surrenders in openness completely, gone in the force of blissful fullness, vanished in the ecstasy of boundless love. She can allow herself to surrender fully because she feels the depth of your consciousness. She can trust you because you are so present, so open, so sensitive to her. She feels the massive love-force of the entire field of consciousness pervading her and opening her. She happily lets go and swoons in the absolute love she has always wanted to receive, the same love that flows from her deep heart, magnified by sexual surrender in the effortless surge of deep being.

FOR HER

The way to a man's heart is actually through a place quite lower than his stomach; his penis is his bodily root. The flower of his heart opens widest when his root is planted deep in your body.

We are not discussing the mediocre lover. For him, the penis is simply an appendage of pleasure, a sensitive tongue or finger with which to enjoy your juicy friction. But as a man continues growing in his sexual capacity, his penis can help ground his consciousness in his body and yours.

Most men tend toward being heady and disembodied. Your man probably thinks, plans, and mulls things over in his head all day. Then, for a few moments of sex with you at night, his energy goes to his genitals, from whence it spews. You might enjoy this time with your man; for a few minutes at least, he isn't glued to work or TV. Your sexual ministrations draw him briefly into his body, where he feels a lot more present with you than when he was in his head.

When a man first starts practicing to grow sexually, he will probably be rather heady—if only because he is trying so hard *not* to be.

He exerts effort from his head. He tries to breathe right, remain "conscious," and stay present with you, all from his head. The antidote to this is your dance on his penis.

Nothing brings a man into his body faster than a firm yank or wet pull on his root. (Most men over thirty years old need direct genital stimulation to achieve and maintain an erection.) There certainly are times for motionless loving and gentle touch, but there are also times for a healthy grasp with your vagina, mouth, ass, or hand. Most women touch their man's genitals too lightly, too hesitantly. Grab him firmly and really pump him. As he approaches ejaculation, slow down or stop so he doesn't ejaculate. Let him relax for a few moments before continuing.

Create an arc of energy between his head and genitals so that his heart is aroused. Remember that it takes great practice for most men to open their heart while having sex. Your stimulation should be intense enough to keep him in his body rather than in his head, thinking about what he is supposed to be doing to be a "superior lover."

To prevent a premature ending to the sexual occasion, remain sensitive enough to slow down or stop the stimulation before he ejaculates, and then rev it back up as his penis begins to soften. You will only open his heart as wide as yours. If you are pumping his penis mechanically, he will simply gasp and spew. But if your body is surrendered open and your heart is fully exposed, then as you draw him down from his head into his body your love will resonate his love.

The art of deep sex lies in your capacity to relax in your body and receive your lover so deeply that he is drawn beyond himself into your love. Open yourself as love so wide that he falls into you, over and over. He will try to pull himself back, to get control, to practice some technique or another. All the while, you are plying his root, drawing him back into his body, and opening your heart and body as wide as you are willing to trust, evoking his fledgling love with the power of yours.

Naturally, you want your man to love you during sex. But he must first learn to decondition his masturbatory habits of mental sexual fantasy. To help him stay present and in relationship with you during sex, remember that most men find a woman's pleasure more attractive than their own.

When men watch a stripper dance on stage or an actress have sex in an erotic movie, they are most turned on by her display of pleasure. To you, her exaggerated moans and pelvic self-pleasuring may seem ridiculous. To most men, her responsiveness and sexual delight are entrancing. (Remember that the exaggeratedly suave or charismatic presence of your favorite movie actor—the leading man who entrances you and makes you swoon—seems equally ridiculous to your man.) Whereas women are most turned on by a man's depth of presence, men are most turned on by a woman's radiance and energy: how she moves, moans, smiles, and opens in love.

What men get from a good sex show is the *energy of feminine openness*. Watching a bored woman have sex is no turn-on at all. Watching a woman touch herself with the enthusiasm of a dead fish is not interesting. But when a man beholds a woman who is truly enjoying her feminine sexual embodiment, he is smitten. His attention becomes absorbed in the radiance of her happiness and pleasure.

A good actress or dancer can give a man this feminine energy, just like a good actor's presence can make you swoon or weep. True acting is a real art; the emotions expressed are authentic. To offer a man the gift of your feminine energy, relax into your authentic openness and pleasure, then allow your body to be moved by the deep flow of bliss.

Your feminine energy and your man's masculine presence can grow in strength together. As he becomes more and more skilled at pervading you with his penis, heart, and the force of his consciousness, sex will become boring for him unless your capacity to open in pleasure grows equally strong—just as you will be disappointed if your unbridled bliss is met with his half-cocked distraction. As he practices permeating you with love-consciousness, practice absorbing him in the fullness of your love-energy.

Relax, open, and trust the sexual pleasure that moves through your body. Your natural desire to surrender your heart in love draws your man's consciousness into you, just as the natural form of your feminine body draws his penis into you. Then, if you continue to open and surrender as love, he is drawn entirely beyond his fears, surrendering with you as a shared openness, both of you undone in love.

The bliss of this mutual sexual surrender is intense beyond words. It far exceeds your need for emotional reassurance from your man. Your childhood needs for security and adoration are entirely dissolved in deep heart-bliss, a love beyond personal acceptance.

Likewise, his need for physical gratification or mere stress release is yielded into love. He is drawn to you in a way that opens his heart in absolute vulnerability; commingled with you in body, heart, and spirit, he realizes he has nothing to fear. He can let down his effort, unguard his heart, and surrender in love with you for real—without holding back.

Keep his penis hard and your heart open so that he has the opportunity to yield into your soft convulsions of pleasure like a tongue entering the skin of a juicy peach. Your natural feminine flavor—who you are when you are full of sex, relaxed as bliss-body, radiant with the energy of love—attracts him more than anything on earth. When his depth of consciousness matches your brightness of love, all boundaries dissolve between tongue and peach.

6

LET GO OF
THE BODY

She is often more courageous than I am in our loving. But right
now, for some reason, she is restrained by a veil of fear. We are
making love, on the verge of total surrender, but she will not let go.

I hold her against me, so she can feel my love through and
through her. I gaze into her eyes, so she can see my love. I want
her to feel that surrender is letting go of everything, of all fear, so
that only love remains. I want her to remember and trust her own
depth of love.

I can feel her gripping her body. Every time we reach the point
where we could simply let go, she tenses her body, holds her breath,
and clamps down as if to fasten herself to a strained anchor, fearful
of drifting away into the open sea.

She doesn't trust love. Not in this moment. She doesn't trust
that as her body dissolves, her heart will shine. She's afraid of
losing who she is. She has spent so much of her life building up a
part of her—her sense of strength and self-reliance—that this part
is now reluctant to let go. To this part of her, such surrender feels
like it would be a loss of power, a way of being swept away.

The larger part of her hasn't yet remembered that, in trusting
love, all that is swept away is the tension of grasping onto her
little sense of self. What remains when her body and mind dissolve

is an immensity of love and energy of which her body was only
a pinch. This immensity is who she truly is. Remembering the
fullness of this love in every cell, she can relax as love's radiance.

A t some point in your sexual practice, you will experience a dissolution of the body, leaving a seamless intensity of energy and open consciousness. As this fullness, you realize what you always have been, even before the birth of your body. As this fullness, you are without borders, not limited to a separate sense of self, and yet you *are,* unbounded, like the clear space in which all occurs. This space is love.

During sex, let go into this space and relax as this space. Don't cling to control and self and body. Be openness itself.

If you are holding back, if you are resisting being love, then simply notice what you are doing and relax. Take your time. Be compassionate with your own fears. When you are ready, even though you may be afraid, practice letting go a little bit into the endless opening of love. Practice trusting love itself. Allow yourself to free-fall into the vast open of love, at first for just a moment, and then for longer and longer periods of time. Anything less than this free-fall into love is only fear, and it should be released, over time, bit by bit, in the practice of loving surrender.

FOR HIM

Suppose you are lying on top of your woman, making love with her. Feel her body and emotions as if they were dough that you were kneading with your breath and love. If you feel her belly become tight, then breathe your soft belly against hers, smoothing out her tension, "kneading" her lumps and knots into one fine consistency with your breath. If the muscles of her face tighten, kiss her gently on the lips or cheeks, reminding her to ease into relaxation. If you feel fear or resistance in her heart, breathe her emotional closure—actually inhale her tension—and then relax more deeply into her while you exhale. Continue kneading the texture of her body and heart with your loving breath.

As you open her physically and emotionally in this way, now and then she may suddenly contract. But when she does let go, she may often surrender more fully than you. You will feel your own tension against her openness, your guardedness against her vulnerable trust. Allow her depth of love to draw you beyond your own fears. Let go more than you ever have before, moment by moment. Surrender yourself utterly in a free-fall of love, holding onto nothing, giving yourself completely.

Do this practice over and over. It's not always easy. Sometimes you won't be able to let go—too much is on your mind. Or perhaps tensions in your intimacy need to be worked out by other means before you and your lover can practice this kind of surrender together.

Face the challenges in your life and relationship directly. Letting go doesn't mean being passive or lazy. Practice letting go while also skillfully working with the real ups and downs of your relationship, like a snow skier surrendering to gravity while also navigating the vagaries of the slope. In your everyday life as well as in bed, practice opening yourself, leaning gently through your fears, and giving your deepest gifts in the midst of moment-to-moment challenges. In any moment when you are giving yourself without holding back—in your work, with your children, or with your woman—then you are practicing surrender. You have ceased curling inward in doubt or fear.

Eventually, your practice reaches a point of sudden realization: nothing has ever made any difference and never will. Who you are at depth is always who you have been, as a little boy, as a youth, as an adult, throughout all your challenges, successes, and failures. With practice, you recognize that you are this depth, this blissful openness, even during sleep. You may come to sense that the birth of your body was not the beginning of this one.

The depth of who you *are* stands larger than time and space; this openness of being includes all the experiences of your life but is unchanged by them. All experiences come and go, appear and are dissolved, in the openness who you are. To do sex from this depth—to commingle with your woman in fully embodied love while rested as eternity—is a practice of incomparable joy.

FOR HER

Men prefer nothing to something. To them, zoning out in the "nothing" of TV is often more refreshing than emotional conversation and sharing. Men are more at home in the empty peace of post-orgasmic slumber than on the energetic roller-coaster of taking the children on a vacation. They seek the moment when everything else disappears while they are absorbed—in a sporting event, a vagina, or a fishing trip. Men are more naturally inclined toward approximating the absorptive "nothing" of consciousness than the fluctuating "everything" of life, although a really good man embraces both fully.

Women prefer something to nothing. They prefer a shelf full of trinkets—dried flowers, collectibles, photos, seashells—to one that is empty. They want to be filled by sexual love more than emptied of desire. Feeling stressed, a woman is more likely to fill herself with something—chocolate, ice cream, conversation—than release herself into TV or post-orgasmic depletion. Women seek to fill the empty spaces in their closets and hearts because they are more naturally inclined toward approximating the "everything" of life than the "nothing" of consciousness.

As a woman, therefore, you are particularly attracted to the sensuality of sex—not only to the sex act itself, but to the fullness of the whole situation. Candlelight. Music. Scents. Touching. Tasting. Luxuriating in water together, lips to lips, hot breath on moist neck. A rose petal drawn slowly across your body from breast to thigh.

Most women don't have any trouble merging with sensual delight. Many men do. That's why men often need exaggerated sensual experiences—direct stimulation of the penis, ten naked ladies touching each other in a sex show—to reach the place that women approach through more subtle, rainbow-like enticement. Women are at home in their senses; men often need to be seduced or enchanted into remembering that they *have* a body—and then they let go of it as soon as they can, drifting off into sleep after hurriedly consummating the sex act.

Therefore, the road toward sexual depth is very different for men and women. Men first need to learn to get into their bodies, then to feel their partner deeply, then to remain fully present and conscious while enjoying extreme pleasure, then to dissolve into openness with their partner in love. Women need to learn to receive pleasure deeply into their bodies and to open their hearts in love, but this is relatively easy for most women. They enjoy caresses, flavors, fragrances, and tingles. They want to exchange deep love with their partners. The problem for most women is that they take it too personally.

As sexual love expands, it includes the personal relationship but goes far beyond it. The special way your lover looks at you, his smell, all the ups and downs you've gone through together with your children, your house, your health—the sharing of these experiences make personal love rich and rewarding. However, they have nothing to do with the love that will open your heart beyond suffering.

You have probably enjoyed many moments of fulfilling personal love. Your man surprises you with a special gift. Or, he ravishes you in a vacation cabin in the tropics. Perhaps he puts aside his own preferences to nurse you to health because he loves you. In many ways, he shows you over and over, year after year, that he is devoted to you and truly committed to your family together.

Then he meets another woman and leaves you. Or perhaps he is still with you, but something feels like it is missing. You can't complain; you know he loves you. But you begin searching for deeper meaning, greater fulfillment.

Sooner or later, no matter how satisfying your personal life is, you long for something more, something deeper, something that fills your heart in a way that your current life does not. It doesn't matter how good your relationship is or how much money you have—we all know of wealthy movie stars or close friends with "ideal" relationships who end up depressed or divorced. We all know—or will know— what it feels like to have everything we want and still feel unfulfilled, incomplete, yearning.

No matter how much your man loves you, no matter how often he goes down on you or covers you in rose petals, at some point you will realize it is not enough. You still yearn for a deeper kind of love. You may even feel guilty about this yearning.

Men and women both feel this need for more than they are getting in their lives. Men want to feel more release, more freedom, more relief from burdens. Women want to feel more fulfillment, more love, a deeper joy in their body and heart. Although seeking through different routes, men and women are actually wanting the same naked intensity of perfect bliss, which is their own true nature. They want to enjoy the absolute fullness of life pervaded by the absolute openness of consciousness. In any moment you are able to *be* who you *are,* deeply and without effort, fulfillment is perfect, love is complete, freedom is endless.

Great sex is a place where most people taste this bliss, to one degree or another. You can taste it any time—during meditation, dance, prayer, sports, picnics, childbirth, death—any time you are willing to be totally present and relax all hold on yourself while surrendering open as unlimited feeling.

If you are like most women, however, the sexual occasion becomes wrought with personal concerns. "Does he like the way I look? Do I smell OK? Does he feel distant because he doesn't love me or because I'm not a good lover?" Although these concerns are real—every woman and man feels them—they are to be practiced through rather than indulged.

Your man whisks you off to a romantic hideaway with an antique bed and a roaring fireplace, unbuttons your blouse with his teeth, and rubs warm oil into your skin, from your feet to your head, before leading you to a huge bathtub filled with scented water surrounded by flowers and candles. A few weeks later, he forgets your birthday and goes out with his friends instead. One situation makes you feel loved, one makes you feel unloved. Neither has anything to do with the deeper love for which everyone yearns.

Both of these situations are starting points for the practice of love. In the midst of flowers and romance, can you open your heart so wide that the personal aspects of your relationship are consumed in the radiance of your love? Do you even want to? Or, would you rather luxuriate in the sensuality of the bath and your man's affection without bothering to open wider in love (just as your man might prefer to luxuriate in your vagina without bothering to connect more deeply in love)?

In the midst of feeling abandoned and rejected by your man, can you open and be the love who you *are* deep in your heart? Or, do you act like a little girl, pouting, angry, waiting to punish your man with your bad mood when he returns from his outing? The real practice of love goes beyond satisfaction and dissatisfaction. Pleasure can be just as limiting as pain if you choose to luxuriate in the slop of your senses without also opening your heart beyond the pen of your personal emotional needs.

The fullness you seek as a woman is only approximated by filling your body with sweets, children, and a good man. Unless you also practice opening directly as love, you will oblige sweets, children, and your man to give you something they cannot give you. Even shopping cannot fill your heart's emptiness—at least not for very long!

Don't submit merely to your man's love or your children's love or the love you feel when you eat your favorite foods, although these wonderful experiences are not to be avoided, either. To find true and lasting fulfillment, submit to the eternal love of which these are only approximations that come and go.

No matter how hurt your heart feels, surrender open. No matter how adored you feel by your man, surrender open. Open your heart, relax your body, breathe down to your toes. Feel the force of life move through your body and open your kinks and closures.

Sexually, allow yourself to surrender so fully that you feel "fucked" in your deepest parts, physically and emotionally. Allow your heart to be ravished by a force of love much larger than the penis of your man or the details of your relationship. When both you and your man let go completely during sex—while he practices invading you with consciousness and you practice opening your body to flow wild with love-energy—the true union you both want is consummated. Emptiness and fullness fuse as love, the open radiance of being. No want is left to suffer.

And when yearning returns, in daily life or in sex, appreciate it. Enjoy it, for it is a reminder for you to practice deeper relaxation, deeper openness, deeper surrender. Again and again, through pleasure and pain, practice living as bright love, radiating love, breathing love, until romance and rejection are but ornaments you wear to suit your mood.

7

UNGUARD
YOUR HEART

Yesterday I made a mistake and said something stupid, hurting her emotionally. I apologized and tried to talk with her, but it made no difference. Now, we lie in the same bed, and she is hiding behind a cold shell of protection. Her body is unmoving. Her face is frozen, etched with tension, anger, and hurt.

I love her, and so I gently touch her shoulder with my hand. No response. I begin to lightly massage her shoulder and arm, giving her as much love as I can. She begins to relax and breathe deeper. I continue touching her, caressing her, feeling her emotions and responses. Eventually, after a long while, she reaches over toward me, smiling, and pulls me closer.

I surprise her and roll on top of her, pinning her beneath me. I am totally relaxed. My belly is soft against hers. My breath is open and full. I am looking into her eyes, giving her love through my eyes, belly, and breath.

For a moment, she closes down again, as if my actions have violated the residue of her mood of resistance. But I'm not forcing anything. I am simply persisting as love. Pressing love into her, slowly, softly, like unrelenting warmth penetrating her skin and reaching finally to her heart.

She begins to open more. Her chest and belly relax. I sink more deeply into her. Her tension releases and tears roll down

*her face. She holds me tightly against her. From my heart I feel
into her, as if my heart were sonar and I was feeling into the deep
ocean of her being. My breathing and hers become one.*

*Her openness is so inviting, so pure, so attractive. I yield more
fully into her. Now, I could feel a subtle tension around my heart. It
is the tension of being in charge. I am still trying to serve her, rather
than simply being love in communion with her. So, I stop trying
to "fix" her or myself, realizing that even this supposedly well-
meaning intent is acting as an obstruction to our unimpeded loving.*

*Her heart has become completely unguarded, and now mine
lets go of all effort. There is no me to help, no her to save. Our
hearts unguarded, all effort wide open, we are gone in the large
undoing of love.*

L earn to have sex with a completely unprotected and vulnerable
heart. But to start with, the heart may be closed. So, you can use
sexual practice as a means for opening and unguarding the heart.

There are two forms of heart closure. One is long-term closure. If
for years you or your partner have lived with a closed and protected
heart, it may take many months of practice to undo the fear and tension that have become stored in your body.

The other form of closure is short-term acute resistance. Something happens—for instance, your partner hurts you—and you close
down. You don't want to be hurt any more. You are in no mood to
give love. So, you guard your heart to protect yourself and withhold
your love to hurt your partner back.

Both of these forms of closure, long-term and short-term, can be
undone in sexual practice. You can actually use sex to de-ice the frozen
heart. Use the heat of sex to melt the rigid protection of fear. Use the

love of sex to invite your partner into yielding his or her separative position. Use the humor of sex to bring laughter into every wounded pore.

In this process, all sorts of emotions may be released. As the heart is unguarded, the stress that was used to form its barricade is released in emotional expressions such as rage, laughter, tears, baby talk, striking out, and unadulterated hate. That's entirely as it should be. Take whatever precautions you need to in order to render the situation physically safe, but expect long-suppressed emotions to boil off as the guard melts. Even if both of you are emotionally hurt to the core, you must, eventually, lean into this practice of lovingly unguarding the heart.

The alternative is to continue protecting yourself by closing down and separating from your partner. Sometimes this is a necessary gesture. You may not be ready to open. You may feel you will lose yourself if you open to your partner. And this is true. With practice, you *will* lose yourself. Into love. Into ragged love.

If you are a weak lover in the moment, you will lose yourself into your partner's needs. If, in the moment, you are a middling lover, you will protect yourself and hold onto yourself, never opening completely to either hurt or love. However, you can grow as a superior lover by practicing to give yourself fully, opening without limit, even while suffering whatever hurt is inflicted on your open heart. This persistence in openness can be felt by others, including your lover. Through your practice of openness, you demonstrate and exemplify the naked strength of love.

You might be tortured by your partner's unlove. You might be weeping in pain as your partner continues to knife your heart with words of unlove. But if you can remain open, willing to suffer in the openness of love, then your partner can feel your strength. Because love is indestructible, you don't need to protect yourself. Your feeling heart can be hurt, dreadfully so, but the profound depth of love always prevails. All hurt is eventually consumed in love.

Over time, this demonstration of love transforms the patterns of your intimacy. Indeed, such a demonstration reaches out and begins to transform the world.

An unguarded heart can be hurt, but not destroyed. It is the "you" of protection that is destroyed, as it must be, sooner or later. Eventually you will have to let go of all holding on to this protection, even if only at the moment of physical death.

But if you let go now and unguard your heart deeply and regularly, your life becomes an ongoing force of love and blessing. The sexual occasion is a powerful setting in which to practice unguarding your heart and the heart of your partner.

Unguard your heart, over and over, even when you don't want to—especially when you don't want to. Continue practicing many short moments of total surrender. Eventually, the habit of guarding wears thin, and your heart is courageously exposed to the world, shining with great brightness and demonstrating a perpetual willingness to suffer others' oblivious rancor without closing.

Love prevails. But it takes practice.

FOR HIM

It's not a nice thing to consider. Certainly it isn't a politically correct thing to say. But it seems apparent: for most men, their "purpose" comes before their intimacy. Some men's purpose is financial: work first, love second. Some men's purpose is artistic: painting first, relationship second. Some men's purpose is political: fight for the country first, spend time with the family second. Some men's purpose is spiritual: meditate first, make love second.

Because the masculine is oriented toward the freedom of consciousness (rather than the flow of love), it chooses purpose over
relationship. "Purpose" in this sense is whatever a man (or woman)
feels is their reason for being alive, the center or guiding principle of
their life. It doesn't matter what a man says, his purpose is revealed in
what he does. He may say that his woman means more to him than
anything, but when he spends 70 hours a week working and most
of the rest of the time recovering from working, you know where
his priority lies. You know the guiding force of his life. You know his
purpose: work, and whatever type of freedom he feels work will give
him, financial, artistic, political, spiritual, etc.

The masculine seeks freedom through accomplishing a mission.
Ultimately, this is the blissful freedom of open consciousness, but most
men only approximate this sense of freedom through large bank ac-
counts or a corner office with windows. If you are a man with a
masculine essence, then freedom—expressed through your devotion
to your purpose—is your ultimate concern. Your intimate relationship
comes second.

Your woman may be the most important person in your life. You
may truly love her. But if you deny your deepest purpose to spend
time with her, your resentment will grow despite your love.

Men don't buy as many "relationship books" as women do because
men don't care as much about relationships. Or, a better way of putting it is that men care more about something else. Freedom.

You have probably had one or more intimate relationships in your
life. You have probably had your heart ripped to shreds by a woman.
You have probably also felt like your woman was an angel, a saint, a
lover beyond compare. She probably has given you more love than
you ever imagined possible, and you have probably felt like you would
do anything for her, even give your life for her, if necessary.

But if your woman could have a video tape of what went on in your head all day she would probably be startled. No matter how much you love your woman, your attention is mostly occupied by concerns about your work, your art, your mission, your quest, your money—not to mention moments of distraction by other women throughout the day.

Which leads to this conclusion: most men aren't motivated to improve their intimacy or sex skills until they realize that in doing so they are actually advancing their true purpose. Your capacity to "fuck" your woman *is* your capacity to "fuck" the world. If you can penetrate your woman with love in spite of her resistances, if you can bloom her heart in happiness, if you can bring her depth when she is superficial, align her life when she feels lost, brighten her with humor when she is dark—if you can learn to give your deepest gifts to your woman, then by doing so you are also learning to give your deepest gifts to the world.

How do you know what your deepest gifts are? You find your deepest gifts in times of solitude and challenge. You discover the vision to guide your life in time by yourself, meditating, walking in the woods, sitting in airplanes, driving to work. You discover what you are made of in the midst of emergency and mastery, rafting through whitewater, building a business, writing a novel, raising a family. In solitude and challenge you discover your depth and cultivate your gifts.

But very little tests a man more than an intimate relationship. There are many ass-kicking businessmen, risk-taking investors, and life-long meditators who crumble in the face of an angry, demanding woman. Most men would prefer to learn a new technical skill at work than improve their sexual skills in bed—they certainly spend more time doing so. Emotional and sexual depth is the weak link in most men's lives. Therefore, most men use their natural inclination toward projects as an excuse not to grow more in their intimate relationship—there's only so much time in a day, and first things first.

Sooner or later, however, every man becomes dissatisfied. Most men don't even bother to discover their true calling. They spend their lives going through the motions hoping that someday things will be different. As they get older, they stop even hoping. They settle for what they have. They learn to live with whatever they have accomplished, justifying their choices one way or another. "At least I'm better off than so and so. Heck, I've had a pretty good life. Actually, I've contributed quite a bit to the world." All the while, they feel a deep sense of unfinished business, as if life has passed them by and they didn't quite do what they were supposed to do.

Nobody gives you faster feedback about your mediocrity than your woman. Ultimately, she wants to feel your freedom in fullest consciousness. But in the meantime, as both of you are still settling for less than your full potential, she'll settle for approximations of true freedom: money, a nice house, going out to good restaurants, beautiful jewelry, wonderful vacations. When material freedom isn't enough, she'll demand emotional freedom. "Why are you always thinking about work? Why don't you spend more time with me? Are you listening to me? I don't feel you love me like you used to."

Because your orientation is toward your mission or purpose in life, your woman's complaints frustrate you. You know she is right, but you don't really want to do anything about it. You actually do want to deepen your love with her, but you'd rather spend the time making money, building your business, creating your art, doing your spiritual practices, or, when you need to rest, reading or watching TV. It's *difficult* to deepen your love with her. As long as you are getting enough sex and things are fairly comfortable, why stir the water? There's plenty of mud at the bottom, and it seems like it's going to take a long time to clear it up.

Eventually, when you have lived long enough to realize that what you *do* or *have* in your life never completely fulfills you, your purpose becomes more direct: How do I live each moment so that I am totally free, at ease, in touch with my deepest soul and expressing my deepest gifts? How do I discover who I really am and live fearlessly based on this knowledge? What is the meaning of my life, and how do I live it? What is death, and how can I prepare myself for it?

It is extremely valuable to explore the answers to these questions in the midst of intimate relationship. You can face your weakest links and find your deepest truths right there, in the place so easy for most men to avoid, the swamp of sex and emotion. You can learn to work with your strongest sexual desires—kinky and straight—as well as your strongest emotional fears, and discover that every situation is ripe for growing. Instead of being satisfied with the challenges of financial success, sports, and saving the world, you also turn to face your most dreaded enemies: your fears of emotional exposure, sexual failure, and the hurt your woman causes you by knowing your hidden weaknesses and secret self-doubts.

More than one man has lived a paltry intimate life while changing history because of his great social deeds. It is common to excel in the public world while remaining retarded emotionally and sexually. With practice, however, you can strengthen your weaknesses and give your gifts from a source of deep love, fearless openness, and profound sexual vitality. Your woman's demands, spoken and implied, can be felt as challenges to grow. She knows your weak spots that you may hide from others. She knows your *real* reasons for doing what you do in the world, and they ain't always so pretty.

She can be your ally or your nemesis. If she is a good woman, she won't settle for your bullshit. You can't trick her for very long with empty promises and superficial accomplishments. She wants depth as well as success, a heart-warrior as well as a good husband. She wants your deep being and real presence—which is exactly what you need to give to the world, if you are to feel complete at death.

To unguard yourself completely—including sexually and emotionally—is to offer your deepest truth and give your deepest love, to your woman and the world. They will both hurt you in the process, no doubt. They will test you and challenge you. Lesser men will just plain quit at a certain point, only giving so much of themselves. When they die they will feel incomplete. A superior man doesn't quit.

Failure and success come in cycles, and any experienced artist, businessman, spiritual practitioner, or lover knows this. Behind these cycles is your true depth of being, which never changes. Practice relaxing into and as your deep being, again and again. When your woman refuses you sexually, relax as your deep being. When you are on the verge of ejaculating, relax as your deep being. When your gorgeous colleague suggests you have a drink with her, relax as your deep being.

Always practice relaxing as your deep being regardless of your situation. Practice relaxing your body so you can breathe from your deep belly rather than your upper chest. Practice relaxing your mind so you can act spontaneously from your gut. Practice relaxing your attention as the openness of space, remaining aware of the sounds all around you, the motions of everyone in the room, and the subtle shifts of energy in your body. Unguard your heart during sex, again and again, so that your deepest being is fully exposed to your woman, and so you can receive your woman's love deep into your heart. Learn to live as this freedom of openness ever more deeply and you will die complete.

FOR HER

Unfortunately, most men are sexual dorks. The height of sexual expertise in many men's minds is being able to give a woman multiple orgasms through oral sex. There's nothing wrong with multiple orgasms or oral sex. But for most women, in addition to physical pleasure, sex is a doorway to profound emotional fulfillment and spiritual surrender— and most men just don't know how to open this door completely.

The way somebody dances tells you a lot about how they make love. The ease with which they move their hips, their capacity to express musical rhythm from toes to nose, their connectedness or oblivious-ness to their dance partner, all reveal aspects of their sexual capacity.

A woman who is married to a man who can't dance often longs for a partner who could glide her across the dance floor. This reveals more than her predilections about dance; it shows what she is lack-ing in bed. If a man can dance well, it means he can enjoy his body, feel the energy of the music, and match his partner's rhythm. If he is a really good dancer, it means he could move her *beyond* what she might do on her own. Most women are turned on by a man who can take them to new places, not only on the dance floor but in bed and throughout life.

However, there is a big difference between energy and consciousness: a man could be a great dancer—with all the right moves—and yet not be very deep in his daily life. That is, a man could be good at moving energy but not be very conscious; he can take you to new places of physical plea-sure, but not to greater spiritual depths and emotional fullness.

The deeper or more conscious a man is, the more trustable he is. You can feel his commitment to truth. You can trust what he says. His life is aligned by a profound sense of purpose that you can count on. Yet he may still be a lousy dancer.

A good dancer may be able to sweep you off your feet physically, but in day-to-day life he may appall you. He may lack a sense of purpose, flit from one woman to another without commitment, and orient his life around having fun, disregarding the daily cultivation of depth and meaning. Yet his smooth moves might trick you into lust.

Ideally, a man embodies both depth of consciousness and physical grace. He is guided by true purpose and is also able to move spontaneously with energy. He is a man of integrity and style. But, if you have to make a choice, a deep man is a much better intimate partner in the long run than a superficial fancy dancer, a Mr. Suave.

If you happen to be with a good man who can't dance—who is, therefore, probably somewhat of a dork in bed—don't despair. He can practice "dancing" with you in bed or on the dance floor. It is much more likely that a deep man will become better at dancing than a superficial man will develop depth. But even if your man remains a clunky lover, you can continue to open.

Allow love to enter your body with or without your man's expertise. This is a crucial practice. You are built to grow spiritually by receiving and opening to the force of love-consciousness in your body, and you don't need a man to do so.

You have probably felt "filled" or "swooned" by a force of consciousness at one time or another in your life. Perhaps you felt guided by the wisdom of a teacher or professor, "fucked" by his intelligence, in fact. You may have actually felt an erotic intensity in his vicinity. Perhaps you felt opened by a therapist's empathy or bloomed by his understanding. Even the directional power of a horse between your legs could be more than merely sensual. The reason women often develop sexual feelings in relationship to their teachers, therapists, and even strong animals that "guide" or "take" them is that they feel penetrated, flowered, or carried by masculine consciousness or directionality.

As a woman, you may find yourself growing through three stages in relationship to the masculine force. First, you feel this force as something outside of you, something that is more powerful than you. You look to an other as your savior, whether he is a husband, therapist, teacher, or close friend. You may find yourself depending on his guidance, support, and knowledge, afraid to lose it, worried that he might leave you for another woman he finds more attractive. You may find yourself playing the helpless victim to his ways, either grateful for his wisdom or tolerating his abuse—or both.

Eventually, you may grow into the second stage, where you "come into your own." That is, you discover and cultivate your own masculine directionality and consciousness. You may start a new career or pursue higher education. You learn to make your own decisions, independently of a man or other outside influence. You refuse to be a victim—but you may also miss the pleasure of opening to a man's loving presence. You become more whole and autonomous as a person, but as a side effect of guarding yourself, you may also feel less fulfilled sexually and emotionally.

The third stage begins when you know that you don't depend on a man, that you can make your own decisions and guide your own life, and yet you are tired of keeping up your guard; you want to relax in your feminine body and emotions. You want to stop protecting your heart. You want to swoon in the bliss of utter surrender, spiritually, emotionally, and sexually.

At this stage, you want to maintain the freedoms and capacities you've developed, but you also long to be entered and opened by massive masculine love. You want to be ravished, swept off your feet, by a trustable man, sexually and emotionally, as a consort, an equal, a partner—not as a victim. Eventually, as you grow, you may realize that you can be ravished by masculine force, bloomed physically and emotionally by a tangible invasion of love, *whether or not you are with a man.*

When you want feminine energy you go to nature. Feminine energy is the force of life. You can be rejuvenated by feminine energy in the ocean, the woods, your garden, or your bath—anywhere you connect with untamed life force, with sensual pleasure, with enlivening radiance and bodily relaxation. On the other hand, masculine force makes you feel entered, blossomed, swooned, or guided into blissful surrender—with a therapist, teacher, lover, horse, career, suave dancer, or even by the thrilling presence of your favorite movie star.

In the first stage, you seek this masculine force in a man on whom you could depend. In the second stage, you seek to depend on yourself for this masculine force. In the third stage, you don't depend on others or yourself: you practice opening directly and being permeable to the ever-present force of divine masculine consciousness itself.

You can practice this while meditating, praying, dancing, or even while sitting right where you are, reading. Relax your body as much as possible. Relax your lower body, your feet, calves, thighs, anus, and vagina. Relax your middle body, your belly and chest. Relax your face, especially your eyes, tongue, mouth, and throat. Remember a time when you felt pleasurably invaded by masculine force, perhaps while you were making love with a deeply trusted man. Or maybe you felt ravished by masculine force while masturbating, or while receiving bodywork or therapy, or in the arms of a great dance partner. Some women have received a swoon of transmission that penetrated their body while looking into a powerful man's eyes. In any of these kinds of situations, you have a sense of being "fucked" by a force of consciousness that opens you deeper and swells you in fullness.

It may feel like a force descending upon you, filling your throat and opening your heart, pressing you down and open, down and open. Or, you may feel it moving up between your legs, filling your womb with warmth and fullness, as your body surrenders in waves of ecstasy. This force of consciousness may pervade you in many ways, all of which involve your trust, relaxation, and capacity to open your heart and yield your body in bliss. Even if your man is just beginning to grow in his sexual capacity, you can still practice, intentionally opening and receiving masculine force.

Opening to this force of bliss is not always a pleasant experience at first. If you were sexually abused in the past, you will naturally resist trusting masculine sexual penetration—by a man or by divine consciousness itself. If your body is chronically tense—perhaps you have spent two years concentrating on a business project with very little time spent dancing, making love, or exercising—then you will feel pain as the force of bliss invades and opens up your tight spots. Masculine force is like a deep tissue massage: it hurts if you are closed, and it deepens your ecstasy as you open.

Men who are good at moving with energy but are not very deep are more like a gentle sensual massage. They will give you pleasure but won't be able to open your closed places, physically and emotionally. They will want to have fun rather than go through the pain of opening with you.

Even if your man is a sexual klutz, he is a good partner if he is willing to stay with you through your pain and continue to practice deepening love through difficult times. A good sexual partner may not be as good a dancer as you, but he is willing to learn and remain fully present while you practice receiving the blissful invasion of consciousness in your body. You don't need a man to do this. You could do it alone. But a trustable man who is learning to grow in love with you can make it a lot easier.

Every day, whether you are alone lying in the grass or in bed making love with your man, practice allowing yourself to be "taken" by the deepest, most loving masculine force you can imagine. As a young girl, you may have fantasized about unicorns and horses. As an adolescent you probably dreamed of the high-school quarterback or the motorcycle bad boy. In your early adulthood, you may have pined for a professor, a "genius" type, or a therapist/teacher who could save you and take you to a new place of understanding and happiness. As a grown woman, you have probably sought for a lover whose strength and integrity you could depend on and trust—and who would also ravish you into bliss.

Now, it may be time to practice opening directly—to be lived *by* and *as* the love-force you hoped for in previous forms. Your exquisite permeability to your lover's sexual flesh and emotional needs is but an innuendo of your divine permeability—your openness to, communion with, and surrender as the force of unbounded love.

PART II
OPENNESS

S exual intimacy—like money or meditation—can be used to express your deepest love and openness. Or, it can be used for childish reasons.

As a child, I remember lying on the couch next to my parents. My face was turned toward the cushions so I could feel the cushy material against my lips and cheeks. The sound of TV and household conversation burbled softly in the background, though I didn't give them much attention. Mom and Dad were so close, right there, on the couch with me. I felt taken care of and could really relax. I felt so safe, so protected, and so peaceful. I could just swoosh in fuzzy oneness with my homey numbness.

In moments when my childhood homelife was not so comforting—for instance, when my parents yelled at each other or my father threatened to hit me with his belt—I would go to hide in the darkness of my closet, surrounded by well-known smells, precious trinkets, and familiar clothing. Or I would seek refuge in the basement, playing with my toys and living in a fantasy world of great adventure. Other times I might retreat under the covers of my bed and meld into softness and undisturbed quiet.

These were childish comforts, providing a false and temporary sense of protectedness that I would eventually learn to outgrow—sort of.

Even as a fully functioning adult I have often yearned for such false and temporary immunity to disturbance. In my life, I've been pretty good at achieving a tenuous sense of buffered security in numerous ways: in a high-paying career and a well-furnished home; in an easy chair, a few beers, and a big-screen TV; in a warm bed snuggled next to my lover; and with certain types of meditation and breathing exercises.

But all of these methods are temporary or partial. I could lose my money and home through chance or catastrophe. The effects of beer wear off. My lover may leave me, or may find another she prefers, or die. And even after profound meditative experiences, I'm still suscep-tible to extreme pain and loss: my body may be crushed if my car's brakes wear out at the wrong moment, or a drive-by shooting may inadvertently ablate half of my brain.

I may partially succeed at buffering myself from ongoing and under-lying anxiety, the fear of loneliness, and the terror of death by absorbing myself in warm flesh and family love, the adventures of career, the chores of playing house, or the closet of spiritual inwardness. But the consola-tion doesn't last, and even while it does, it's rather thin.

Sometimes a deep uneasiness manages to break through the trance of my daily drone of comfort. Unless I am very clear, I may try to remedy this swell of fear and anxiety by seeking a secure place in which to absorb myself, as I did in my childhood.

To assuage my pain, emptiness, and loneliness, I may hope for a deeper or better love relationship, one that I can truly depend on. Or perhaps I labor to accumulate more money, toys, or friends with which to occupy myself. I may zealously search for a parental God to save me: a therapist, an organization, or a teacher who will take care of everything if I follow the rules, do the practices, and go to meetings once a week. Or maybe after a moment of feeling that I am alone, unfulfilled, and on my way to certain death, I go back to the comfort of my everyday tasks, pick up a magazine, or watch TV.

Occasional safe havens are necessary. There are times to go forward and times to rest. And each of us has our limit; we are only willing to look the lion in the face for so long. Sometimes the stark tooth of life and death is just too much to deal with and we seek solace in places of comfort. Then, when we are ready, we continue to grow at our own pace.

To grow in freedom is to develop the capacity to remain open as love even in the most difficult—as well as the most pleasurable—circumstances. This growth involves combining yourself entirely with the actual emotional texture of the present moment. It involves feeling your fear of emptiness and loneliness, your yearning for love, and your denial of death. It involves noticing when you try to absorb yourself in TV, professional and family occupations, or meditative inwardness in the childish hope of security and emotional tranquility. To grow in freedom and love involves developing your capacity to be a true adult: to stay open even as sorrow rips through your heart, terror nauseates your gut, and anger inflames your passions.

To grow, you can't hide like a child from your own emotions. True growth involves the capacity to feel into, as, and through your emotions, exactly as they are, without trying to make them go away or pretend they don't exist. Feel fully *and* open. When hurt by your lover, you grow in love by keeping your wounded heart open, rather than closed. When threatened by intense pain or impending pleasure, you grow in freedom by breathing the sensation fully rather than by clamping down and holding your breath. When your heart is exposed to an unloving partner, you grow by relaxing the body and staying in the ache of relationship with your partner rather than by turning away and closeting yourself behind a shut door of tension.

To be sure, sexual intimacy will bring out the best in you as well as the worst. To continue growing, feel into, as, and through all of it, while remaining open in love. Sex reaches down into the dregs of your dark hidden past. It exposes your strange and secret kinks, fears, and desires that developed through your life as you curled your private passions inward. Sex also reaches up to the brightest light of your being, giving bodily expression to your deepest love and highest truths.

Between our most dark and light qualities, sex often reveals our typically middling character: essentially childish, seeking comfort and security, opening when our home feels safe and peaceful, closing when relationships feel threatening or hurtful.

Your growth as a lover involves counter-practices to your childhood habits of withdrawal, closure, and self-absorption. Instead of seeking peace and safe comfort by curling inward, feel through everything, inside and outside, so that nothing is avoided at all.

Feel every emotion and relationship exactly as it is, and relax open as the entire moment, accommodating every passion, scuffle, expectation, and snuggle in this fundamental openness of love and trust.

This practice of openness is not always fun. It can really hurt. But even the hurt—discovering that your lover desires another more than you; realizing that your life is near its end—is felt through so that the spacious nature of this moment remains obvious as your home.

All your experiences are temporary and unique waves in this ocean of openness: the raggedness of your sadness, the perkiness of your lover's nipple, the smell of coffee, the eyes of your child looking at you from a hospital bed—all experiences wash through this openness, coming and going, tragic or ecstatic, remembered or forgotten, and yet the openness remains, always and only, a home from which you cannot leave because it is your very nature.

Sex—like money or meditation—is best used to realize and express your natural openness, rather than to build a false home of childish security. How do you practice this recognition of openness during sexual intimacy?

8

Do Sex As
Open Feeling

We were in the kitchen. I was standing near the counter and she was sitting at the kitchen table. She began eyeing my crotch with snake eyes and a smile. I walked toward her. She unzipped my pants and began mouthing my penis.

She was really into it. She sucked and sucked, looking up into my eyes, slurping and gulping. Her hair fell in her face as she slid closer to me, taking me completely down her throat. She was ravenous, snorting and gasping as she swallowed me whole.

She began furiously pumping me in and out of her mouth. I was feeling intense pleasure, my hard-on blazing, my whole body seared by shards of yes. I could also feel her. I could feel her desire. I could feel her energy building, moving like light through her veins.

I wanted to help her energy radiate more brightly from her heart. I felt into her, as if I were moving through her body, pervading her every cell with love, breathing her entire body with my breath, and feeling her emotions with my heart. Combining my love, breath, and feeling with hers, I open with her as one edgeless oh.

But then I noticed that my feeling had stopped short. I was luxuriating in the intense pleasure of love, light, and energy. Here I was, snuffled in our bliss, as we were dying. I saw the wrinkles of age forming around her beautiful lips. Slowly her face transmogrified into an old, haggard woman, gumming the withered appendage of my moldy destined self. I was seeing the movie of our life at superfast speed, she and I growing old, everyone growing old, losing everything, our bodies and minds and children and parents and friends deteriorating, disappearing, gone forever.

As I felt this quickness of life—fragile, wrought with moments of pleasure and miles of pain—my heart opened more fully. I relaxed into the sacrifice that is life. I was alive as love—why not? Why not give myself completely in love as I live and change and die?

And so, there I was, penetrating her with unbridled love. Her whole body seemed to open more. Still sitting on the kitchen chair, her legs began spreading and coming together like frantic butterfly wings, and tears began to stream down her cheeks as she kissed and mouthed me. We were dying, in love. We were a living sacrifice in love.

I felt how God is alive as us: an infinite fire a few licks of which undulate as our bodies and minds. We quivered as those waves, temporary, tragic, blissfully evanescent, as our edges whitened and flashed gone. She began to come in waves of orgasmic sobbing, even as she continued sucking.

Her body was vibrating and convulsing as she looked into my eyes. Through her eyes I felt the love-fire that moves the world, that lives as all beings as they themselves spark and shine and come to ash. I felt through our sexing, through our bodies, through our loving, until only love was lucently obvious. Love burned as the only light. Our sacrifice had come to One.

Eventually, she released me and slid off the chair onto the floor, shaking, weeping, smiling, her hands splayed wide open, our eyes vulnerable in the ageless vision of love.

There are three basic steps to converting conventional sexuality into a means of communion.

1. Feel your own sensations fully.

Whatever you are feeling, feel it completely. Feel the sensations on your skin and the energy moving through the inside of your body. Feel your emotions and thoughts come and go, without adding anything to their natural flow. Feel your body, mind, and emotions completely and without distraction.

2. Feel into your lover's sensations fully.

Feel through your own sensations, and feel into your partner fully. Feel your partner's breath. Feel the energy moving through your partner's body. Feel what your partner is feeling on every surface of skin, mouth, vagina, penis, anus, and even between his or her toes. Feel your partner's heart, emotions, and desires. This will take practice, but eventually you may be able to feel your partner's entire body, emotions, and thoughts almost as clearly as you can feel your own.

3. Feel *through* your lover into the divine.

Feel even through your partner's sensations, feeling beyond them, until you can feel the nature of feeling itself. This isn't about trying to understand something intellectually, but is actually a matter of feeling, like when you feel the soul of a great musician through his or her music—you don't just hear the music, but commune with a quality that lies through and beyond every note and pause.

Feeling through your own sensations, feeling through your partner's sensations, you become aware of the spacious quality of feeling itself. Within this spaciousness all things transpire. Every thought moves. Your lover's flesh glistens. Sweet and sour tastes fleet. Every itch and dread and succulent delectation is self-manifesting, spontaneous, evanescent, and alive. Full yet empty. Glorious yet gone as it arises.

You'll know when you are feeling *through* experience in this way, sexual and otherwise, because you will cease adding tension, fear, or closure to the present moment that is openness itself. Sex will drop through the hole of the moment suffused as the oneness it is trying to achieve. All urgency for sensation and pleasure will be reversed in a bodily utterance of fullness. The moment will consume itself in love and the remainder stands without time.

FOR HIM

You can change yourself a little bit, but for the rest of your life you will remain pretty much as you are, whether red headed and short tempered or tall and anxious. You can diet and lose weight, work out and gain muscle, cut your hair or grow a beard, but your friends will probably still recognize you; the changes you create in the way you look are small compared to how much you stay the same. You are stuck with yourself more or less as you are. Whatever your characteristics of mind and body, they won't change too much no matter what you do.

No matter how much therapy you do or how many years you meditate, your personality and thinking patterns remain more or less as they are, as recognizable as your face. Sometimes a traumatic event may occur later in life that severely alters your body or personality, but more often the friends you meet at your 30-year high school reunion will recognize an older version of the same character you were in high school.

Up to a certain point in our lives, growth is based on changes in our bodies and minds. As children we grew taller and eventually sprouted pubic hair. As young adults we learned skills to earn a livelihood. Perhaps we went to college and studied French, Shakespeare, or accounting. It's easy to understand why many people think that spiritual growth is based on changes of the body and mind; that's the kind of growth most of us have experienced so far.

For the most part, spiritual growth is not based on changes in your body, mind, or personality. Your brown eyes don't need to become blue in order for you to see God. If you enjoy opera and fine cigars now, you probably will continue to enjoy them as you grow spiritually. Your sexual fantasies—which are likely to be pretty much the same now as they were when you were sixteen years old, though perhaps less intense and less frequent—won't change too much, either. If you have a taste for blonde women with large breasts now, you probably will have the same taste if you become enlightened.

Spiritual growth involves recognizing deeper aspects of who you are, not changing the surfaces (although the surfaces may change somewhat as a result). As a child, your attention was occupied, say, with toy trucks and tree houses. As a teenager, your attention, freed from toys, became obsessed with girls and cars. As an adult you are probably preoccupied with earning a living and perhaps caring for a family.

You may still play with toys occasionally, though they are probably bigger and faster than your childhood playthings. You may still be turned on by fine cars and young girls, but a good portion of your attention has moved on to other things. Toys, cars, and girls seem somewhat more trivial than when they constituted the entire world of your youth.

What constitutes your world now? For most of the day, what are you concerned about? What are the objects that now bind your attention? Money, career, a social cause, a mistress, TV, a family? As long as these things are fulfilling, there is no problem. Life seems good, or at least good enough.

Adolescent hormonal changes freed your attention from toys so you could invest it in girls. Spiritual changes free your attention in the same way. If you continue to grow spiritually—and everybody does, at their own pace—sooner or later the things you have invested your life in seem empty and trivial. They no longer give you the fulfillment that they once did.

This can be horrifying. You may be in the middle of a great marriage, surrounded by glorious children, succeeding at your career, and whammo! Suddenly you lose interest in the whole damn thing. Or at least it begins to feel like you are just going through the motions without wholehearted enthusiasm. The same thing can happen in the midst of a life committed to social activism or religious pursuit. Suddenly you feel done. Ready to move on. But you don't know where. And the baggage you've accumulated can be immense.

The good news is this: *Where* to go is deeper into the bliss of your very being, and you don't have to change your relationship, family, or career to do so (although they will be imbued with new depth as you grow, possibly changing as a result). The bad news is that spiritual growth, while deepening your consciousness and bliss, can be as painful and difficult as growing from childhood into adolescence or making it through medical school.

Teenage growth is mostly driven by physical changes. Growth as a young adult is mostly based on developing the mind. Spiritual growth depends on cultivating a depth of attention or awareness, *in spite of the condition of your body and mind*.

You can be well-versed in Shakespeare or barely literate; you can be a marathon runner or confined to a wheelchair; you can be homosexual, heterosexual, celibate, or polygamous; you grow spiritually when your attention is no longer bound to its present objects—money, women, thoughts, desires—and is free to relax more deeply into its source.

The source of your attention is consciousness itself, the openness of being. When you are in deep sleep and begin to awaken, if you are very sensitive you can feel attention "come out" of a deeper, blissful consciousness and "carve" a world of thoughts, objects, feelings, and relationships that you call your life. Out of the silent, blissful nothing of deep sleep, suddenly you are aware of—and absorbed by—whatever world reflects your current fears and hopes.

As an infant you probably woke up into a world consisting of breast or bottle. As a teenager you woke up with a hard-on and thoughts of what the school day would bring. As an adult your first rising of attention may bind your consciousness to noises coming from your children's room or to the documents you don't want to forget on your desk.

Even now, your attention is still occasionally wrapped up in objects like breasts, hard-ons, and perhaps school. But you are no longer so locked into these objects; your attention is more free and so has grown wider and deeper. It is *wider* because it takes into account so much *more* than it used to as a child. It is *deeper* because your understanding of what these objects *mean* has grown. You know deeper suffering and deeper joy than you did when you were younger, so certain things—dolls, toy trucks, The Beatles, financial victory—don't mean as much as they used to, though you may still enjoy them. Now, other aspects of life seem more meaningful.

Just as age developed your body and school developed your mind, spiritual practices develop your depth. You grow spiritually by letting go of your attachment to certain objects, which happens naturally, and then relaxing your attention more deeply into its source, the openness of being. This development of attention from superficial to deep can be practiced in many ways, including prayer, devotional contemplation, meditation, and studying scripture.

Since so much of our attention is tightly bound by our sexual hopes, fears, and desires, our sexual life is usually one of the last parts of us to grow spiritually, no matter how much we meditate or pray.

But at some point we realize that sex isn't all we hoped it would be—we suffer because our sex life is not satisfying. It might have seemed satisfying yesterday, or ten years ago, but it is not now. Just as we may find our career or relationship suddenly unfulfilling, we may naturally become frustrated or even bored with our sex life; though perhaps still physically pleasurable, sex begins to feel empty. And this is a sign of growth.

Our culture only supports growth up to a certain stage. We are allowed to liberate our attention from childhood and adolescent concerns, but then we are supposed to be satisfied by occupying our attention with "adult" concerns of money, family, sex, sports, and affection, with a little bit of social do-goodery, artistic appreciation, and religious belief thrown in. But when we grow beyond these objects of concern—when they no longer interest us—our modern culture offers very little advice beyond therapy, TV, drugs, divorce, changing careers, and trying to search for meaning in the world.

Meaning is not to be found in the world, but in the depth of being, which then recasts the world in a new light. When your family and career no longer fulfill you as they once did, don't leave them. If your lack of fulfillment is due to spiritual growth, a change in family or career will make absolutely no difference in how deeply you are fulfilled. Your only true choice is to go deeper: relax as the openness of deep being, even while you continue to skillfully deal with the things of your life.

It's best to regularly practice this deepening in a formal and undistracted situation such as meditation. But ultimately you practice this deepening in *every* situation, and especially those situations that *most* bind your attention, the places in which you get most caught up. From your teens throughout middle life, sex is one of these places. Your attention—and the energy of your life, which follows your attention—is distracted by and absorbed in sex. Not just sexual intercourse, but the whole sexual world: relationship, love, lust, orgasm, rejection, fantasy, need, masculine push, feminine pull, the whole whopping, fantastic mess, in your bed, at work, at home, on the street, and in your head.

Feeling through your sexual experience is a way to liberate your attention from sexual objects and feel more deeply into the source of attention, which will reveal itself little by little as you practice. Enjoy the hot, wet friction on your penis as much as you want; just feel through the sensation as you do so. Argue with your woman until you are red in the face, all the time feeling through the waves of emotional intensity. With practice, you can feel into the deeper openness and profound bliss of sex instead of being bound merely to its superficial sensations and emotions.

Until you discover the depths of sex for yourself, whatever any-body says about it will seem meaningless to you. You will settle for great orgasms, an emotional connection, and fine tits and ass for as long as they fulfill you. You shouldn't even *try* to make sex deeper until the best oral sex you've ever had feels like suffering. Physically it may feel great, but something is missing. It feels superficial, trivial, unsatisfying, like your favorite toy from childhood would now feel to you.

At this point, it will be natural for you to practice feeling through your sexual sensations and emotions since they don't fulfill you much anyway. Don't stop having sex. Continue doing all your favorite sexual activities with your lover, but do them with deeper aware-ness. Practice *feeling through* your most physically pleasurable sexual moments, relaxing as the openness of deep being, again and again.

In this way you will liberate your attention into a deeper bliss of being, an openness of consciousness in which you abide even now, but which you don't tend to notice because your attention is bound by more superficial objects. For now, the total release, absolute freedom, and unshakable bliss of deep consciousness may still be less interesting to you than your favorite forms of sex—just as in childhood, sex was less interesting to you than your favorite toy. Sooner or later, though, everybody grows up, and their needs deepen. As a practice, meet every moment of unfulfillment as a call to feel through the present objects of attention and relax more fully as the openness of deep being.

FOR HER

If you have a feminine sexual essence, then you want to look and feel good. The earrings you wear—gold or silver, beaded or feathered, huge or tiny—affect how the energy flows through your body and how people experience you. The color of your clothing and the style of your shoes affect how you feel—and how others feel you—all day. Most women are excruciatingly sensitive to the way they look and feel, to themselves and others.

Most men, on the other hand, care far more about how successful they are than how they look or feel. Advancing their mission and accomplishing their goal is their priority—quite often at the expense of how they look and feel. In fact, men often take pride in exhausting themselves and looking like crap because they have been working so hard.

The differences between men and women can be interpreted from many perspectives: Their genetics are different. They are exposed to different hormones as embryos. They are treated differently as children. Societal expectations influence men and women differently. All of these differences are real, as are many other factors that may affect how men and women feel and act. One of the biggest differences, yet one that is hardly acknowledged or understood, is the difference between masculine and feminine sexual essences—what can be called a spiritual difference.

As described in *Intimate Communion,** the sex of your body and the gender of your essence need not coincide. For instance, perhaps 10% of women (and 80% of men) have a more masculine sexual essence. These women find more bliss in challenge and competition than in sensuality and relationship. At the movies, they would prefer an action adventure to a love story. They would prefer to quickly scarf down their food and get back to work than relax and enjoy fine cuisine with champagne, candles, and intimate conversation. They would more often prefer to ravish their lover than be ravished by their lover.

Ultimately, the divine is one, but manifests as two: masculine and feminine divinity, or consciousness and light. A person with a masculine sexual essence identifies with the freedom of consciousness. If you are such a person, you struggle to feel free, which requires that you are clear in your priorities. You are not really happy unless you know what you want to do and you are free to do it, financially, emotionally, politically, and spiritually. Free consciousness comes through the body as presence. If you are "on purpose" and therefore free in your consciousness, you are also very present.

Generally speaking, the more someone is clear in their priorities and able to stay consistently on purpose, the more money they are able to earn. This is why money is sexy: money is a stepped-down version of free masculine consciousness, and every woman feels this. A man who is very conscious, present, full of humor, and wealthy is sexy. These qualities—consciousness, presence, humor, and wealth—reflect different levels of the attainment of masculine freedom; a person with these qualities is sexy to you if you have a feminine sexual essence.

If you are a person (perhaps 80% of women and 10% of men) who

---

*David Deida, 1995. *Intimate Communion.* Deerfield Beach, Florida: Health Communications, Inc.

has a feminine sexual essence, then you identify with love and light (rather than freedom of consciousness). You want to be seen. You want to be radiant. You want your hair, eyes, and skin to shine, but mostly you want your heart to shine. That is, you want to give and receive love. *Love is the way light feels.* When you are truly loving, your inner light shines as a perceptible radiance regardless of your age, and this radiant love flows from your heart as an expression of the feminine divine.

Just as freedom fulfills the masculine essence, love fulfills the feminine. Whereas a truly free and conscious man is full of presence and purpose, a truly open and loving woman flows with the forces of the universe. She is full of intuition and light. She radiates love-energy. Gloriously radiant women attract men who are very conscious, and vice versa.

At a superficial level, this is why financial wealth and physical beauty are so often found attracted to one another. A rich man can almost always find a physically radiant woman, and such a woman can almost always find a man of means to marry. At a more profound level, a woman of deep radiance and intuition whose heart is founded in divine love is attractive to and attracted by a man whose presence is founded in divine freedom. A superficial but wealthy man doesn't interest her as much as a man of profound consciousness, humor, and depth—and if he is wealthy too, so much the better!

You know how powerful your radiance is. You can turn it on and wrap a man around your little finger with it. Men are suckers for a woman's radiance, and the more her radiance shines the more a man is willing to do for her—the more his consciousness is attracted into her. Some women are born with great physical beauty just as some men are born with wealth. This kind of attractiveness is very real, but relatively superficial. Eventually a woman's body ages and withers, and a wealthy man who never develops depth loses his charm real fast.

As you grow spiritually, your feminine essence identifies with more and more profound depths of love and light. In your feminine youth, you probably spent substantial time beholding yourself in the mirror, learning to brighten your eyes with various shades of eye shadow, trying on different clothing to see how it lightened or darkened your energy. Little girls—if they have a feminine essence—don't have to be forced to play with jewelry, make-up, and clothing, as many mothers can attest. In the same way, most little boys—those with a masculine essence—love challenge and competition. They don't have to be taught how to whack things with sticks or fight with their closest friends—they love it.

Genetics and social conditioning certainly play a big part in this difference. But spiritual differences—the differences between the masculine and feminine essences—must also be comprehended so men and women can understand how to grow spiritually, in addition to growing biologically and socially. Masculine and feminine spiritual growth occurs in different ways.

Playing with dolls and make-up as a young girl is the beginning of your spiritual growth as a woman. You learn how to cultivate love and energy. Caring for your doll is the beginning of learning how to open your heart—regardless of your mood—and embrace the world in love. Looking at yourself in a mirror and feeling the difference between what a red skirt and a blue skirt "does for you" is the beginning of learning how to feel subtle flows and work intuitively with energy, and how to heal, enliven, and bless the world with your bodily expressed radiance.

A big part of sex for you is about feeling attractive because your feminine essence identifies with light. The feeling of light is love. In your heart, you know that you *are* light and love. You know that you have the power to bless others with your light and love by shining energy through your body. You want your radiance felt and acknowledged.

Your sexual essence is always shining, though surrounding this essence may be all kinds of physical blocks, psychological kinks, and emotional resistances that can limit your shine. Sex is one place where you discover just how open your body and heart are. As you make love, do you shine as the bliss of love-light? Or, do you close your body and heart to some degree, allowing less of your radiance to shine, denying energy and joy to yourself, your lover, and the world—and then doubting your self-worth?

Nothing is more important to the feminine than love, which shines through the heart as light, through the body as radiance, and through relationships as care. You grow from superficial to deep forms of love. As a teenager, you obsess about your physical appearance; what is most important to you is how others see you. If you grow beyond this level of feminine concern, as a young adult you begin to learn to feel your own radiance; what is most important to you is how you see yourself. If you grow from this self-concern into a greater fullness of feminine expression, your concern is with light or love itself: "How surrendered am I as the absolute light of love that shines through the heart of everyone and through my body to all others?"

Learning how to dress and put on make-up is a full-fledged feminine art. Most women in our culture participate in this art to a greater or lesser degree. Some women master it, others only dabble, but most women spend a significant amount of time concerned about and adorning their appearance, becoming artists of energy ("Does this or that earring make me feel better?") and of light ("What color blouse brings out the shine in my eyes today?").

Eventually, if you grow, this kind of concern may begin to feel superficial. Some modern women have chosen to jettison the feminine art of light altogether when they grow beyond this level of concern.

But as you grow spiritually, your feminine art and mastery can deepen. In addition to superficial energy play ("Plaid or solid?") you learn to intuit and move energy more deeply.

Through the arts of dance, yoga, massage, and many others, you can develop the same kind of expertise you have with clothes, but with your internal energy flow itself (as well as with that of others). You can learn how to breathe and move so that your body opens to your deep flow of internal energy, and thus your radiance grows. As your bodily obstructions are released, the love-light in your heart is able to shine more and more through your entire body as a blessing force in the world, regardless of your age.

Your intuition and radiance of divine love-light grow deeper as you learn to feel, breathe, and surrender more fully. Is there a subtle tension in your heart? Are you guarding your heart, hiding the depth of your love, attempting to disregard your constant yearning to give and receive deep love? The deepest form of feminine beauty is love itself, shining freely from the heart, radiating through the body and into the world, unobstructed and unguarded.

Our culture doesn't support this depth of energy: your mother probably spent more time teaching you how to dress than how to love. She probably commented more on the way you should do your hair than on the way you should breathe in order for your energy to move blissfully through your body and enlighten the hearts of others.

At their deepest level of expression, feminine love is the same force as masculine freedom. They are one openness of being. Nevertheless, the masculine and feminine journey of growth are quite different. The feminine essence identifies with the love-light of being ("How do I look? Am I loved?") and the masculine with the freedom of being ("What is my purpose? How can I be more free and successful?"). Spiritual growth, for women and men, involves growing from superficial to deeper levels of these identities.

Feminine spiritual practice involves surrendering as and express-ing the deepest light and love that flows through your heart, devoting your body to dancing love's dance, breathing love's bliss, and radiating love's light, moment by moment, regardless of how bad you feel. You don't need to deny your emotional ups and downs or your physical pains while you practice being love in their midst.

Your body is going to rot, no doubt. Sooner or later—usually sooner than desired—you will look in the mirror, see your wrinkles, gray, and flab, and your heart will sink. This is the equivalent of a man's mid-life crisis, when his family life or career suddenly seems empty to him. The masculine part of you can experience the same mid-life crisis that a man does. But the feminine part of you goes through a very different kind of crisis, not of purpose but of light: "Am I still radiant?"

Because the feeling of light is love, when you doubt your radi-ance, your heart doubts love—unless you are able to grow in feminine depth. This requires learning to identify more with the radiance that shines from your heart through your body, rather than identifying with the superficial shine inherent to youthful flesh.

At a certain age in middle life, it is entirely natural for you to feel like your body is "betraying" you. Once you have learned how to cultivate physical radiance through dress, make-up, jewelry, and the sensual sashay of a feminine body, you have made your youth obsolete. Your young body—which is naturally radiant with energy—has served its purpose for the sake of your spiritual maturation. It is now time for you to con-tinue growing and *deepen* your feminine art of love-light.

Locate the love in your heart and practice shining it through your body. This involves the practice of allowing the full spectrum, the en-tire rainbow, of love-energy to flow through your body. What might this practice look like in relationship with your man? While making love, you can practice giving him the energy of a mother, your body transmitting nurturing and comforting love. You can give him the energy of a wild animal, your body transmitting love through untamed, dangerous, bestial force. You can give him the energy of a whore, your body transmitting love-energy in its slutty, lusty, "dark" form.

If your body is resistant to flowing with some aspect of feminine energy, then you will limit the force of love that can shine from your heart; you will weaken yourself. Practice flowing with the energy of love that you most resist. If you are comfortable giving tender motherly love but resistant to humping your man like a drunken slut, then you have more to learn in the art of transmitting love and light. The feminine grows spiritually by learning how to let every shade of love-energy flow from the depths of your heart to the tips of your tongue, fingers, nipples, and toes, into and through all of your relationships.

Spiritual growth means growing in your capacity to incarnate love. Your body learns to flow with the entire spectrum of love-energy, savage and pristine, sisterly and witch-like, bitchy and saintly. Ultimately, your love embraces the whole universe, the entire display of energies, every possible form. To love this big, you must be willing to feel every possible emotion, allowing your body to flow with every possible energy, whether you like it or not.

Whatever energies you are unwilling to incarnate in your own body you will resist in others. Your very resistance will attract these energies into your life so you can learn to love in their midst. For instance, if you are resistant to being uninhibitedly happy and sexy in every inch of your body, you will despise women who you think are "bimbos," attracting them into your life. If you deny your own power to influence others through your energy, then you will disdain women who seem manipulative, attracting them into your life.

To grow spiritually, learn to embrace and express every energy *in love.* Your body grows in its capacity to shine every kind of light, ugly and beautiful, cosmic and infantile, pastel and dark red. To open yourself like this takes practice. It is easy for a woman to surrender as love in the forms she finds comfortable: your man massages your back, fixes you dinner, and then ties you to the bed with velvet ribbons in order to torture you with his tongue—you can probably handle that. But when you are angry—your man lies to you about something important—can you allow the energy of rage to flow through every cell of your body *and at the same time keep your heart open to his heart?*

Can you feel through your anger, stay with your man heart-to-heart, and feel the depth of love and yearning that churn in your open heart? Can you breathe love—inhaling and exhaling love as if it was air—while also shouting at your man, demanding his integrity, tolerating nothing less than what you know is true of him?

Developing your capacity to shine love through different shades of energy takes time, as does learning how to put on make-up. Your body learns to incarnate every form of energy in the universe, ultimately, while your heart remains surrendered to the radiance of love that shines in its depth.

Once your body and heart have learned to remain open, then you can practice relaxing into the source of light itself, the very love that you are, the deep bliss of being. More and more, as you learn to surrender, this force of love lives *as* you, beating your heart, moving your limbs, speaking your words, flexing your vagina, and beheading any fool who stands in the way of love.

Enjoy the interplay of masculine consciousness and feminine light at every level. Your glowing smile and eyes draw your man's one-pointed purpose to you, skin to skin. His presence penetrates your body, intermingling with your wide feeling-radiance. His unwavering consciousness permeates the force of love shining from your heart, and this fusion combusts as love absolute. Overwhelmingly full and sublimely free, this ecstasy is the deepest joy of sexual love a man or woman can discover, the open bliss of very being made palpable through the heat of flesh surrendered.

9

FREE ATTENTION
IN THE MIDST
OF PLEASURE

I am on the verge of ejaculating. She is pulling me deep within her, milking my penis in the grip of her vagina. Her need seems unquenchable. "Harder," she cries, smashing her vulva against me. Twisting my organ tight in her velvety grasp, she begins to come in waves and shakes, extorting my spew through frictional torture.

But I do not want to ejaculate. I do not want the occasion to end. I do not want to be reduced to a spent sperm vessel.

Instead of being led by the pleasure, I feel into and through the pleasure. I don't allow myself to be drawn into a frenzy of spurt, release, and depletion. Rather, I reorient my attention. I feel through the intensity of pleasure, like a lion jumping through a ring of fire, into the openness that lies behind the pleasure. Feeling into this openness, the sensation suddenly shifts, as if the fire of pleasure were a mirage, or a heat wave, rippling in a huge ocean of radiant naught.

The pleasure has not decreased, but it is no longer the pivot of my attention. It is but a small gleam, a transparent shimmer on the surface of an ocean of depth. As I allow my attention to relax into this wide source, the urge to ejaculate disappears. Instead, the intensity of sensation increases and flows up my spine in an eruption of brain light.

We are still forcefully coupled. Her legs and pelvis are now vibrating like an engine about to explode. She has never allowed herself to be filled with so much energy. And I have never sustained awareness so deeply in this violence of pleasure.

I can feel her trying to draw me over the horizon of consciousness into the whorl of her quivering love. It is as if she is testing me: Will I lose it? And yet, as I sustain awareness through the vortex of her pleasure, our energy increases, our surrender deepens, and new levels of mutual bliss arise and disperse, again and again, each more perfect than the last.

The attractiveness of her bodily ecstasy demands an almost absolute penetration of consciousness. If I contract the openness of my awareness for even a moment, my attention is sucked into the whirlpool of genital stimulation and I may unwillingly spurt quick joy in one last convulsion of lost cognizance. I must keep my recognition strong in the force of her profound sexual arousal. The more stable my persistence, the deeper her surrender. The wider the space of my recognition, the more intense the display of her rapture.

In this revelation of true "fuck," she and I are awed in God.

Understand the difference between energy and consciousness during sex. The feminine error is to lose yourself in energy or pleasure. The masculine error is to suppress energy by rigidly holding to consciousness or separative effort. Rather than making these errors, practice feeling energy fully, but feel it *as* consciousness, as a ripple of who you are most deeply.

The feminine partner will tend to get lost in energy first. If the sex is really good, he or she will tend to forget all else and become the energy, the pleasure, and the sensation. Then the masculine partner will tend to either hold back and resist or get swept away by the feminine partner's pleasure.

If you allow your inherent spaciousness of consciousness to be narrowed by mere sensory pleasure, then you will be corralled toward orgasm. Without spacious consciousness, orgasm tends to lead to a collapse of energy and awareness. A swift ride to a mediocre null. Instead of falling prey to this common grunt of stimulation and release, re-orient your attention so sex goes beyond mere satisfaction.

Many people have experienced only the most meager of sexual pleasures. They have habitualized to a sexual routine of stimulation leading to intolerable excitement followed by an explosive release of tension through ejaculation or clitoral orgasm. This kind of sex is like pigs feeding in the pen of neuronal exhilaration, stuffing themselves with energy to the brink of explosion, unconscious of a path beyond such shallow slaughter.

If you are the masculine partner, don't lose the open space of consciousness for the sake of momentary pleasure. But don't resist the force of pleasure either, like a rigid twerp trying to maintain control. Sexual pleasure itself has a natural magnetism that can draw awareness into its open source like a moth to a flame. Attend to the pleasure (as you will in any case). Feel into it, but don't stop there.

Feel *through* the pleasure, as well as through the space around it and behind it, into the ocean upon which it shimmers. Feel the sexual sensations fully, as well as the openness in which the sensations hover. Feel the excitation, as well as the sharp clarity that cognizes every throb and pulsing intensity. Be feeling itself, extended to infinity, through every thing.

Allow your attention to be attracted by the velvet torque or molten throb of your lover's genitals, and feel through it. Allow your attention to be drawn by the siren rhapsody of your lover's moans, and feel through it. Rather than being swept over the edge by your lover's currents of abandon, meet this untamedness with your ferocity of consciousness. The more wild your lover becomes, the deeper you must feel through your lover's energy.

In some moment, you will feel through it all. Openness sex, without circumference. Openness itself, without difference. Love. For this apparency to ease itself plain, you must practice freeing your attention in the midst of extreme pleasure.

As if waking up while still dreaming, practice feeling the entire sexual occasion arising in the open of consciousness. This recognition transports the pig to the palace. Suddenly, you are aware of what is always true: You are consciousness-radiance itself. Everything that happens, including sex, takes place in this openness and is a creation of conscious light. Except you forget this, and get lost in the drama of hope and desire, in the dream of fulfillment and release, in the vision of flesh and grind.

While humping in the bedsack it is easy to forget who you really are: consciousness-radiance, the natural love, openness, and depth of being. Always practice to remember who you really are, even amidst the slosh and smell of sex.

FOR HIM

You probably use your woman to stimulate yourself. You like the way her thong bikini cuts between her ass cheeks. You get off when she wears leather, or whips you, or kneels before you. Her gentle massages, wispy lingerie, and cinnamon-caramel-tangy fragrance turn you on. Then, through sex, you ride your own excitation to the brink of release, and in a flash of intense pleasure it's over.

Women are probably the most beautiful, sexy, and attractive inspiration of your life. That's good. That's how it works out; women reveal to men the beauty of existence. Without women, this would be a sorry life indeed. But your relationship to feminine attractiveness doesn't have to stop with sexual titillation.

Suppose you are on a beach and you see a woman who attracts you, whether she is your lover or a total stranger. Perhaps she attracts you because her skin is soft and smooth and shines with oil in the sunlight. Perhaps you can't keep your eyes off her cleavage, front or rear. Perhaps it is her elegance, her grace, the way she walks, or the relaxed depth of passion in her eyes.

The feeling of "wanting" a woman is the feeling of wanting to merge with her, to take her and make her yours, so that for some moments you are absorbed in her beauty and delicious woman-ness, released of desire because you have exactly what you want. But what is it that you want?

Most men know the feeling of wanting a woman, having sex with her, and then feeling done with her, at least at the energetic level. You have gotten what you wanted: stimulation to the point of ejaculation. You are released of desire. Though you may still cuddle with her in love, you are already drifting away, into sleep, reverie, or the TV on the other side of the room.

Some men come to a point of feeling shame or guilt about this kind of sexual relationship. So they try to find other ways of relating with their woman. More civilized ways. Besides earning a living and raising a family, the first attempt at coupling in non-sexual ways usually involves finding common interests. Foreign movies. Bird watching. Discussing ideas. Reading by the fireplace. Collecting wine, antiques, or rare something-or-others. Some men consider these to be more "mature" forms of sharing, and they certainly do transcend the quick in and out of sexual desire and release. They last longer and aren't dependent upon youth, energy, and physical attraction.

If you are like many men, you quit at this point. Besides working and caring for your family together, you enjoy being with your woman sexually as well as watching movies, going to concerts, and discussing international politics. Together, you lust after great orgasms, discussions, and vacations you both find interesting. In bed, you enjoy fleshy intercourse; in museums or galleries, intellectual exchange. Secretly, you crave just one night with your eighteen-year-old next-door neighbor who suns herself in the backyard. Or, you fantasize about being with the brilliant and provocative woman at work with whom you could share things that your partner couldn't even begin to understand.

If raising a healthy family, having sex three times a week, and shopping together for great deals on Persian rugs completely fulfills you, then enjoy it while it lasts. It won't for too long. Consider sexiness itself: no matter how appealing your woman's body is or how interesting her mind is, you will probably grow to a place where it isn't enough. Your first impulse may be to find it elsewhere. In some instances, another woman *can* give you the bodily energy or intellectual brilliance that your current woman lacks. But even so, you will eventually become as disillusioned with her as you have become with every woman before her.

Great sex is alluring, and then you grow to a place of depth where that isn't enough. Your interest becomes piqued by the special kind of woman who can "share a life" with you. Hopefully, this kind of woman is also sexually attractive to you. Then you grow some more. Whether you stick it out with your current woman or try for greener pastures, it doesn't change anything fundamental. You must liberate your consciousness from old habits and reorient to a deeper sexual truth if you are to find life and relationships meaningful.

Become sensitive to where your attention goes when you are interested in a woman. Perhaps it goes to her breasts and legs. Or maybe you think about what a good mother she would make. Or perhaps you imagine relaxing on a ranch together, watching the sun set while you sip coffee and your woman puts the finishing touches on her latest work of art. Unless your consciousness continues deepening, you will feel unfulfilled when these things lose their oomph. You will end up feeling, "So what?" You will slowly starve in quiet desperation or chuck your current relationship and start from scratch, both of which will leave you short of true happiness.

Eventually—and don't rush it, you'll know when the time comes because you will have no choice—suffering compels you to greater depth. Then it is time to practice easing your attention through its things—as if feeling through the deck of a boat into the deep rhythms of the sea, or relaxing your gaze through the objects reflected in a window pane so you can know the vast landscape behind them. Every object of your attention floats in a boundless space of being. Who you are *is* this entire depth of being, including the "reflected" things. Ease your attention through every experience so you can know and feel this depth of openness.

Feel through stiff nipple and wet crotch as if feeling through images and sensations in a dream, feeling through their transparency into the inherent spaciousness in which they shimmer. Feel through the waves of household sounds—the children laughing, the phone ringing, the dog barking—as if feeling into an underlying ocean of silence. Feel through your sense of satisfaction while lying next to your woman after a long day of hard work, relaxing into the openness of deep being, the "who" in which arises, "I'm satisfied."

Feel through everything into the "who" of your feelings, the deep silence behind the sounds, the open space in which the images of your life move. You will probably notice that you can't do this for very long. In a second or two you will have forgotten depth and become riveted to the surface, to the sights, sounds, and feelings of your life—and these things don't fulfill you for very long. Practice again, anew in the present moment, feeling through everything to which you pay attention, opening as the depth of being. Over and over, practice for many short moments all day and eventually even during your dreams at night.

Especially practice when you are most attracted or repulsed by life, which probably happens quite often with your woman. Use her attractiveness (or her problems) to pull your attention off your own body and mind into her body and mind. But don't stop there or you will end up feeling depleted, bored, and unfulfilled. Feel to her and then feel through her to the depth of existence itself.

For instance, while making love, your attention will naturally be drawn to the warm grip of her vagina around your penis. Feel your attention actually move to this sensation from wherever it was a moment before. Then, using the momentum of your attracted attention, feel right through the sensation, into the space of sensation itself.

A rainbow takes place in the sky. A movie takes place on a screen. What is the background against which you feel any sensation? Find out. Feel through the pumping, slippery heat of your woman's vagina around your penis. As good as it may feel, it feels better when you also feel the empty space in which the energy of the sensation appears, like the air in which a mirage occurs. This simultaneous realization of fullness (hot, wet, silken, throbbing) and emptiness (the space of sensation) liberates bliss from the merely physical into an unconstrained infinitude of openness and depth.

Sex—as well as raising a family, sitting by the fireplace, or collecting cars—is only as deeply fulfilling as you are willing to feel. The capacity to feel through the surface into the depth of any moment is learnable. Its strength grows with practice. When you can feel through the sensation of a mosquito bite, the moment is as blissful as being massaged by five naked women. The smells, tastes, touches, sounds, and sights are different—and certainly most men would prefer one experience to the other—but the bliss of the moment is identical. The depth of the moment is identical. The degree to which you feel fulfilled—open, free, alive, and complete—is identical.

When you can practice feeling through experience, then you no longer hope for the impossible: that this or that particular experience will fulfill you. Nor are you depressed by the facts: sex is passing you by and you still haven't totally *done it;* your woman is sometimes loving and sometimes bonkers; your daily life is filled with endless chores and picayune. You feel through it all, and in doing so the very bliss of being dawns overwhelmingly obvious, suffusing all experience.

If your practice grows strong, you might still complain about your aching back or curse at your broken car, but the inherent bliss of being remains unbroken as the tangible, underlying "substance" of every moment. You might feel sorry for yourself, but you also feel through your own self-pity, and thus relax as open depth even while you bitch and moan.

After you have located and relaxed as this deep bliss of being, you can practice allowing it to pervade every aspect of your daily experience, moment by moment. Your family life becomes permeated by the openness of your being. Your professional life becomes an expression of your depth. Your woman is swooned by the force of your presence transmitted emotionally through your body and breath.

You no longer use sex simply to release tension and desire; rather, you release yourself utterly in the *feeling through* of sex. You allow yourself to be attracted by smooth skin and fetching smile. You use the attractive momentum to "feel" your attention right through the sensations and emotions into their source and depth, the "who" of experience itself. Then you allow the depth of this "who," the force of love and openness of being, to arise as all your experience and the entire world around you. You are made free not by woman or orgasm, but by relaxing as the bliss that you are, over and over again, until fear and desire lose their hold in the fullness of unfettered emergence, realized anew every moment.

FOR HER

When love is flowing in your life and relationship, you tend to feel open and happy. When love is not flowing, you tend to feel depressed and tired. So it's very natural for you to try creating a flow of love in your life and relationship in the hope that you will feel good.

If you assume that the source of love is in others, then you will do whatever you think will get their love. You may bend your personal desires in order to cater to the needs of those whose love you want: your family, your man, your friends. Eventually, if you really go out of your way to please them, you might end up feeling abused, a victim of their whims. The truth is, in many cases, you are tolerating their abuse because of the love you also hope to get from them. Otherwise, you would simply stop making yourself available as a potential victim.

If you really feel unloved and unnoticed, you may actually crave abuse. You probably don't think about it this way, you just feel hurt and angry. Your man sits in front of the TV drinking beer. He has ignored you for weeks. You try talking with him and he doesn't respond. You do something special—make him dinner or wear an especially beautiful outfit—and he doesn't even notice you. You are in the kitchen and, frustrated with his apathy, you suddenly throw down a plate and break it. Or, you pull your car into the driveway and feel like "accidentally" driving right into the garage door.

You know such behaviors aren't going to make your man love you more. But they will get his attention. When a relationship gets really bad—in the sense that your man doesn't even notice you—then his angry attention is better than no attention at all. His abuse is better than total lack; in his anger at least you can feel his presence.

This is a very low level of "presence" indeed, but, nevertheless, most women have at moments desired it from their unresponsive man: "I'd rather break his stereo so he notices me than continue on this way." You can at least feel his responsiveness in his anger. He may be yelling, but at least he's talking with you. Receiving his heated anger may be as close to receiving his passion as you've gotten in a long time.

Love is so important to the feminine essence that some women will do just about anything in the hope of getting it, including giving up authority over their personal lives in the hope of receiving love from their family, lover, or friends.

As you grow spiritually, you realize how unfulfilling it is to always depend on another for love. You realize that whether or not your man gives you love—whether or not anyone gives you love—you are worthy of love. You don't need to please others to feel the flow of love that you desire in your life. You can love yourself.

This transition is very difficult and rewarding: to grow from depending on others to giving yourself the love that you want. Learning how to love yourself is a big step in life. It makes you whole and independent, a true adult able to make your own decisions without setting yourself up to be a victim. You can choose your own course and live life on your own terms and let others do the same.

To some, this kind of autonomy is the achievement of a lifetime. After years of being in a relationship with a man who expected you to do everything his way, finally you have grown into a relationship of equality, mutual respect, and independence. You share love with your partner, but you also know how to give yourself love. You take care of your partner, but you also take care of yourself. For a while, this may seem like an ideal relationship: friends and lovers rather than oppressor and dupe.

The next transition occurs when this equality isn't enough. Your relationship is safe and supportive, but something feels missing. Your man gives you love and also respects your freedom, but the ecstasy of total surrender isn't a frequent pleasure. You no longer would "do anything" to be with your man, but you are beginning to feel you might do just about anything to feel the bliss of absolute love penetrating deep into your heart and body—yet you know that to surrender to another for this bliss is a prescription for abuse, victimhood, and weakness.

As the next stage of spiritual growth unfolds, you learn to open yourself completely without losing yourself in another. You no longer suffer the hurt of dependence nor the pride of independence. You stop pulling and pushing your lover and simply breathe as love.

When you were dependent, you practiced sacrificing yourself for the sake of pleasing your man. When you were independent, you practiced strengthening yourself so you could please yourself, with or without your man. Now, you practice true spiritual surrender, which involves opening to the love that lives the universe, flowing as your body, mind, and emotions. Your pleasure lies in this submission, neither to your man nor to your self, but to the very flow of love for which you yearned all along.

This kind of submission makes you stronger, not weaker. Surrendered to love itself, moved by love itself, you are a force to be reckoned with. As love moves through you, your man better straighten up or watch out. In fact, *you* better straighten up or watch out. Love is a force that strips you of false comforts and aligns your life to love's demands.

Most women choose physical comfort and emotional security over true love. Their lives are aligned by the demands of nice homes, good jobs, and their relationships with family and friends. Only after submitting to both dependence and independence are most women ready for submission to love. Only when a woman is willing to be moved by love—not by her man's desires or by her own dreams—is she ready to take this next step in spiritual growth. This step involves "marrying God," becoming love's woman, rather than your man's woman or your own woman.

When you are ready to take this step you will know it because you will have no choice. Perhaps you will be sitting in the kitchen, your beautiful children eating at the table, your devoted man looking into your eyes, and you feel fulfilled—almost. There is still a "God-shaped void" in your heart.

You will notice a tension in your body and a yearning in your heart. You may try to keep yourself busy to avoid feeling it. You may try to convince yourself that you have no right to feel this subtle lack; after all, you have everything you ever wanted, certainly more than many women are lucky enough to have. And yet, somewhere, somehow, something is missing, though you can't quite put your finger on it.

Some women try to analyze their ennui through therapy or talking with friends. Other women seek the ecstasy of "losing themselves" in the rush of something "greater." They give their lives to a spiritual leader or a social movement and experience the bliss of self-surrender that they lost in developing their independent emotional stance.

But this kind of bliss is temporary and dependent on their chosen beloved person or purpose. When they are rejected by their spiritual teacher they feel as bad as when they are rejected by their lover. Or, if they have chosen to lose themselves in merger with a larger social issue—for example, ecology, feminism, education, or worldwide health—they suffer the eventual success or failure of their mission; again, they yearn for something more.

Ultimately, the only surrender that is truly fulfilling is to the love that is the substance of every single moment, the love that moves as you and the universe. If the love you are surrendering to is love "of" something or someone, then you have more to learn. You will never be completely fulfilled by something or someone. Never. You may have moments of relative happiness, but these will be stretched between moments of relative unhappiness, and this cycle of getting and not getting love in your life, day by day, eventually becomes barren. Futile. Exhausting. An authentic spiritual teacher, teaching, or movement turns you directly toward the bliss of love itself, and then helps you to serve the world *as* love.

True spiritual surrender is submission to love itself, the love that breathes your breath and beats your heart, the love that dances alive as this moment. Spiritual growth involves going through whatever you have to do to recognize this love, open your heart and body to it, and live *as* it, expressing it through your life. You may choose to express love in relationship to a man or as a celibate nun. You may choose to express love by giving birth to many children, by adopting, or by living alone. You may choose to be a political leader, a doctor, or a fund-raiser. You are free to choose the life you want—but you will only be fulfilled if you are practicing to live as love moment by moment.

Without this practice, your life will eventually come to desolation. Many women have loved a man, raised children, and made great social contributions, yet still felt lonely by the end of their life—or even in the middle of it. Many women have joined spiritual teachers and social groups and yet have died unhappy, exhausted, and bereft of true fulfillment. There comes a point when the only thing left to do is surrender directly as the flow of divine love—you have tried the other forms of surrender and, however benevolent they have been, you have remained wanting, yearning for more.

Giving yourself to another is a beautiful thing, but eventually unfulfilling. Giving yourself to your own direction is a beautiful thing, but eventually empty. The yearning deep in your heart can only be penetrated fully by the love that is the nature of your very being.

In this present moment, practice opening your body to bliss. Breathe love in and out with every breath. Learn to relax your muscles—your heart, your belly, your thighs—so that the energy of love can flow through you without obstruction. Practice feeling the love that flows through your heart and body regardless of your emotion in the moment: surrender open and live as love while you are hurt, angry, or afraid. Open yourself as love, through your breath, throughout your entire body, over and over, whenever you can remember.

You will discover that parts of you may resist surrendering as love. Your belly hasn't relaxed completely in years, so love-energy can't flow fully to your genitals. You are afraid of losing financial support, so you are reluctant to stop trying to please your man. You have been single for so long that you are afraid to let down your guard and feel the pain held in your heart.

Learning to surrender directly to love is often an agonizing process. You will be disillusioned of your dreams of comfort, security, and romance. Every emotion that you have stuffed into your body without feeling fully will emerge for you to re-experience. Years of loneliness and ache will be exposed as your heart unfolds. Yet, when the time comes, you have no choice but to go through this process and learn to surrender as love, receiving and giving the bliss of deep openness with every breath.

This bliss is born of your true nature—an eternal love that cannot be lost. The force of this love cannot be beaten or victimized. This love fills your body and heart with a pleasure so deep that even your own thoughts and emotions cannot sway your fundamental happiness. Your loneliness is filled with a bright immensity of joy. This love-energy flows from your heart through your body and out your feet, hands, and eyes like beams of beauty. You live in love's rapture, even as your day-to-day life continues in the form that you choose.

Sex becomes literally making love, magnifying love, from the boundless depth of your heart through every inch of your body and in merger with your man. You are so full of love and pleasure that it is impossible to give it up in an effort to please your partner. You are so open in bliss that you no longer need to guard your heart for fear of being hurt or taken advantage of. Your love is larger than your man or your self. You have nothing to fear or protect. Love has already worked its way through your secret hopes and dreads and opened every speck of you as light.

You are neither possessed by your lover's needs nor by your own. You *are* love. You live *as* love. And when you find your heart yearning still, practice surrendering more deeply as love. While washing the dishes, picking your child up from school, or firing an employee, practice allowing love to flow through your every gesture, word, and breath. In every moment, practice receiving love deeply into your body and giving love from every cell. You are thus transfigured, breath by breath, from a needy woman looking for love, to a self-sufficient woman who loves herself, to a woman always and already full of love's bliss and blessing power.

10

GO OUT,
NOT IN

She had an old habit of going inward during sex, especially when she wanted to have an orgasm. She would close her eyes and withdraw, going inside herself to experience her own sensations. It was as if I wasn't there any more. Although I was the source of her stimulation, as she turned inward she became completely unaware of me or anything else outside of her own body of excitation.

She asked me to help her remain more open during sex; she wanted to learn to feel through our sexing into a larger love. But first, she had to learn to feel through the cave of her own sensations. So we decided that whenever I felt her withdrawing into herself I would stop moving. Then, she would open her eyes, feel through her own pleasure, and reconnect with me, heart to heart. Then I would begin moving again.

Sometimes this exercise was very frustrating for her. But she wanted to continue. Over a few weeks she retrained herself to remain open throughout the sexual occasion. Even while she was approaching orgasm, she remained open and felt through the waves and thrills rather than closing down and going inward. She allowed her orgasm to move outward, like a gift to the universe, through her body, through my body, and far beyond. She gave herself in pleasure rather than keeping the pleasure in herself. Her

openness deepened our mutual surrender, wherein we both gave
ourselves so fully in love there was no inward left to go.

D o your best not to dissociate from your partner and go inward during sex. Rather, go through the vehicle of your embrace and open as love. This takes practice. At first, it's very easy to close your eyes and go inward, especially in moments of intense pleasure or pain.

Instead, practice to stay open. Gaze into your lover's eyes, and feel into the deepest love you can feel. Breathe your lover, and then breathe through your lover. Let your attraction to your lover undo the torque of your inward curl. And then, once your feeling is uncoiled enough to be stable in the contemplation of your lover, feel through your lover into the love that moves the universe, the love that is alive at the heart of all beings.

There are times to go inward during sex. There are moments when it is appropriate and natural to close your eyes and separate your feeling from your partner. But most often, practice opening outward, feeling into and through your partner further and further, until there is no horizon to the expanse of your loving.

FOR HIM

During sex, it is very easy to turn inward and get lost in the pleasure of your own body or erotic thoughts. Instead, stay in direct relationship with your lover. Look into her eyes. Practice feeling the subtle currents of energy flowing through her body. Is her breath full or shallow? Is her belly tense or relaxed? Are her eyes open or closed? Are her toes curled or splayed wide? Learn to feel the rhythm of her motion and stay with her, loving, breathing, and navigating both of you into deeper ecstasy.

Eventually you will learn to feel through your lover as open depth without limit. For many, depth means going inward. But eventually it becomes obvious that depth underlies inside and outside. The thoughts in your head and the clouds in the sky are both perceived by *you,* who *is* depth. This "who" of depth (who you are) beholds both inward and outward objects: emotions and automobiles, thoughts and chairs, energy rushes and river currents.

Introspection or inward meditation is one way to delve into the depth of who you are. Sex is another way, a two-person way. If you are going to go inward during sex you might as well do it by yourself; there are far less complications in solitude. But if you choose to delve into depth sexually, practice feeling into the depth of your lover, the depth of the entire universe. It is the same depth who you are most truly.

Sex is a natural way that depth can recognize itself in another. This depth is openness or love. You open with your lover as love and relax in the depth of sexual embrace. Her body has holes that fit your pegs. She loves to receive what you love to give and give what you love to receive. Sex is a way to celebrate the give and take of love with the whole body, lips, genitals, and breath, allowing depth's openness to permeate flesh, thoughts, and emotions. The whole-body bliss that results from this perfect fit and dissolution in open depth far exceeds the pleasures of tensing up, going in, and losing yourself in physical intensity for a few seconds before releasing in ejaculation and being finished.

FOR HER

Throughout the sexual occasion, and especially during orgasm, open outward rather than curling inward. Instead of sinking into yourself, enjoying the solitary pleasures of your body's waves and ripples, open outward as if your pleasures enveloped your man and the entire world.

Some women (and men) need time to become sensitive to their inner energies by closing their eyes and learning to feel within, either with a lover or by themselves. This is a good preliminary practice if you have lost touch with the flows and pleasures that move within you. Any time you want to gain awareness of your own body, it helps to temporarily close your eyes and go inward for a moment.

But when you have reconnected with your own bodily flow and pleasure, don't limit your love to yourself. Love is magnified by inclusion. The more you embrace in your love—your body, your lover, and beyond—the greater the bliss of your loving. Once you are sensitive to your inner feelings and sensations during sex, remember to become equally sensitive to your partner's.

Stay with him in love. Even when you are hurt, weeping, angry, or in the middle of a catastrophically blissful orgasm, stay with him. Do not close, withdraw, or hide. Practicing love means staying in direct relationship—eye to eye, body to body, breath to breath—as much as possible during sex, including when you are bursting with pleasure, shyness, fear, or shame. There are times to close your eyes and go inward, but most often remember to go out, not in. Stay in relationship with your lover through thick and thin and ouch and ooh; in this way love works its deepest magic.

II

ALWAYS MAKE LOVE
WITH THE DIVINE

*I am entering her from behind. Her ass is gorgeous. I love the
way her back narrows into a slender waist, and then widens out
into her full hips and butt. I reach around and hold her breasts.*

*Suddenly I realize that I have become absorbed in her body.
My attention has been reduced to the adoration of her form.*

*There is nothing wrong with this. She is beautiful. Her form
makes me happy. But I have forgotten the larger picture. I've
forgotten the expanse of awareness that is the foundation of this
moment. I've forgotten the depth of love that is the basis of our
sexing. I have been reduced merely to adoring her body.*

*And so, without taking my attention away from her
sumptuous form as we make love, I deepen it. I feel through
my joy, through the space around my joy, through her body, and
through the space around her body. I feel through and through
the openness of love that is alive as us. I rest wide as the
cognizant openness of this moment. And all the while her ass is
still as beautiful.*

*She presses closer to me, offering herself to me for deeper
penetration. The sweat from my chest runs down my belly, into the
crack of her rounded butt, and then slowly, in rivulets, down the
inside of her flushed thighs.*

We breathe deeply, receiving the divine through every pore on the inhale, giving ourselves to the divine through every pore on the exhale. We breathe the entire moment—its colors, smells, sounds, heat, space, and boundless depth—as the moment breathes us. We sex in the open of no difference, vanished in love, making love, being made by love.

While having sex, be careful not to allow your attention to be narrowed for too long. It is easy to focus on a perky nipple, a luscious kiss, or inflamed genitalia. It is easy to reduce consciousness to the targeting of attention. But the consciousness that is your deepest truth is much more than this.

What is true of you at heart is always true of you. The deliciousness of sex need not distract you from the depth of your being, but can provide you with a doorway to feel more deeply into it. Sex can loosen the blocks of energy in your body and emotions and liberate your attention from mundanities so that you are free to feel what is real and profoundly true—through and through—rather than merely focusing on one event and experience after another.

Bliss and pleasure and lips and thrust are good. But they are only fleeting wisps, as gone as all your past sex is now.

In moments of sexual intensity, practice to recognize what is *always* true, what is always the depth of this moment. You make love through, not merely to, your bodies. Your bodies are simply vehicles through which to feel and express your deepest truth, your unbounded openness, your divine nature, the love who you are.

Practice being love, using the sexual occasion to make love with love through the body—embracing, feeling into, inhaling, exhaling, penetrating, and being penetrated by divine love. This is an actual practice to be consciously engaged during sex, without avoiding the rainbow of fleshy pleasure that also hangs wet in the space of love. Do it nasty, do it fine, but always feel through the colors of desire and make love with love divine.

FOR HIM

For many men for most of their lives, sex is their actual religion. In church, their attention is occupied not by the sermon, but by the exotic woman with the nice legs two pews over. They spend more time watching women's bodies on the street and bikinied actresses on TV than contemplating the glory of God.

At a strip joint, they may shout their praises, "Oh my God! You're unbelievable! Yes! You're fantastic!" And in bed, too, orgasming with their woman, "Oh my God! My God, I love you." Yet, outside of the sexual realm, most men remain uncommitted in their praise of the divine mystery alive as all.

Divine praise during sex is not an accident. Our bodies are built so that sex stimulates our energies and opens our hearts. Our sense of aliveness is heightened, our perception of beauty and perfection is glorified. Sexual exultation is as close as most of us get to religious awe.

If we are too obstructed physically or are afraid of deep love in relationship, then money may become our religion. But sex is a more primal possibility for the bliss we hope our lives can give us. Sex affords us the opportunity for letting go of ourselves without reservation and merging with our woman in pleasure and love.

This feeling of two merging into one is the epitome of sacred and secular pleasure. As babies we merged with our mother. As children we merged with our toys and friends. As teenagers we merged with our thoughts, drugs, cars, and music. As adults we merge with the slope while we ski, with the road while we drive, with our children while we hold them, with the TV while we relax, and with our hobbies as we are absorbed in them. But few of us experience the intensity of pleasure and love anywhere else as consistently as we do during good sex.

Because sex and its pleasures are so intense, some people substitute the communion afforded by sex for divine communion. As long as genital stimulation is more pleasurable than our experience of deep being, our sex lives will take precedence over our spiritual lives. We will devote more energy to sexual pleasure than to the bliss of spiritual depth.

You can suck your woman's breast and feel blissful like a baby merging with his mother. This is comfortable and safe but not very deep. You can merge with your woman's waves of orgasmic delight and feel the same kind of bliss you would while surfing the ocean or getting a great massage, but it doesn't last too long. You can merge emotionally with your woman, relishing each other's feelings in a kind of emotional telepathy of vulnerable sharing. The pleasure of this openness and trust can be truly sublime, but it is difficult to enjoy this merger while at the office the next day.

Merging with the divine—the mystery and depth of open being— has very little to do with infantile oneness, losing yourself in athletic flow, or merging with your woman emotionally. Whereas all these mergers are with a particular state of pleasure, excitement, or empathy, divine merger is not with any particular state at all, but with the deep openness of *all* states.

Suppose you have sex with your woman. Your body merges with hers. Your emotions merge. You move and feel together as one. This can be extremely pleasurable, but temporary. The flow can be ruined by a bad fart or a sudden foot cramp. You can remember a phone call you were supposed to make earlier but didn't. Your woman can tell you about wrecking the car, or your children can knock on your bedroom door. Physical and emotional bliss are easily broken. Divine bliss is not.

Practice opening as the depth of being in the midst of sex. Then, spiritual bliss will include and exceed the merely sexual. If you have made use of sexual openness to help you relax as the depth of being, then bad smells and raucous children only change the landscape of experience, not the depth of bliss.

There are deep and shallow blisses. Most people settle for the shallower ones. The more shallow a bliss is, the more it can be disturbed. A good game of golf or watching your angelic children sound asleep can be truly blissful. But this kind of bliss is totally dependent on conditions. A cold, wet, lousy game of golf is hardly blissful. A child who resists going to sleep night after night can be quite a test of patience.

With practice, we relax as an openness that is not dependent on conditions. As beginners, it is easier to relax as openness under certain conditions—such as during meditation, in beautiful natural surroundings, feeling the unconditional love of our children, or during fantastic sex with an adoring lover—but these are only portals into a depth that is always here, that is our true nature, regardless of conditions. We might realize this depth and enjoy its bliss in a moment of grace or when conditions are just right, but then we can practice realizing this depth over and over, when things are good or bad.

One measure of your depth of spiritual practice is this: throughout what range of conditions do you remain aware of and relaxed as the bliss of your deepest being? The story of Jesus says his heart was wide open in love even while being crucified. Tibetan monks in prison and Jews in concentration camps have reported deep compassion and spiritual openness while enduring the most excruciating tortures.

True spiritual depth, true divine freedom, requires practicing the recognition of your deepest nature in every moment, while being pleasurized or tormented. Feel through every condition and merge with divine openness—your true nature, the true nature of everyone and everything—over and over, until conditions no longer keep you distracted into the shallow events of life, which are always changing.

This is a very different kind of merger than that of an infant or an athlete. It is not dependent on a breast full of milk or a sunny day. As divine openness, you are alive as what is already blissful, right here and right now, without needing to change anything. But you can forget this depth of being by habitually locking on to the shallow changes that catch your attention: bowel movements and taxes, deadlines and bedtimes, fantasies, thoughts, hopes, and fears.

Your attention is absorbed in things that change, and thus your deep bliss remains undiscovered. You won't sink into the depth of bliss until you are ready. As long as the pleasure you get from the ups and downs of money, TV, work, family, and sex is greater than the pleasure you have thus far experienced relaxing as the inherent openness of being, then you will continue attending to the more superficial aspects of life rather than the deep.

Eventually—as you earn and forfeit money, care for and lose family, come and go sexually—you may suffer the shallow changes of life enough to loosen your attention. You may "fall through" conditions into the eternal depth of being. Then, free as the openness of deep bliss, it will be as if nothing has ever happened at all, even in the midst of a life full of happening.

FOR HER

Divinity schminity. If you don't feel deep love in your heart and body, who cares if you are living a devout spiritual life or debasing yourself, eating chocolate with a lover wrapped in furs? The feminine gravitates toward whatever feels like love, whether it is ultimately healthy or not. An abusive man who passionately ravishes you into multiple orgasms and buys you diamonds and gold can be more attractive than a caring and supportive man who ejaculates prematurely, hates giving oral sex, and is stingy with his money.

The divine doesn't mean anything to you unless you feel it in your body. If you don't, then you will substitute sex, food, shopping, and other sensual pleasures for the divine. You will try to fill yourself with emotions, flavors, and textures if you are not already full of love. What do you turn to when you feel empty inside? Coffee and conversation, or the bliss of divine love?

The masculine is attracted to the freedom beyond experience, but the feminine is filled by love transmitted through relationship. Sexual "nothingness" is hardly attractive to most women, though men seek it every day through orgasmic release. Likewise, experiencing the spaciousness of divine freedom doesn't pique a woman's interest as much as feeling divine force passionately enter her heart and ripple through her body like waves of intense love more pleasurable than any orgasm she's ever had.

You especially enjoy love in embrace with a man who loves you, or with friends and family. Relational ecstasy is the genius of the feminine. Relational blessing is the domain of the feminine divine. The joy of family, the colorful web of life on earth, the circle of friends and community—the feminine divine is most strongly expressed through the body in relationship.

If a woman cannot feel the divine in her body, then these relationships become her hopeful resort rather than the recipients of her blessing. She attempts to be satisfied by filling her life with family joys *rather* than opening as divine bliss. She settles for the sights and sounds of a walk by the lake *rather* than receiving the ravishing force of divine energy deep into her body. She devotes her time to community and friends *rather* than swooning in the divine love that swells as all bodies.

Devoid of a deep heart-connection to the divine, her natural feminine energy may begin to dry up even if she is surrounded by friends and family. Disconnected from the deep source of joy and love she yearns for, her body may begin to wither. Her genitals or breasts are often the first areas to suffer the lack of deeply sourced feminine energy, showing signs of discomfort or disease.

Eventually, she may collapse into a sense of emptiness and bodily vacancy that not even her family—let alone a double cappuccino and chocolate truffle—can fill. Chronically depressed and weary, she may seek to simulate a sense of devotional surrender by opening herself to abuse or self-abuse rather than to divine love.

However, when you are filled with divine love—when your body is overflowing with abundant light and bliss—then your family, the earth, and your community are all recipients of your blessing force. Your body communicates power, relaxation, and joy. Your vagina knows pleasure. Your face shines devotion. Your limbs move with the grace of certain love.

Sexually, your body relaxes in the full range of divine expressions, including all forms of life in heaven and on earth. You can be an angel, smiling serenely between the sheets. You can be a tiger, pouncing on your man and clawing him into submission. You can be a child, cuddling in innocence. You can be a demoness, tearing your man apart. You can be a whore, making him beg for more. You can be a sorceress, sucking the energy out of his gut with a few choice words or gestures. You can be a goddess, revealing more love to your man than he has ever felt before.

When you open to the divine, your body opens. Your energy flows with fullness, pleasure, and strength, including your sexual energy, whether you are celibate or sexually active, married or single. Your energetic flow is made as large as the power in your heart.

Most men, however, tend to withdraw energy from their body and their sexuality as they become more spiritually oriented. Therefore, in general, as you and your man grow spiritually, you may become more sexually powerful as your man becomes less sexually energetic. It doesn't have to be this way, but this is how it often turns out.

Since a woman's heart and genitals are directly connected, when her heart opens, her entire body flows with love-energy, including her genitals. Her sexuality is full of genuine love and care. Because a man's heart and genitals are often disconnected, his heart may be wide open and yet his body may remain limp and empty, or simply lusty without any emotional connection to his lover. His genitals may still "have a mind of their own" unless he has practiced sufficiently to connect them with his open heart.

When a woman grows spiritually, love-energy fills her body naturally; in fact, her spiritual growth is largely a matter of consciously practicing to receive love-energy into every part of her body, so that her body opens, relaxes, and flows powerfully as an expression of deep love-energy. Most men find it more convenient to ignore their body's energy—as well as their family's, their community's, and the earth's.

The spiritual doorway for most men is through their mind. For most women it is through their body, which is perhaps why relatively few spiritual texts have been penned throughout history by women. Spiritual texts are often a primary means to carry men's attention to the bliss of the divine, but women are more often transported via the revelation of love-bliss through the openness of their body, via means such as dance, touch, sexuality, childbirth, and communion with nature.

The feminine naturally orients toward the flow of fullness or love; the masculine toward release or freedom. Spiritual growth is lopsided unless it enlightens our capacity for bodily love as well as our ability to let go of our body in freedom. Neither aspect of divinity—neither love nor freedom, life nor death, the energy of the body nor the space of awareness—can be ignored for long without serious imbalances occurring.

In recent history, men and masculine versions of divinity—God "out there"—have taught us much about spiritual life. A new cycle seems to be emerging, during which we will learn much from women and feminine versions of the sacred grounded in the fullest divinization of the body, family, community, earth, and sex.

Meanwhile, we can't throw out the masculine; that would make us as lopsided as we have become by ignoring the feminine. Sacred sex, for instance, is as much about deep pleasure as it is about death or letting go. It involves massive flows of bodily energy and relational love as well as feeling through the energy and yielding as a timeless openness in which the body is transparent.

Since their hearts and genitals are more likely to be connected, women are more naturally inclined to grow sexually than are men. Women are more at home in the realm of pleasure, energy, emotion, and relationship. But without the masculine penetration of consciousness, feminine sex can tend to emphasize sensual pleasure and emotional connection *only*, without depth to the point of vanishment in the openness of love's bliss.

These days, some women have become as disembodied as the average man, lost in a world of projects, plans, goals, thoughts, and schedules—one-pointed, rigid, and relatively pleasureless. For these women, finding the divine starts with finding their body, feeling their breath, freeing their emotions, and allowing themselves to be wracked with unbearable pleasure. Dance, massage, and yoga are a few of the ways to start this process.

Sex is sometimes the last place you are willing to practice receiving the divine in all your parts. You may allow yourself to dance full of sweaty ecstasy. You may welcome your children to fill you with abundant joy. You may invite your friends to be a constant source of love and support. Yet, in bed with your man, you suddenly become aware of your limitations—and of his. Sex is usually where you can feel your energetic knots most clearly: which parts of your body are open or resistant to orgasmic pleasure? Sex is where you can feel how full or empty of love you are: when your lover rejects you in some way, does your heart remain open in hurt or do you shut it down?

Sex is often the place you most desire and resist the infiltration of divine love. Until you are ready, you will give priority to all kinds of needs rather than your deep desire to live as a body of love. You probably put much more energy into learning to communicate with your man than into learning to breathe love's bliss through your vagina. You probably are more concerned about whether your man desires you than whether you are surrendering your body open as the fullness of divine love-radiance.

You are probably much more attached to your lover, friends, and family as sources of comforting love than you are devoted to living with them *as* the force of love—that is, until a crisis occurs in your heart. Your man may leave you, your children may turn from you or perish, or you may simply realize that you want to give and receive more love than your body and emotions presently allow: your sexual energy is blocked, your bad moods collapse the household, you snap at your children because your deep heart is frustrated. Or maybe no specific crisis happens in your external life, but due to the inexorable force of deep yearning, you find yourself wanting to devote more time to surrendering your heart and body open in the flow of deep bliss.

There are plenty of ways to do it, from Buddhism to Christianity, from gardening to dancing, from celibacy to raising a family. However you choose to practice opening, do not ignore your sexuality. It can be a key to incarnating love-energy throughout your body, and therefore can serve your capacity to flourish spiritually while blessing others with your heart-force of radiance and love.

12

WHEN YOUR PARTNER HURTS YOU, GIVE YOUR PARTNER LOVE

I hadn't seen her for a long time. I missed her. My heart yearned for her. My body desired her. I knew she would be back from her trip this day, and I was awaiting her call.

She called. She told me she was back. She had a lot of work to do. She couldn't see me until tomorrow.

She came over the next day. She was beautiful. We embraced each other and wept. We held each other for a long time. We lay down, she gave me a wonderful massage, and I caressed her gently. Then, abruptly, she told me she had errands to run and had to leave.

My heart was ripped. We were so open, so loving, why the sudden change? She told me she had just looked at the clock, noticed the time, and now really had some important things to do.

I knew that, like everyone, she occasionally popped out of her heart into her head and needlessly busied herself with tense and superficial thoughts and tasks. But, this time, I could feel my own neediness. I really expected her to fulfill me. And she would not. Could not. Never would, it seemed.

The next day she called and told me how much she loved me. Then she told me she would be spending the evening out with friends. Didn't she know how bad I wanted to see her? Didn't she know how much I missed her?

I decided not to insist on anything. Although she might have been avoiding love and intimacy with me, I most strongly felt my own neediness for her love. I felt my own need for a "mommy," for a partner who would always be there for me, upon whom I could depend for love.

My heart was aching. When I finally did see her I did my best to give her love, rather than allowing my need for her love to collapse me. She felt my wounded heart and persistence in love. She opened into my rawness. Tears came to our eyes as she melted against me. We were totally undefended, our bodies merging into one, our hearts melding without separation. Our loving was original joy.

Of course, in a few hours, she got up and told me she had other plans for the evening. Again, I could feel a sense of betrayal welling up inside me. How could she be so cold when we had just been so loving?

This cycle continued. Eventually, I was walking around heart-exposed, tender, expecting no fulfillment. My need for love that remained unmet was now obvious to me as a need that could not be met by any woman. The only "woman" who could meet my need for love was the one who is always appearing. This "she" is the very experience of this moment. The form of this "lady" is the shape of this moment. "She" is always dancing as whatever sights, sounds, textures, thoughts, and emotions flicker in the field of consciousness. And love is the music that dances her.

My misplaced desire for perfect unity, for the realization of utter non-separation, had led me to believe that union with my lover could fulfill me. But no matter how deeply I might merge with her or any woman, in other moments we would be separate. Inevitably, we would hurt or close to each other in moments, and finally leave each other, if only at death.

Her momentary love for me, whether she expresses it a lot or
a little, is not enough to quench my deepest need. My only option
is to practice love itself: opening as love, being love, giving love,
without chasing after the mirage of her promise. Opening as love
most fully, I receive this moment as my lover, feeling through "her"
in our unity, transparent in the space of love's One. My heart is
spread home and no longer waits for future relief.

One of the basic lessons of spiritual growth occurs when you realize that you will never be fulfilled for very long or very deeply by anything in life. Even things you work really hard for, when you get them, are just another moment. There are some tremendous moments of happiness in life, but they pass. And even while they last, there is always the tension and fear that they might not last too much longer.

Your lover is a concentrated dose of this lesson. He or she will never truly fulfill you—not for good, and not even that deeply in the best of times. The depth of love you might share is quite fragile, so that a wrong word or even a misinterpreted gesture can collapse the most sublime moment into a craving hole of hurt and need.

At first this seems to be bad news—a good excuse for having a few drinks, or eating a box of cookies. But getting this news is crucial. It allows you to stop wasting time in the hope of being fulfilled once and for all by relational love. Instead, you can devote your relationship—and your entire life—to realizing the truth of this and every moment: this moment is spacious, full, aware, and luminous, regardless of the love you feel you are getting or not.

In any moment, even if you are not being treated like you wish you were, you can do love and give love because you *are* love. You are consciousness alive as love, dancing as the fullness of this moment. You are already one with the love you seek. By aligning your breath, body, and mind with this truth of love, your life becomes a vehicle through which love can enter the world and your relationship.

If you remain closed when you are hurt, love doesn't have a chance. Your practice of openness, however, even when you are hurt, gives love a channel through which to infuse the moment, including difficult moments of relationship.

How do you practice love when you are hurt, afraid, or angry? First, relax your entire body. Let go of all your tension, especially any stress in the front of your body. While breathing fully and smoothly, relax your belly, chest, throat, and face. It's fine if you cry or yell, just return to a full, open breath and relaxed body—especially a soft belly and chest—as soon as you are able.

If possible, look directly into your lover's eyes. As you continue breathing fully and easefully, feel as if you are breathing your lover. Feel as if you are breathing his or her breath. Then, feel as if you are breathing *through* your lover. Be willing to experience your lover's pain, anger, hurt, fear, and tension. Inhale it all into your body and then release it all, exhaling love into and through your partner.

It's fine to cry or tremble, but do your best not to collapse. Keep your body open and softly relaxed. Practice keeping your breath and body full in this way even if your emotional pain makes you want to close your heart and cave in your chest. Keep your heart and body open through the openness of your breath.

With every breath, feel the entire room—in front of you and behind you, to your left and right, above and below you—and use your breath to "carry" love outward from your heart, spreading out in all directions, pervading and embracing the entire room and your partner.

In this way, practice receiving your lover, breathing love, giving love, and magnifying love, especially in the midst of your hurt. When your lover denies you and your heart is torn apart, make love by breathing love. Make love through your every action. Through each word. Through your tears and smiles. And, if the occasion should become appropriate, make love sexually in this way, through open breath and feeling.

This practice can be torturous. It doesn't allow you to curl up into yourself and mope. It prevents your childish pout from taking hold. When your heart is really ragged and ripped, to stay open and give love feels like you are going to die. Nevertheless, the practice is actually to give love through your breath, body, and feeling even when all you want to do is close down and be given love, comfort, and adoration.

You will never be given enough love so that you no longer want more. You want love because you have misplaced your attention, and you are starving. You attend to events and relationships in the hope that they will eventually fulfill you once and for all. They won't. Instead, attend *through* events and relationships until you notice what is always true. Attend through them until you can feel the ever-present openness in which they take place. Feel through your pain and your pleasure, feel through your angry lover and your day at work, until the openness of feeling itself is more noticed than the things you are feeling through.

What is the nature of your primal openness? How spacious does it feel compared to the release you wish for at work? How full does it feel compared to the love you hope to receive from your lover? How intimate is this openness compared to your lover's body?

All substitutes dissolve when you rest open as love. They reappear, but with no need to fulfill. Rather, your work and your lover are either enjoyments of openness or tests of your capacity to breathe love and be love even when your personal needs are unmet. Your work and your lover are like your own body, the form of your life, the form you have been given to infuse with love for as long as it lasts. It all rots in the end, and it even stinks a little now. To expect it to fulfill you is foolish.

When your lover denies your needs, do not deny love. Open your body. Breathe love, radiate love, pervade all space with love. In doing so, you live the truth that you *are* love, and you allow love to continually infuse your relationship even if pain is the texture of the present moment. It takes time to work out the stuff that comes up between you and your lover. As the drama of your relationship (or your career) unfolds through time, remember that this practice of love is always available—and expressive of your deepest truth—right now.

FOR HIM

Imagine that your woman is waiting for you to have sex. She stares at you with the look in her eyes that says she really wants you badly. Her desire turns you on. Her sexual openness excites you. You hug each other and she rubs herself against you. She falls to her knees, grabs your penis, and takes it in her mouth. You ejaculate almost immediately. She's upset you came so fast. You feel bad, too. What to do?

Practice fullness even when you feel depleted or ashamed. What your woman really wants from you sexually is to be taken to another place, to feel your presence and be filled by your love so she can trust you and surrender utterly in full-bodied bliss. You don't need an erect penis to do this, although filling her with your penis—in addition to your consciousness and passion—is a delightful way to overwhelm her in love.

With or without an erection, you can find the fullness that you *are* already and transmit it through your whole body. It's one thing to fake it and act strong even when you are feeling weak inside. It's another thing to locate the depth of your being and relax as it. Allow its deep energy to manifest through your breath and body. Then, pervade your woman with this love-energy. Such practice is always possible, even when you are feeling physically defeated or emotionally down.

Locate the beating of your heart. Actually feel each beat begin and end. Notice that "you" don't have anything to do with your heartbeat; it goes on whether you are sleeping or awake, whether you are a sexual adept or failure.

Notice your thoughts about ejaculating so soon. Feel your thoughts moving through your mind like leaves in the wind. Instead of being wrapped up in your thoughts, simply notice them come and go.

Where do you feel your sense of failure? Is it in your belly? Your chest? Does it have the flowing amorphous energy of an emotion or the linear conceptual clarity of a thought?

How is your woman reacting? Does she seem open in love or closed and angry? Where in her body is she holding tension?

Witness the beating of your heart, the coming and going of your thoughts and emotions, the tensions in your body and in your woman's. You don't have absolute control over any of it. Who knows why you ejaculated so soon? Maybe you ate too much meat or salt. Maybe you were nervous or needed to release tension. Maybe you have a lot to learn about sexual loving. Right now, it doesn't matter. What matters is whether your presence is full.

Your presence is determined by how relaxed you are in the fullness of your being. Are you shrinking, curling inward, caving your chest, shortening your breath, averting your eyes? All of these actions serve to lessen the extent to which the fullness of your being can flow through your body—and this is the erection your woman wants most.

Men know they are "supposed to be strong." It is an inner feeling against which they often measure their worth as a man. There are three stages to this growth in masculine strength.

In the first stage, a man wants to be strong in other people's eyes.

He tries to walk and talk and act in whatever way he thinks others will consider powerful.

In the second stage, a man seeks inner strength. He often tries to "do things his own way" because to listen to others would be to admit his dependency on them. He realizes that whether others approve of him or not, he's got to be true to his own thoughts and emotions. He develops an inner confidence that gives him strength regardless of what others tell him. He no longer cares so much how he looks. He doesn't act with macho posturing and stoic bravura like in the first stage. Rather, he is calm and equitable. This kind of inner strength is based on self-knowledge: he knows his limits and his gifts, and he lives as true to his own beliefs as he can, regardless of how he is viewed by others.

In the third stage, a man opens to the strength inherent in deep being. To do this, he opens beyond what others think of him—as well as what he thinks of himself. Even self-confidence is an obstruction to relaxing as the force of open consciousness. His own beliefs and opinions—which guided his second-stage life—become as if transparent in the fullness of deep being.

This effortless strength is as obvious and recognizable as first-stage macho posturing and second-stage integrity and self-confidence. A man who is practicing third-stage strength is trustable because his actions are not influencable from the outside or the inside; even his own sense of accomplishment or failure can't derail him from living spontaneously as the love-force flowing from the depths of his being.

Sex to a first-stage man is about "acting like a man." Therefore, premature ejaculation is very embarrassing—not something he wants to talk about.

Sex to a second-stage man is about sharing and honesty. If he ejaculates too soon, he is not afraid to talk about it. He can find other ways to please his woman sexually, through oral sex, caressing, massage, and even using sex toys. His confidence is not deflated because he knows that he has other things to offer his woman besides his erect penis. She values his emotional sharing, care, sensuality, humor, and companionship as much as his sexual capacity. Besides, she secretly enjoys all the attention that he lavishes on her when he ejaculates too soon.

Sex to a third-stage man is about surrendering the whole body to the force of consciousness and allowing the depth of being to pervade through his body and breath, into his woman, and beyond, as love. If he ejaculates too soon, he and his woman may not even notice. The depth of his presence and the strength of his love are not depleted, for they are rooted in consciousness, not physiological arousal. His attention remains free of concern—his own and his woman's. He can continue to ravish his woman, penetrating her heart and invading her body with his passionate love-force. Her orgasmic response may be just as full as if his erect penis was inside of her body.

In a first-stage moment, his energy would have collapsed in shame and his attention would have been occupied by fear that his woman may think him inadequate. In a second-stage moment, his energy would have gone into sharing with his woman sensually and emotionally while his attention was already concerned with how to improve his sexual capacity in the future.

A man practicing in the third stage sometimes experiences shame and is also concerned with improving his sexual capacities to share love with his woman—but his energy is not lessened and his attention is not absorbed by these things.

His unwavering presence isn't a matter of macho rigidity, a need to impress his woman, or self-confidence. It is rooted in the depth of being, rather than in an image of himself or a desire to connect with his woman. He may very well have an image of himself and also desire to connect with his woman, but these things do not compromise his practice of locating, relaxing as, breathing, and transmitting the consciousness or love that is deep being.

Even while your practice grows, you will still hurt when your woman ignores you, closes down to you, or laughs at your weaknesses. But the hurt just becomes part of your practice. Feel through it and relax as the depth of being, allowing your breath and body to be moved by depth, not by hurt.

You won't always be able to do this. Sometimes you just hurt too much. Your energy collapses and your attention gets trapped in misery. Continue to practice feeling through. Do your best to relax your belly and chest. Allow your breath to deepen. Loosen yourself as the space around the pain rather than allowing your attention to become locked in it. Feel your woman and breathe with her into greater openness.

Even if you continue to collapse and withdraw into your own sulk of shame or fear, practice this way. Practice even just a little bit. Relax a tiny bit more. Breathe a tad deeper. Listen to the farthest sounds you can hear to help liberate your attention from your own strife. Feel your woman's emotions and energy just a smidgen more than you were a moment ago. Many tiny moments of practice add up to enormous transformations over time.

To be strong as a man is to give love even when you feel hurt. Not because you want to look good, and not because you will feel that you are growing if you do so, but because *not* to love is more painful than practicing to relax as love. As you grow, the love springing from the depth of your being demands to flow strong, regardless of how much you or your woman would rather slump and take a break or sit down and have a civilized chat. The tide of this love is threatening as long as you hold on to the security of another's love or your self-love. But when you are ready to grow beyond the false safety of dependence or independence, the free force of unbound love is the river that will move you.

FOR HER

Most men are not at home in their bodies or emotions. They need to be attracted into life and relationship, and you are probably the paramount source of your man's attraction. He is attracted into the openness of your love and the radiance of your feminine energy. Among his favorite forms of feminine energy are probably the nurturing energy of "mother" and the sexy energy of "whore." He is attracted to many other aspects of you, but these are among the energies that most men feel lacking in their lives. They want to be sustained and aroused, rejuvenated and seduced.

But when your man does something that lacks integrity, when he doesn't carry through with what he tells you, for instance, then you feel hurt, angry, and frustrated. If he doesn't do what he says he's going to do, then you can't trust him fully. You can't let down your guard. You won't allow yourself to fully surrender with him sexually. Nor will you feel inclined to feed him with your mother energy or ravish him like a hungry vixen. You will probably feel more inclined to lop his head off.

This too is one of the natural energies of the divine feminine. In effect, this energy is saying to your man, "I know you are capable of greatness. I know how deep and strong you are. I won't tolerate your lack of commitment and your lies. I won't tolerate your backsliding. Live up to your own fullness or I'll have no choice but to destroy you and your false weakness!"

When your man hurts you because he lacks direction, integrity, or clarity, you can love him without supporting his weaknesses. Loving your partner when he hurts you *includes* not tolerating his bullshit. Don't surrender to his hurtful ways; surrender to the love that lives as you and him. And while you are flowing as love, you may also be very angry and demanding of your man's best.

You are exquisitely sensitive to your man's alignment with his own truth. You know when he is betraying himself—and you—before he knows. You feel the slinkiness in his posture. You hear the ambiguity in his voice. You know he is deceiving himself before he is aware of anything. Your feedback can be a great gift to him.

He will only trust your feedback if he feels your openness as love. You can't disconnect from the love deep in your heart, tense your body in fear and anger, and then expect that he will believe what you say. He'll think you have some kind of problem. He'll either criticize you or try to fix you instead of hearing the reality of your communication. Your unlove will hurt him and he will close even more.

To help your man sense when he is "off" you must remain full in love or he will attribute your feedback to your own problems. When your man has hurt you, keep your breath full and deep, as if walking in a garden enjoying the scent of the flowers. Keep your body as relaxed as possible, especially your belly and chest, as if you were pressed against your lover's naked chest. Feel into your man and find the deep place in him that you *do* trust and that you hope will come more to the fore. Tell him about this place in him that you trust. Show him love through your open body and breath. Tell him how you lose some of your trust when he acts a certain way.

Remember that he probably doesn't know what you are talking about. He probably can't feel his own weaknesses as easily as you can feel them. He probably feels he is doing his best in the given situation. But what you are talking about is more likely *how* he is going about doing something rather than *what* he is doing. You can feel when his actions are no longer aligned with his truth. You can feel when he hides his weakness from himself, and that scares you. You can't trust him. Nor should you.

Don't tolerate your man's bullshit, but always practice love by cultivating the fullness of love in your body. It is very difficult to keep your body and breath open and full when your man has betrayed your trust; it is just as difficult for him to remain open and receive your criticism—especially when he can see that you are coming from a place of closure rather than love. So, practice communicating from a place of love, even if you are also, at the same time, screaming wildly with rage. When you are open, then your love can be expressed as compassionate anger, an anger without hatred.

With practice, love flows freely through your body and breath even when you are angry, frustrated, happy, excited, shut down, or feeling betrayed. Love embraces all emotions and shines through them, expressing itself through the *full* spectrum of emotional energy.

You and your man can both practice living as love while you are hurt. While doing so, you will learn how to breathe and relax as love even when you feel betrayed. Ultimately, as you grow in your capacity to live love through your body, you will no longer *depend* on your man to "be there for you." He will no longer *depend* on you to give him comfort and rejuvenation. These are real gifts when they are given and received freely, but when your ability to relax in the bliss of love depends on them, then they become expectations that limit growth.

If your man wants the energetic colors of "mother" and "sex goddess" to flow freely through your body, he's going to have to learn to deal with all your other free energies, too. This includes your "wild woman" energy that won't settle for anything less than a man willing to examine his faults, find humor in them, make whatever changes are necessary, and live a life committed to practicing deep love and undiminished presence—without collapsing when you don't feel moved to nurse him with dinner or coddle his genitals.

13

FEEL THROUGH
THE TENSION
OF ATTENTION

*We have been making love for about half an hour. Our energies
are flowing fully. Our hearts are open. The front of our bodies
are soft and pressing against each other. Our breath feels like one
breath. We surrender more deeply, and the boundaries of our bodies
become diffuse.*

*The atoms of our flesh and bones spread out in space. Thoughts
feel like waves of space. Attention itself feels like a tension in the
open space of consciousness.*

*I can attend to many things while we make love: The
commingling of our breath. The sweat squishing between my chest
and her breasts. The love I feel in her heart and see in her eyes.
The hot merger of our genitals. All these experiences can be objects
of my attention. Yet, this attention feels like a tension. The very
attention to experience feels like a kind of tension, a collecting
of space into a bundle of form: a breast, a sensation of heat, an
emotional feeling.*

*Who I am, most deeply, is not this attention. This attention—
and the whole sexual experience that attention carves in the space
of consciousness—takes place within the dimensionless openness
who I am. The blissful open of being is not a thing that can come
and go, but I can forget it or ignore it. I can be distracted by the*

things of attention, by tits and ass and money and pain. I end up assuming I am like these things, solid, limited, and temporary. I become tense and afraid because I forget who I am most deeply.

Minutes, hours, days sometimes go by, and I can be totally lost in one experience after another, working, eating, sexing, and fretting without profoundly relaxing as the infinite depth of being that I am. In order to not get lost in merely attending to experiences, I practice recognizing and relaxing as who I am most fundamentally, whatever experience waves in its deep.

This is especially true during sex. Sex seems to be the summary of everything I want to experience, everything to which I want to attend. It is the most seducing illusion, promising fundamental fulfillment, always around the corner. But, as I rediscover again and again, no experience, even the most pleasurable sexual experience possible, is completely fulfilling. It doesn't last. And, even while it does last, it is always more shallow—and threatened by loss—than I hoped.

When a hoped for moment of experience finally comes—the peak of orgasm, for instance—it's just another swift moment of experience, a tension in the midst of open being. A sexual experience might feel great. Or it might feel lousy. But open being, the bliss who I really am, who my lover really is, doesn't change because of any experience, good or bad. And this openness of love—unlimited, spontaneously alive, and cognizant—is the nature of every single moment, now and in the future, while sitting on the toilet or while crying with my lover.

Paying close attention to all your sensations and to your lover during sex is a good start. But this practice can actually get very depressing! Nothing amounts to much, nothing lasts, and everything is always changing. Unless you realize love, it is easy to mistake attentive clarity for a deeper practice.

Beyond bare attention is the mystery of love: the effulgence of bliss as all forms. Naked as this moment, with no edges, you are alive as love, as the open of being. Being undone in this openness is the ultimate orgasm, leaving not a trace, as if nothing has ever happened at all and love is the only history.

Attention is a tool, an action, a limit. The open of love is what is, whether attention acts one way or another or not at all. And sex is a primary darling of attention. To feel through attention during sex is to be free in the midst of one of the strongest, most attractive snares of attention, so that your true depth may burgeon outward through the flesh of the moment.

FOR HIM

What you do with your attention determines the quality of your life. Three men in the exact same circumstance—a brothel, for instance—would have different experiences depending on where they placed their attention.

One man might pay attention to his thoughts: "What if my wife finds out? What if I get a disease? I wonder how much this is going to cost." The texture of his experience is anxious, tense, and jittery.

Another man's attention might be absorbed in his visual perception: "Check out that tall woman in the corner dressed in red leather. Wow! Look at the tits on that woman covered in glitter! Man, those two blondes dancing together are gorgeous!" His experience is exciting, enlivening, and full of color.

The other man's attention might be focused on genitals: "I'll bet she's really tight. I'd like to put it in her really deep. I'll bet she could milk me with the muscles of her tight pussy." The texture of his experience is throbbing, animalistic, urgent.

Where you put your attention determines how you feel, to yourself and others. Women are especially sensitive to where a man's attention goes. If he is wrapped up in his own thoughts, she feels it. If he is checking out all the other women, she feels it. If he is a "walking genital," she feels it.

The primary quality that makes a man attractive to women is the freedom of his attention. When his attention is not tightly bound to this or that, then the force of his consciousness is free to transmit as the strength of his presence. When a woman walks into a room full of people, she quickly notices the man with the most presence and freedom, just as easily as you would notice the most radiant woman.

Men, too, can feel your presence or lack of it. If your attention is free, not convoluted and scattered, then men can trust you. But men won't trust you as much if you are "not all there" because you are distracted by your thoughts, emotions, or genital need. A large part of business success is based on how trustable you seem to others. Most men who succeed at business are very present; you can trust that their attention is free enough to focus on the task at hand and carry through with it. Their depth of commitment and clarity is easily felt.

The more free a man's attention is, the more he can handle in life. The attention of some men is so trapped that they can barely deal with waking up on time, remembering to feed the cat, and doing what they are supposed to do at work all day. The attention of other men is more free. They decide to wake up early to practice their martial arts skills. On the way to work they narrate their latest project plans into a tape recorder, or meditate on openness. At work they not only do what they are supposed to do, they devise creative ways to improve their performance and bring humor and happiness into their co-workers' lives. All the while, the quality of their presence is strong and full, yet relaxed and spacious.

One way to look at spiritual growth is as a progressive liberation of your attention. The more free your attention is, the more free you are as a force of creativity and blessing in the world.

With practice, train your attention to take into account more and more with greater ease. Eventually, while having sex, you practice to notice your own thoughts; feel into your woman's emotional flows; sense the currents of energy moving through both of your bodies; enjoy her fragrance, the smoothness of her legs, and the fullness of her lips; open your heart to merge with her heart; breathe together; redirect your orgasm so it shoots up your spine and through your heart in a rush of colors and mind-blowing intensity; relax your attention to feel through your woman and outward through the room in all directions; collect the "field" of consciousness with your breath and penetrate your woman's soul with it; ravish your woman with the force of your deepest love; allow your love to move through your body, your woman's body, and outward to all beings; and recognize the open depth of being, moment by moment, resting as the spontaneous force of bliss that dances as you and your partner and everything else.

To do this, your attention can't be locked on to the unpaid bills waiting on your desk. Liberating your attention requires that you take care of unfinished business and continue to deal with the duties of your life as impeccably as possible. As you grow, you learn to take care of everyday details while simultaneously opening your attention to deeper things. In fact, you won't even be interested in deep sex until you have grown enough so that your attention is free and, in effect, you ask, "What's next? What's deeper? How can life and sex be even more fulfilling and free?"

Your attention is progressively trapped by deeper and more subtle things, and therefore the experiences of your life become deeper and more subtle as you grow spiritually. Any bozo can guzzle some wine and enjoy getting drunk; someone who has cultivated a taste in wines can pay attention to the fruity bouquet and the undertones of cinnamon, wonder whether the wine had matured long enough, and all the while also enjoy getting drunk. His attention is less constrained than a drunkard who is only concentrating on getting as much wine down his gullet as possible. In other words, a connoisseur's attention is trapped by more subtle enjoyments than is the drunkard's.

Spiritual growth is like becoming a connoisseur of awareness and its objects, which include your thoughts, feelings, sensations, perceptions, and emotions. As you grow, your attention is more and more free to notice very subtle things that most people don't. Other people who are less free in their attention think you have secret powers: how can you tell what someone else is thinking? Or, they think that you are crazy and imagining things, making it all up. After all, they can't sense the subtle energies and perceptions that you seem to enjoy, so either they are blind or you are crazy—and most people don't like to think of themselves as disadvantaged.

But even the more subtle things of life are eventually felt as a trap of attention—just like, over time, a pair of large breasts that you initially couldn't keep your eyes off of become more familiar, less exciting, and eventually boring. As you grow, you continue to feel, "So what? What's next? What's deeper and more free?" Eventually, the act of attention itself—attending to anything at all, no matter how subtle—is no longer very interesting. All the flavors and colors of life, even the ones that most people can't even sense, are simply not enough. You still feel trapped—exactly as you might feel trapped by a job that no longer interests you.

The only place to go that is more fulfilling is deeper. What is deeper than attention itself? Can you feel where attention comes from? What happens when you relax *as* the source of attention in the middle of a sexual occasion, while your attention is also moving toward your pulsing hard-on, your woman in the throes of ecstasy, and an emotional expanse that reverberates with everything from your childhood need for mommy to your darkest fantasies of rape and domination? Your practice will naturally answer these questions as you grow.

Eventually, everybody grows in their need to untrap their attention from whatever happens to be the focus of their life. The feeling of this need is underlying dissatisfaction.

When you feel that aspects of your life don't completely fulfill you, when the glow has worn off the things that used to really turn you on, it is time to move your attention to more subtle things. And when more subtle things no longer make life worth living, it is time to move your attention to deeper things yet. And when the deepest things no longer mean anything special to you, then allow yourself to feel even deeper than things, before attention makes a thing.

You can do this even while attention is involved with sexual things. Slowly, over years of leisurely practice, pleasure, and inevitable dissatisfaction, expand your capacity to open as deep being even while embracing and convulsing in sexual love. Allow the union of bliss and openness to alleviate the tension of attention.

FOR HER

Your man's attention is riveted by certain things that draw him in a specific direction, such as financial success, political freedom, or artistic expression. He is like a train headed down the tracks. If you want to go where his train is going, then get on; he's a good partner for you.

But if you are interested in going toward another direction, then the relationship isn't likely to work.

There are many things you can share with your man in a relationship. You can raise a family together, build a house, start a business, and work together for bettering the world in many ways. So it is good to choose a man who is interested in the same direction that you are. If you want to move toward creating a large family, for instance, it's best if your man does, too.

More subtle than your shared direction is the relative depth of shared attention: are your man's concerns as *deep* as you want your concerns to be? Even if you agree on how many children you want to raise, you won't be able to fully relax in intimacy together if his notion of parenting stops at making sure the children grow up to be able to support themselves and yours includes helping them develop a deep sense of compassion and universal love. You won't be able to trust him completely as a father, and at times your differing priorities will create seemingly unsolvable conflicts in the way you each parent your children.

Nor will you be able to fully enjoy sex with a man whose concerns are more shallow than yours. If your attention gravitates more deeply than your man's, then you won't trust him with your heart and body. The way he uses his attention—and therefore his "vibe" or his charisma and presence—will seem relatively superficial to you. You may not be totally clear on why you don't trust him. He may seem to be a good man. He means well, anyway. All you know is that you can't sexually open yourself as much as you would like to. You can't surrender with him absolutely. You don't trust that he will take you to the deep place you want to go.

Little turns your man on more than your trust of him, which means you can open deeply with him and give him the fullness of who you are. But if you don't trust your man's direction during the day, you won't open with him at night. If your attention gravitates more deeply than your man's, you won't want to surrender sexually with him. His "fuck" will feel superficial and won't satisfy what you know is possible in your heart. He will feel your reluctance to surrender and try to demand that you give him more sexually, though his demands will be fruitless. Over time, you may begin to feel disappointed, resentful, or bored with the entire relationship.

On the other hand, if his attention gravitates *more* deeply than you are interested, then the depth of his attention and commitment may threaten you. You want a more comfortable home; he would be willing to let any home go in order to take the next step dictated by the convictions of his heart. You want him to commit to spending more time with you; he will only spend time with you to the extent it allows him to fulfill the deepest purpose of his life, which includes but goes far beyond your relationship.

If you are with a man whose attention gravitates more deeply than yours, you will feel a constant pressure to open, grow, take more risks, and be more expressive of your true gifts. If you want to grow in depth, then the relationship can work out fine. But if you want to stay more or less as deep as you are, then you will be exhausted by feeling the constant demand of his forceful presence. It's not so much what he says to you but the way he lives his life that will threaten the emotional security you long for.

You can only "count on" a man to be concerned about his current depth of attention. If your heart yearns for a fulfillment that can only come with deep sharing and trust, but your man won't stop watching TV long enough to connect with you, you'll probably feel disappointed. You may find yourself wishing that his interests weren't so superficial. On the other hand, if his attention is on negotiating a peace settlement between two warring countries—or he is making plans to go on a month-long meditation retreat—and you want him to "care enough" about you to take you on a romantic getaway for a weekend, you may also be disappointed. You may wish his concerns weren't so deep.

If you want your relationship to work, make sure that where you want to go in your life is also where your man wants to go. Furthermore, it's best if the depth of your heart's motives matches the depth of your man's.

Direction and depth: these are the qualities in your man that will most determine how fulfilled you are in relationship with him. Many other factors certainly influence your enjoyment, including how your man smells, what kind of father he is, his level of income—everything from his height to his sexual style to whether he likes country-western music will influence the quality of your time together. But if your direction and depth do not match, then no degree of similar interests will make the relationship very fulfilling.

If he is going where you want to go in life, and his depth is as profound as you would like to live, then the relationship is workable regardless of how much your other interests jibe or not. Your lives can weave together in spiritual bliss, as well as in sexual embrace and emotional trust.

PART III
DESIRE

H ello, my friend," Mykonos said when I opened the door, answering his knock.

He stood outside my cabin, grinning a horse's smile, wearing shorts and a tank top.

"Hi," I said, welcoming Mykonos into my small home. "Come on in."

The one-room beach cabin had no furniture. Mykonos stepped inside, looked around the room for a moment, and sat on the wood floor.

"I didn't expect to see you, Mykonos."

"Well, I just thought I'd stop in. Is that OK?"

"Of course. I'm just surprised that you're here."

I had met Mykonos twice before. The first time was a few years earlier, after Mykonos had been ousted by his spiritual teacher and shunned by his fellow students who he had, supposedly, threatened to beat with a baseball bat.

Then, a week before his appearance at my cabin door, I ran into Mykonos on the beach. We sat together and talked about God, who Mykonos called the "Great One." We watched women walk by, and Mykonos expounded on the spiritual capacity of women's genitals, which stunned me.

When I joked that he seemed obsessed with women, he said, "What would you rather consider besides sex and death?" Not much, I admitted, and Mykonos nodded slightly, looking deep into my eyes.

ˈDavid Deida, 2005. *Wild Nights.* Boulder CO: Sounds True, Inc.

For a moment, everything stopped—no sounds, no motion, even my breath stopped—and then Mykonos got up to go. From the beach, I pointed out my cabin to Mykonos, but I never expected him to actually show up.

"Do you have any cold ones?" Mykonos asked, looking toward my refrigerator.

I figured he wanted a beer. But I didn't have any beer. I didn't drink. My life was very strict. I did three to five hours of spiritual practices in my little cabin every day, and I was a die-hard vegetarian.

"I don't have any beer," I told him.

For a few minutes, Mykonos made some small talk and then got up and left. I regretted that I didn't have any beer to offer him. I knew that Mykonos had a lot to offer me.

Mykonos was a man as ugly as he was tough. I had heard that he grew up on the streets, playing hockey, boxing, and getting into more than his share of trouble. He was also a decorated Vietnam veteran. After recovering from nearly fatal battle wounds, Mykonos, still a very young man, turned from the world and wholly devoted himself to spiritual growth. He spent twenty years studying at the feet of his spiritual teacher before being kicked out, ending up in the same coastal town where I lived.

I knew that he spoke from an enormous wealth of spiritual knowledge—what I didn't know is that he walked his talk with a vengeance, and that he was about to walk into my life and change it forever.

The next time Mykonos showed up at my cabin door, I was prepared. A six-pack waited in the refrigerator.

Mykonos came in and sat on the floor. He seemed particularly animated.

"Do you have any cold ones, my friend?" he asked.

I went to the refrigerator, secretly smiling, and grabbed two cans.

One for me, one for him. I handed Mykonos a beer and sat down in front of him. He popped the top and raised the beer high.

"To the Great One," he toasted.

"To the Great One," I replied.

We both took a sip. I couldn't believe it. I was drinking beer. In my spiritual efforts to live a healthy life, I viewed alcohol as poison. But I had to trust Mykonos. If he wanted to drink beer with me, then there must be a reason. I was willing to go along with him and find out.

He took out a pack of cigarettes and lit one. I swallowed. Cigarettes? I had been pure for so long. I hadn't eaten meat, or even drank tea, for more than fifteen years. I didn't want to throw away years of devout purity for a few hours of chatting with a guy who looked like a cross between an ax murderer and a car wash attendant. Mykonos was not a big man, though you wouldn't want to mess with him. Between his knees and his shorts, scars from shrapnel wounds crisscrossed the flesh of his thighs. He had a certain look in his eyes, as if he knew death—from both sides.

As soon as he lit up his cigarette, I was sure Mykonos felt my fear and resistance. He placed the pack within my reach and nodded toward it, indicating that I could help myself. I didn't.

Mykonos took a long drag on his cigarette, and then exhaled very slowly. Smoke filled the room of my clean cabin. He took another sip from his can of beer.

"Ah yesss," Mykonos sighed. "The lady is all around us." He made a sweeping gesture with his hand as if to indicate the beach, or maybe the entire world, outside my cabin. "She is beautiful, is she not? And she'd just as soon kill you. Eat you alive. What a bitch. What a beautiful bitch. Do you have any idea what I am talking about?"

Startled by his vulgar language, I nodded, hoping he would tell me more.

We both continued drinking beer in silence. I waited. Then Mykonos spoke of seemingly random things: books, sports, schemes to make money. I felt he was testing me. Seeing if I would bite. Finding out if I was ready to receive what he had to give, or whether I would be satisfied with small talk and common chat.

Meanwhile, I was starting to feel the effects of the alcohol. By then we had each drank almost three beers. Having been a long-time teetotaler, I was beginning to spin a little bit. I was losing the thread of the conversation.

"Breathe it down, my friend. Suck her down your front. Breathe her down to here," Mykonos said, firmly grabbing his crotch, which frightened me. "Why separate yourself from her? Hmmm? Why not take it to her? She wants you. She's gonna get you one way or another. She's gonna chew you up when you die. And after you die? On the other side? She's waiting for you there, too. You can't escape her, my friend."

Mykonos took another drag off his cigarette. I was wordless. Reeling.

"No amount of your so-called spiritual practice can save you from her," Mykonos continued. "You can't get away. You can only love. You can live in fear, or you can dance with her. And when you love her without holding back, when you see her as she really is, through and through, she dies in bliss. You know? Only bliss. But if you can't get her to spread her legs, if you won't even drink a beer, if you are too uptight to breathe her down to here, then she's just gonna laugh at you. We are talking about a *big lady*. A *very* big lady. Your agenda doesn't mean shit to her."

As he spoke, I felt dizzy, and my gut tensed. His words were crude, but he was right. I had equated spiritual practice with squelching my desires, denying them, suppressing them. I could sit in a clean room by myself and meditate for hours, but I wouldn't dance with what

Mykonos called "the lady." I was afraid of life. I was afraid of death. I was afraid even to drink a beer and lose my purity.

I wanted refuge, not chaos. I wanted peace, not passion. I was trapped in my little room of sanctity, in my meditative stillness and solitude. This wasn't true freedom. Nor was it love. As Mykonos pointed out, I wasn't penetrating the world with my love and opening "her" into bliss. Rather, I was pulling back. I was obsessed with myself.

Maybe the beer was loosening me up, or maybe it was just the right time, but as Mykonos spoke, my entire life strategy began to unravel. I had believed that by keeping my body balanced and my mind clear, then everything would work out. But meanwhile, I was dying anyway. The "lady" was eating me. The whole world was a massive, chaotic woman who terrified me, so I tried to seek safety and refuge in my spiritual inwardness and purity.

"What is a vagina, anyway?" Mykonos suddenly queried. "A lotus of delight or an ugly cut of mucous? Why do you want to poke it so bad? You like to see it in bed, all prettied up, but do you want it as bad when it's on the toilet, shit coming out of the ass? Hmmm? The body is what it is. Usually you like to hide it behind your underwear. You keep the bathroom door closed. Genitals!" Mykonos laughed. "They can be beautiful or disgusting. It's no big deal either way. Love has nothing to do with all that. And, believe me, the big lady doesn't give a damn about your genitals one way or another. If you are going to love the big lady, it's going to take a lot more than your pecker. And the same goes for loving your woman."

I thought of Gia, who was going to college, and wouldn't be able to join me at the beach for several months.

Mykonos smiled and lit another cigarette. Then he offered the pack to me. This time I took a cigarette, put it between my lips, flicked the lighter, and inhaled. The sharpness of the smoke caught me off guard, but I managed to quell my cough. I took a sip of beer, a drag off my cigarette, and tried to relax into the situation.

When we finished the last beer we walked down to the local store to get some more. Then we went to the beach. We sat on the sand, drinking and talking.

Mykonos tilted his head toward a gorgeous blonde tourist walking by in a bikini. I saw smooth tanned skin, narrow waist, and full hips. I saw upright breasts and nipples showing through the fabric of her bikini top. I saw legs to die for. I felt Mykonos regarding me.

"You know what she is?" Mykonos asked with a smile. "Years of arguments, snotty-nosed children, mortgages, and bad smell. You look at that thing every day, day after day, and you just want to run. You know what I mean?"

I did know what he meant, but I didn't say anything. I thought he was talking a little too loudly.

At that moment, we saw another woman walking on the beach. She was about 35 years old, dressed in jeans and a T-shirt. She was a friend that Mykonos and I both happened to know. She was a good person—though, to my taste, she wasn't particularly attractive. I certainly wouldn't call her sexy. She walked up to us and said hi.

"Hello, ma!" Mykonos responded fervently. I assumed that Mykonos developed this habit of speech from spending time in India, where, as a matter of love and respect, women are sometimes referred to as "ma," living facets of the Great Mother, the Goddess of the Universe.

"You are looking very happy today, ma!" Mykonos said.

"I'm doing OK," said the woman, with a shrug.

"You are looking very beautiful. Very radiant. Would you like to have a beer and share the shine of your heart with us, ma?" Mykonos asked her.

"Sure," she said, already visibly happier. And definitely more attractive.

I realized that Mykonos's manner, as outrageous as it seemed, was revealing the limits I put on love. When a woman entranced me, his words disillusioned me. When I was indifferent to a woman, his words unveiled her beauty. Either way, I was trapped by the caprice of my desire, and Mykonos's words, as crass as they were, showed the possibility to open in a way I had never allowed—to offer love without holding back in fear.

"Have either of you ever really been fucked? I mean, *really* fucked," Mykonos asked us.

Before we could respond, he answered his own question. Looking at us, drawing back his lips to expose his front teeth, he shook his head and said, "I don't think so."

He sat in silence, gazing at the ocean. I waited for him to continue, but he didn't. I felt I had to say something.

"Mykonos, what does it mean to be really fucked?" I asked.

He sat for several more minutes without answering, smoking his cigarette, looking out over the water, as if remembering another time and place. Eventually he looked at our friend and smiled.

"Ma knows what fuck is all about. Don't you, ma? Hmmm?"

She grinned, a little shy, a little hesitant to admit it, but definitely like she knew exactly what Mykonos was talking about. He continued.

"You know what it's like to take the Great One so far into you there's nothing left to do but give it all up to the Lord, don't you? Maybe you've never done it. But you know what it would be like. You can feel it. You know you want it. You want to be fucked into God, don't you? Do you know what I mean, ma?"

Now she was smiling, beaming, nodding her head. Mykonos went on.

"Sure you do, ma. You know what it's like because you *are* love. Your heart is love. Your mind is love. Your pussy is love." As he spoke

Mykonos looked at her heart, her head, and between her legs. The expression on his face was one of blatant veneration, but without the slightest hint of pretense. I couldn't believe that Mykonos was looking at her crotch this way, without guile and full of virtue and love. Meanwhile, she seemed to be drinking in his praise, basking in his adoration of her form.

"Our poor friend here," Mykonos said, nodding toward me, "He is afraid to fuck. He is afraid to dance with the lady, ma. He wants to stand back and watch, like a scientist. He's afraid to leave his room, to lose his purity and peace that he has worked so hard to attain. He's afraid to lose his precious stillness. He's afraid of the wildness of woman. Everything has to be all tidy for him. He wants the pussy, but he doesn't want the slop. He wants the tit, but not the tooth. Oh, he is a good man, alright. Look at the light in his eyes."

Mykonos put his arm around her shoulders and sat back so both of them could look at me.

"The light has guided his entire life. This boy might just make it. But not until he learns to embrace the lady, ma."

Then, the air around us shifted. A dense rapture grew down upon us, descending into our bodies as thick love, permeating us, impregnating us and the space between us with a blissful pressure. Mykonos continued to speak, his craggy face glowing in beatitude. He began addressing our friend as if she *were* the big lady. He began speaking to her as the Goddess.

"Our boy here won't know love absolute, he won't know what real freedom is, until he can fuck you, and be fucked by you, so that only the Great One shines in his place. And I'm not talking about him wiggling his pecker in your pussy, you know? I'm talking about the heart." Mykonos stroked his heart and the pressure of love seemed to grow. He continued speaking, so tenderly.

"Can you feel it now, ma? Can you breathe love into your pussy? Can you open yourself to the Great One now? Can you feel the Great One everywhere, between your legs, filling your body, breaking your heart wide open?"

Mykonos was looking into her eyes as she began to weep and tremble. Her legs opened and closed as she breathed deeply and gasped, "Yes." Then, more loudly, as her body brightened, she began laughing, without care, full of power, full of sex, full of love. "Yes!" she yelled, ecstatically, fearlessly. She seemed bigger than life, touching herself, opening herself, laughing, radiating fierce energy. Mykonos was right. I was afraid.

"And you, my friend," Mykonos turned to me. "You're going to die anyway. She's going to eat you, sooner or later. Stop struggling. Give it all up now. Give all your love. I mean *all* your love. Why not? What do you think you can gain by holding back? Do you love this woman right now? Can you feel her? Is she not the Goddess? Is she not alive as love unbound?"

She was. Radiant. Open. Alive. Laughing and weeping. Displaying her womanhood without inhibition or pride. Free in her glory. Legs open. Tongue thrust out. Her eyes were wild, full, sexy, unafraid, knowing. She was everything I ever wanted in a woman. Even though I was still afraid, my heart went toward her. My whole body filled with force. The force of desire.

"That's it," Mykonos said to me. "Don't hold back. Don't be an asshole. Love this woman. Give her everything. Feel it all and be free in love. Be open as love. There is only love. Only this Great One, always love, always making love. The Great One is Fuck! There, have I said it? Have I gone too far? There is only the Great One, even in all our seeming twoness."

As outrageous as his words were, Mykonos was right. We were sitting on the beach, fully clothed, not even touching each other, opening as man and woman, alive as love, opening as love, giving love. It was as fuck as fuck gets. And it was clear that every moment was as deeply loving and spontaneously alive as this moment, if we would only consent to give and receive love without holding back or closing down.

"There is only love," Mykonos continued. "There is only this Great One, always churning as love, always making love. Ours isn't a world of angel wings and white spires. Maybe when you die and go to the other side, you'll flit around as golden light. But that's not how love shines in this human realm. Here, in this place of hot blood and rosy flesh, the Great One makes love through bodies of desire. This is the red realm. And the only way beyond it is to feel through it—by loving *as it*."

Although Mykonos is a fictionalized character, various teachers have often pointed out my resistances, my fears, and my refusal to be love. They gave me countless opportunities to practice being love in the domain that I have tended to avoid most through my so-called spiritual life: the feminine domain of women and the world. They revealed to me how in my weakness I allowed the feminine to either entrance or disgust me. And they revealed, time and again, her power to attract me into deeper loving than I would otherwise allow. But mostly, I was taught that desire is not to be avoided. Rather, it is the very nature of the Great One manifesting as two.

When you can remain open and recognize desire for what it is, then desire is felt as the very force of love. Desire is what it feels like to be the very One appearing to itself as another. Love loving love in the form of an other, the nature of the universe makes itself apparent in the timeless desire between man and woman, masculine and feminine. The moveless depth of he and the endless dance of she is consummated. The difference vanished. The Great One *is* Fuck.

Wherever he may or may not be, I thank Mykonos for the beer.

14

MAGNIFY DESIRE
THROUGH SEX

On Monday, I really wanted her. I was thinking about sex all day. I imagined satisfying myself with her. We never got together.

On Tuesday, I could hardly wait. I could feel her body against mine. I could feel myself inside of her. Where was she?

On Wednesday, I finally saw her. We ripped off each other's clothes, and I entered her while standing.

I immediately wanted to ejaculate. The pressure had been building in me for days, and now I could release it in her. I wanted to so bad.

But something felt off. I wasn't making love with her at all. I was using her for the sake of my own release.

So, I began to practice through my need. I felt my whole body, rather than just my genital urge. I felt outward from my heart, into her. I slowed down and deepened my breath, and began to circulate energy through both of us with my breath. I felt into her more and more deeply as my heart opened wider. I relaxed into loving, instead of driving to dump the load of my desire.

As I relaxed more and more into our loving, my desire grew. But it grew in a big, round way. It wasn't sharp. It wasn't seeking release. It was as if a huge ball of desire grew out from my center, consuming both of us in its vastness. Eventually, the universe itself felt like desire: open-ended, not trying to resolve itself, but churning in its own expanding heat.

We made love for several days in a row. I never ejaculated but continued to magnify my desire. In our loving, I smoothed out the edges of desire, so what before was pushy and aggressive was now so huge, so edgeless, so as to be unsizable. It had nothing anymore to do with ejaculation or the need to be released of pressure.

Her desire also enlarged. We walked around in a state of immense openness. We were full of force and at the same time only love without need. We could have sex or not—it hardly mattered.

I learned that the neediness of sexual craving is this vast desire made narrow, focused on a goal, targeted toward release. Penned into a corral of sexual fantasy, it would run wild, generating thoughts and motives of penetrative aggression. But this same desire, articulated as sex, loosed in the space of love, is the motion of all life.

S exual desire should be magnified and smoothed large, not satiated or depleted during sex. As described fully in *The Enlightened Sex Manual*,* once your addiction to ejaculation or orgasmic release is broken, your sex will no longer be for selfish release. Aggressive need will become passionate love.

If you notice that you look forward to sex in order to release tension, practice using sex to round out your energy, rather than to deplete it. Open into desire, and realize your power. The more you magnify desire through sex without release, the more you must match love to the size of your desire. Huge sexual energy necessitates huge love. Otherwise, magnified sexual need becomes

---

* David Deida, 2004. *The Enlightened Sex Manual.* Boulder CO: Sounds True, Inc.

demonic, subverting your relationship into an arena of brutish grasping and expenditure.

But when you relax your desire into the openness of love, its wideness swallows its sharpness. There is plenty of room in infinity, and huge sexuality splays into huge love. Use sex to magnify desire, not to diminish it. Enlarge desire as the edgeless space of this moment.

FOR HIM

Your sexual desire comes in two basic forms, *energetic* desire and the desire for *love*.

Energetic desire is all about wanting a certain *kind* of woman or energy. You may love your intimate partner—you may open in oneness with her—but you happen to see a woman at the grocery store who totally turns you on. There is something about her that you want. Something other than what your woman gives you. Your whole body feels magnetized toward this stranger. It is as if she offers you a different "flavor" of feminine energy than your woman does.

What makes a woman sexually desirable to you, in particular, is her energetic flavor. In your committed intimate partner, you probably also want depth, intelligence, compassion, a good sense of humor, and a number of other qualities. But you have a certain sexual "taste" that may not have anything to do with these other qualities. You might not know a single thing about the woman in the store, yet she can still evoke your sexual desire. Her *energy* alone may evoke your desire.

Some women are hot and feisty. Some are cool and calm. One woman may have the energy of an innocent little girl while another may feel like an ornery slut. One woman may slink like a tiger while another may prance like a gazelle. Some women seem like elegant sophisticates while others appear to be dangerous fiendesses. This woman may have sex with you like a freight train while that one may tickle you with delicate kisses.

Every woman—and every man—can embody, express, and desire any or all of these energies. Nonetheless, each woman predominately radiates a characteristic flavor of energy, and each man has a specific taste in women. Again, there are many aspects to a woman other than her characteristic quality of energy, but this is a very important quality when it comes to your sexual desire. If you don't understand your desire for energy, you may confuse it with your desire for love, a deep sense of oneness, and openness of being.

A woman's devotion—her depth of love—may open your heart and evoke your love, but her energy evokes your sexual desire. Both at the same time is best: a woman who is deeply loving and also able to radiate the energetic qualities you find sexy. But even a shallow woman, a woman who doesn't love you at all—a woman you don't even know—can turn you on sexually if she has the right energy. You may not want to spend the rest of your life with her—or even the rest of the day—but your body wants to taste her energy, sexually or perhaps just through a glance.

The immense and culturally universal history of prostitution, mistresses, sex shows, and polygamy—often in spite of penalties for engaging in such activities—speaks loudly of man's need to sexually experience different flavors of feminine energy. One woman may be enough—*more* than enough—to occupy a man's longings for love, companionship, and sacred union, but his body responds to countless sources of feminine energy day after day.

If a man's energetic neediness grows strong enough—if he isn't getting the specific flavor of feminine energy he needs from his wife whom he loves, for instance—he will seek it elsewhere. For some men, just glancing at a woman in a grocery store is enough. Some men need a more distilled dose of feminine sexual energy, and so they may use erotic movies or adult magazines to drink the flavors for which their taste is greatest.

Other men engage in energetic sex by flirting with co-workers or conversing with women friends. Some men develop rich lives of inner vision wherein they receive the energy of the woman of their dreams through masturbatory fantasy. Some go so far as to hire a professional feminine energy source to get what they need, through sex or through dancing, massage, or role playing.

Many men hire prostitutes or adult entertainers not so much for sex itself, but to experience certain kinds of energies—dominant or submissive, innocent or nymphomaniacal, nurturing or wild. If all a man wants is sexual release, it is far easier and less expensive for him to masturbate in private. But masturbation isn't sufficient if his hunger is for an embodied source of feminine energy.

Men have been known to risk losing the woman they really love in order to get the feminine energy they need from another woman. Of course, when a man really loves a woman and she is also able to give him the feminine sexual energy he needs, then his attraction to her is complete—though this won't prevent his body from being momentarily attracted to random women throughout the day whose energy happens to fit his tastes and therefore magnetize his sexual appetite.

As a man, your energetic needs may change throughout your life, depending on the stage of your spiritual growth, the demands of your career, your health, and even where you happen to be geographically—the kind of women you are attracted to in Paris will be very different from the kind you are attracted to in Hawaii or at home. And as the style of your work changes—from sitting alone in an office to managing a group of 50 people face-to-face, for instance—the type of energy you are sexually attracted to will also change.

This attraction has nothing to do with trust, commitment, or even friendship. It is simply an attraction based on the energetic disposition of your body at the time. The strength of this attraction may be intense—you may find yourself doing something very stupid for its sake—but it is not about love.

For a woman whose heart and genitals are connected, this is not easy to understand. She might find it painful and difficult to open sexually with a man she doesn't trust and love. However, this is not to say that women aren't attracted to strangers or don't enjoy an occasional fling or affair. Sometimes they do.

Sometimes women have affairs for the same reason men usually do: they want to taste a specific flavor of sexual energy. Women especially begin to feel this way when their intimate partner is energetically "dead" or uncomfortable in his body. But what really distracts a woman from her committed intimacy is when she meets a man whose love penetrates her more deeply than her partner's; then, she often becomes confused. When a man moves her with deeper presence and more trustable integrity than her husband—perhaps her therapist, tennis instructor, colleague, or teacher—then her heart may become divided.

As a man, you know that your sexual attraction to other women does not necessarily divide your heart. Often a man discovers during the course of a committed relationship that the woman he truly loves and wants to spend his life with does not give him the energy he wants sexually. And, he discovers that he can continue loving his chosen intimate partner with all of his heart *while* having a sexual relationship with another woman to get the energy he needs. According to statistics on extra-marital affairs and multiple relationships, the majority of men in most cultures on earth seem to feel this way, and more than a few women do, too.

To grow spiritually involves aligning your life with your deepest motive. Although sexual attraction can be extremely strong, it is rarely your deepest motive. In fact, after an ejaculation or two you may be quite ready to ditch your mistress or prostitute and go home to the woman with whom you share your heart. The question to answer for yourself is this: what sexual behaviors most support your growth so you can sink into the depth of your being, relax as the openness who you are, and give your deepest gifts?

There is no single answer to this question that will apply universally. No particular sexual style is "correct" for everyone. There have been highly evolved men and women—great men and women recognized in their time and place for their great gifts to humankind—of all sorts, including celibate, monogamous, polygamous, homosexual, heterosexual, and bisexual.

Some great men have enjoyed the company of whores. Others have had royal harems, or lived alone in caves and jungles, or spent their entire life with one woman. Some great women have had one husband and many lovers, while others lived by themselves, or enjoyed intimacy with women more than with men. If you can imagine it, some man or woman has probably lived it. Since each person is unique, every man or woman manifests their gifts in different ways, from raising a beautiful family with one devoted intimate partner to founding new forms of art fermented by the juices of assorted vamps, skanks, or scalawags.

As you grow, you will find old husks and needs dropping away and new priorities emerging. As this process transforms your sexual life, always commit your actions to your deepest truth. Discipline yourself so that you attend to your deepest desires and allow them to govern your more superficial ones.

However strong it may be, the desire to get laid is relatively shallow, spiritually speaking: you share it with earthworms, fish, and lawyers. Don't have sex with everyone you are attracted to. That reduces your motives to the purely animal level of desire. But also, don't deny when you truly hunger for certain inspirational or healing energies, deceiving yourself for the sake of emotional security.

Cater neither to your body's desire for animal lust nor to your emotion's desire for succor and dependable comfort. Rather, discover how you must arrange the details of your life to manifest the most love on earth. For most people, a long-term, committed relationship affords the best opportunity for spiritual growth while learning to give your deepest gifts and manifest love in the world.

However, no arrangement will end your cravings. So what if your body remains promiscuous and lustful, or if your emotions crave a more cozy and consoling nest of comfort? *They will in any case:* even if you have a hundred lovers, even if you have one lover who adores you, your body will occasionally want others and your emotions will occasionally crave more security. You can never get enough money or affection, sex or security so that you feel complete.

Completion lies in utter surrender or relaxation as your deepest truth, opening yourself as the flow of love, and giving your true gifts. When the unthreatenable presence of your deep being saturates your body, mind, and emotions, then you will know how to express your love, spontaneously and authentically. Until then, the changing tides of your energetic hunger and your need for emotional security will pull you this way and that way, creating divisions within you.

Energetic desire is very real and natural. You are not a bad person because you love your woman but fantasize about spending time with a lady who wears leather and beats you with a whip or dresses like a cheerleader and obeys you like a daddy. Communicate your desires with your chosen and committed intimate partner. Usually, she can find the qualities of feminine energy within herself that you need to heal and grow beyond your current cravings.

If she can't give you that energy, or if you are too embarrassed to receive it from her, then try to get it in other ways, but in her company. Watch an adult movie that gives you the flavors for which you hunger, but watch it with your woman. Make it a shared relational event, enjoyed in love, humor, and intimacy, not a secret indulgence cloistered in guilt and shame.

Most of your sexual desires, no matter how weird or kinky they may seem, are rooted in your need to give and receive love or your need to experience a specific part in the spectrum of feminine energy. These needs are natural, although if denied or hidden they can grow into "pathological" forms that require healing. If you don't acknowledge these desires in yourself with compassion, you can create an inner division that results in an energetic kink.

For example, your natural desire to experience the energy of feminine innocence and vulnerability, like a dew-laden flower opening at dawn, can get kinked into a pathological need to be sexual with an innocent and vulnerable little girl.

To have sex with a girl who is too young virtually always violates her sanctity, confuses her mind, tortures her heart, and creates ripples of pain and suffering that spread throughout her entire life. No man dedicated to realizing his deepest truth and expressing love in the world would do such a thing. But if you are not allowing yourself to receive this aspect of feminine energy in a mature intimate relationship for some reason, fantasies and cravings will begin to attract your attention—if only to have a few beers and watch the topless little bo-peep show at the local men's club.

The more you grow spiritually, the more you are able to feel, acknowledge, and embrace your desires *before* they grow into "demonic" or pathological cravings. Always remember that at your core you want to give and receive love, however tense and disturbed you may feel. Remember that it is natural for you to want to give and receive love through specific shades of the spectrum of feminine energy—usually those parts from which you feel most alienated or separate.

Ultimately, as you grow spiritually, you won't feel separate from any energy. You will live as love in communion with the entire spectrum, and then your sexual desire will become aligned with the love deepest in your heart rather than with your heart-separate pockets of craving. But as long as you have divided yourself from your own desires, those parts will seek acknowledgment, expression, and healing, quite naturally and inexorably. It is your responsibility to find a loving and benevolent way to balance yourself energetically—such as in nature, through massage, with music and art, or in play with consenting adults—before your desires take on a "demonic" life apart from your deep heart-integrity.

FOR HER

Your yearning for love probably never ceases. Occasionally, in moments of absorption in relationships or distraction in tasks, you won't notice your yearning. But sooner or later you realize that you are not deeply fulfilled, blissed to your bones, and happy in the center of your heart. There is an emptiness, a vacuum deep inside you, that wants to be filled with love.

If you are not in a relationship, the first thing you blame is most likely your loneliness. "If only I was with a good man who really loved me."

If you *are* in a relationship, you will often blame your man for your unhappiness, for the yearning still in your heart. "If only he would open his heart to me more, desire me more, and love me more deeply."

Yearning, however, is the natural sensation of the yet-to-be-fully-surrendered heart. Your man, or the man you don't yet have, is not responsible for your yearning. You yearn for love exactly to the degree that you are not surrendered into the fullness of love right now. And even when you are surrendered, yearning can *express* your fullness of love.

Be conscious of the way you may punish your man for your own yearning. When you want to hurt him for not fulfilling your heart, you will tend to give him an energy he can't handle. As strong as your man may seem, you know exactly the energy that will get to him.

Some men can't handle their woman's anger. Other men shrink when their sexual, financial, or spiritual capacities are criticized. Most men crumble when their woman doesn't acknowledge their success in the project that is most near and dear to them. Other men are terrified of their woman's emotional chaos. You know what your man most fears, and you know how to give it to him.

If your man knows how to handle it, your "testing" energy can be a real gift to him, helping him see where he is weak and dependent, thus strengthening him. He can absorb your anger or criticism, discriminate what is true and useful, make the necessary changes in his life, and embrace you with a smile, not taking the non-constructive momentum of your emotions too seriously.

But if he is not yet ready to change, then your heavy, angry, or shut-down energy becomes a pure burden in his life. Whereas the fundamental feminine bad mood is the feeling of being unloved, the fundamental masculine bad mood is the feeling of being burdened.

You want your man to love you, to embrace your moods and enter your heart, to desire you more than any other woman. Your man wants you to relieve him of his sense of burden and give him energy, enlivening his weary heart and body. When you feel your man is not desiring you in love, or when your man feels you are not rejuvenating him with love, the bad mood cycle starts ping-ponging between the two of you.

You punish him by burdening him with more of the energy he can't handle, and he punishes you by withdrawing and turning away in undesire. Eventually, you may feel disgusted by each other, each of you manifesting what the other hates the most. Your man knows how to express his non-desire for you with as much precision as you know how to weaken him with your energy.

Your man can learn to discover the freedom and openness of deep being. Then he won't blame you for burdening him, nor will your attempts at "hurting him back" have much effect on him. He'll embrace you in real love, and if you continue to bitch for too long he will lovingly let you go and move on.

You can learn to discover the love and bliss that flow in your deep heart. Then you won't blame your man for causing you to yearn, nor will his withdrawal of love cause you to collapse. You may feel hurt by his undesire, but you remain open and full of love. If he continues to be unloving over time, you can bring your overflowing love to another man who is able to meet the depth of your love with the depth of his presence. Or, you can stay with your man and surrender directly to the love that moves through you and as you, whether or not your man is able to meet your openness in love. You won't reflexively punish him for not being able to open, though you may continue to test him.

This testing is natural on your part. Testing whether your man can match your energy with his strength of love—whether he can "fuck" you with his presence and desire you in the midst of whatever you can dish out—is a healthy aspect of feminine emotional play. But punishing him with your hurtful energy is a form of misplaced anger; you are blaming him for your yearning, which only you can be responsible for.

Once you have learned to free fall into the moment and are willing to exist, naked, as the depths of your deepest intuition, then your yearning and your love become one. You intuit the huge love that you are. You use the strength of your yearning to bloom the depths of devotion, surrendering your body open so you are filled with the bliss of love.

Feeling the yearning in your heart, you breathe deeply, receiving love-energy into your body with every inhalation and releasing anxiety with every exhalation. Your feet relax into the tender earth, even through harsh floors. Your body softens into a river of energies, hot and cold, swift and calm, angry, hurt, joyous, peaceful, and wild, sourced in the huge ocean of love from which these different currents flow. Suppressing nothing, you surrender wide as the force of this ocean.

From this disposition of devotional strength, you can bless your partner—or anybody else—with whatever energy most serves him. Sometimes you give him energy that tests him and at other times you give him energy that heals or rejuvenates him. Sometimes you use your energy to turn him on sexually and other times you use it to get his attention. But you no longer use the force of your energy to punish him because you yearn for more love than he gives.

You are not a victim of his love disability. If he is not loving you, if he doesn't desire you, that's his problem. You may feel hurt by his unlove or by his lack of desire, but your heart knows that hurting him back is no way to evoke his love or desire. A part of you may want to punish him—and you know exactly how to do that—but the deeper part of your heart is filled with compassion. You know you *are* love, and deep down, so is your man. Your man is going through whatever lessons he needs to open more deeply into love with you. You may want to celebrate this love with him, but if he is presently unable to embrace you, your own fullness need not cease.

When you don't collapse into victimhood or punish your man due to blame, then you remain radiant, full of energy and love. You will naturally attract a man who *does* desire your love-fullness, or you will evoke in your man his desire for your love-fullness, which will help to pull him through whatever lessons of love he needs to experience. If he isn't able to love you, if he isn't able to want you, the softness of your heart may be pained but the fullness of your love remains strong.

15

CONVERT ANIMAL LUST
TO A FURY OF LOVE

She was very wet, I was deep inside of her, and she was bucking like a wild goat. She grabbed my ass and pulled me as if to bring me yet deeper. But deeper I could not go. I was pressed against her, and she was grinding against me. Her wails and moans of need sounded like desperation riding on waves of voracious indulgence. Her breasts were a blur as she rammed her body up and down against me.

Her wild sexual abandon was about to make me come. It wasn't just the physical stimulation; her feminine bestiality was drawing the savage mammal out of me. I wanted to fuck her like an animal.

I began pumping like a wild man, feeling like I would, in moments, pump gallons of semen deep into her hungry body. And then, suddenly, I noticed that we were both merely animals. Humping happily. Lost in the sweat of the moment. Heart eclipsed by fervor.

Recognizing this, I practiced to reclaim my heart. I remembered love and breathed love. I slowed down for a moment and allowed my body to be pervaded by the love emanating from my heart. My rampant thrust and clutch were eased of vicious zeal and rejuvenated by the steady force of love, circulated by my breath.

Heart resurrected, breath wide, and body open, I now loosed
love through the animal of my desire. Her disposition, too, changed
instantly. She was still wild. But now, she was open and loving.
We still clawed and rammed. Our bodies continued flailing and
our sweat continued flying, but the wild force of our surrender
was moved by love. Even while clawing each other, our hearts
communed and our bodies relaxed in the thick spread of love.

Know the difference between surrendering to animal lust and surrendering as love through the play of desire. Lusty abandon is fine. There are times when all you want is the fun of wild sex. But this is a very different way to have sex than giving love *through* the wildness of your sexing.

When you are in the throes of crazed coupling, locate your deepest core of love, and offer this gift through your animal zing and swallow. The masculine partner transforms the static electricity of chaotic excitement into a heart-focused thunderbolt of love. The feminine partner opens as large as the universe, devouring all lesser forces in the fury of love's light. Fuck your lover with as much energy as you can handle, but also be vulnerable. Allow sublime communion and transmission. Remember love, even in the midst of tooth and sweat. Whatever the form of your passion, give love through it.

Use the whole of human being, encompassing both animal and angel, as a vehicle for transmitting your love. Practice enlarging your sexual capacity so you can give love through all forms, whether porcine or cherubic, tiger or deva. Love has no limits.

FOR HIM

Most men have some pretty strange sexual desires. Maybe you mas-
turbated in your closet as a child, and now you get turned on by the
smell of leather or shoes. Maybe your parents' punishment and your
hormonal development coincided to produce in you a sexual desire to
be spanked, whipped, or flogged. Perhaps you dream of savagely raping
a woman, or your fantasies flow with dark images of torture, humili-
ation, bestiality, feces, or urine. If you could see the sexual scenes that
occasionally occupy some men's minds, it wouldn't be a pretty sight.

Why are some men so sexually twisted? Their sexual energy is not
inherently linked to their heart, so it is free to flow into the amoral
nooks and base crannies of their psyche. For most women, sex is about
relationship; it is an emotional matter, a sharing in trust and vulnerable
embrace. But for many men, sexual energy is more related to private
fantasy than relational sharing.

Men are often at a disadvantage when it comes to combining love,
emotion, and sex; most women do this more naturally. But, once a man's
emotional capacity grows and he *is* able to connect lovingly through
sex, then the woman is sometimes at a disadvantage with respect to the
next stage of growth, beyond personal bonding.

Her need for an emotional tie—her desire to be the special woman
who makes an inseparable "love unit" with her man—can limit the fullness and depth of her love. A man, once learning to connect with his
woman deeply in love, is sometimes more likely to feel through the limits
of personal hope and desire and relax open as the love that lives all beings.
At this stage of growth, the fact that for him sex isn't as intertwined with
personal bonding can sometimes work to his advantage. But first a man
has to *get* to this stage, which isn't always easy.

Unconnected to his deep heart, ungrounded in relational sensitivity, a man's sexual energy flows through his body with the force of a

raging river, at least in his early adulthood. Because his sexual energy is not so pulled by the needs of intimate sharing, it is frequently routed in other ways. Sometimes, a man chooses to use his sexual energy for creative purposes, to write a novel, explicate a philosophy, or practice spiritual disciplines. More often, however, this flow of sexual energy follows a strange path in a man's psyche.

This path has been carved by a combination of animal heritage, childhood experience, cultural exposure, and random predispositions shaped by innumerable influences. Sometimes it is possible to trace the causes of a man's sexual desires and behaviors. For instance, a boy who is sexually abused as a child is more likely to be sexually abusive as an adult. But there are plenty of examples of abused children who grow up to be extraordinarily loving adults, as well as well-loved children who grow up to be terrors. Not all of a man's traits are so easily reduced to identifiable causes.

A man's destructive sexual desires and behaviors need to be taken into account by appropriate means. A legal system exists that punishes men for behaving harmfully and also sequesters chronically dangerous men away from those they may injure. Pharmacological methods can be used for regulating a man's behaviors whose biochemistry is unbalanced. Various forms of psychological and medical therapy can be useful for helping impaired men achieve a modicum of sexual health and balance.

But many "healthy" men—almost all men—harbor desires they would be embarrassed to admit. These desires may remain entirely in the realm of fantasy. Perhaps while you masturbate, you remember a girl from a TV show you used to watch as a child. Or, perhaps you imagine that you are a king surrounded by a naked harem. You might be a "normal" and loving kind of guy in your everyday life, but in your private masturbatory fantasies you may imagine being strangled at the peak of an orgasm.

You can probably feel in yourself your own "strange" fantasies. The landscape of your secret sexual desires is carved by all kinds of past and present influences. You didn't ask for whatever shaped your sexual fantasies. You didn't ask for your mother to over-protect you, or for your father to make you feel weak—or for your first masturbatory experience to be with an uncle, or an animal, or while defecating, or inspired by Marilyn Monroe movies or TV re-runs of *Gilligan's Island*.

You may not be responsible for acquiring the secret sexual fantasies and desires that you harbor. But you *are* responsible for dealing with them. As you grow spiritually, your sexual fantasies and desires must be digested, metabolized, and assimilated—not ignored or suppressed—in the openness and love of your deep being.

In addition to legal, pharmacological, medical, and psychological treatments that can be used when necessary to help regulate and heal your sexual desires and behaviors, there is another measure to take as you grow spiritually: embrace your sexual desires—no matter how strange they may seem—in the arms of love, the natural openness of your deep being. When you can stay totally present with your sexual desires—without avoiding them, suppressing them, or acting upon them—they are transfigured by the force of your very presence.

Consciousness liberates energy. When you can fully feel any energy or desire, and feel *through* it without clinging to it or avoiding it, then you can rest as open consciousness even as the desire occurs. The desire arises within your natural openness and is relieved of tension. It is transformed from an anxious pressure into a blessing of energy.

Your sexual fantasies are frequently reflections of your unmet spiritual needs. For instance, you may have lost touch with your deep being and therefore feel disconnected with authentic strength. So, you seek a substitute sense of omnipotency in fantasies of forcefully taking a woman.

Or, perhaps you have spent years identifying with your capacity to take charge and lead others—as a business executive or community leader, for instance—and so you begin to crave other aspects of your essential being that you have ignored. Perhaps you long to experience the bliss of surrender, devotion, and trust, but it's difficult for you to let go of being in charge. So, you find yourself fantasizing about being tied up and made vulnerable at the sexual mercy of a dominant woman.

How do you work with habitual sexual patterns? It is best to work with them immediately as they arise. Imagine you are having sex with your woman. The intensity builds. She bites you hard on your shoulder. First, this elicits pain, then your energy of anger. You smack her lightly, and she smacks you back—quite forcefully—causing your lip to bleed and your nose to ache. At this point, if you are not careful, your rageful energy may flow in a path carved by your past habits.

If you have habitually regarded aggressive energy as "bad," perhaps you will close down emotionally, lose your erection, roll away from your lover, and pout. If you have actively entertained violent sexual fantasies, your incited energy may flow through the path carved by your vicious masturbatory reveries, and you may find yourself "out of control," beating your woman mercilessly.

In spiritually deepening sexuality, your habitual energies are embraced and dissolved—self-liberated in their inherent openness—rather than rejected or acted upon. All of your energies—perverted and virtuous—arise as forms of consciousness in the flow of your deep being. Like ripples on the surface of an ocean, they arise from and dissolve into your depth of openness. When your recognition of the self-releasing nature of your fantasies becomes strong enough, then you can approach them as doorways to greater openness rather than as obstructions to love.

Your woman bites you hard and you are full of intense energy: Feel the flow of energy within you in great detail. Is it hot or cold? Does it flow upward from your belly or downward from your head? Is the energy sharp or round, staccato or smooth? Feel your lover. Is she opened or closed? Is she connected to the love deep in her heart or is she lost in the energies of the moment? What does she need from you so that her love is brought more to the fore: a slap, a bite, or perhaps some soft cuddling?

Stay totally present with your sensations, emotions, pleasures, pains, and thoughts, as well as with your partner's. Even if you feel ashamed, queasy, or weak—like a hole is gaping in the pit of your stomach—stay with the feeling. Even if you are disgusted with yourself for wanting to pummel your lover, stay with the feeling. Don't act on it. Don't think about it, or try to make yourself feel better, or turn away. Simply remain totally present with everything you think, feel, and sense, in yourself and in your partner.

Your presence, the force of your very consciousness, will begin to pervade your energies and desires. You may feel pain where your woman hit you. You may feel hot anger welling in your body causing your head to fill with pressure. But you also remain present with these feeling, re- laxing as they are reabsorbed in the openness of deep being.

If you notice that your breath is tightening, feel it like you would feel a sunset in order to artistically capture its essence or like you would hold an infant to your chest, lovingly. Intimately feel all the qualities of your tight breath. *Love* your tight breath. Remain present with your tight breath. Without trying to change it, your tension will dissolve in mere presence, openness, and love. Your angry urgency will uncoil in the deep openness of being.

Continue feeling any aggressive energy moving within you, push- ing you from the inside, "making you" want to hit your woman back. Feeling this pressure within you, love it, embrace it, and metabolize it in the openness of your being. Once your breath has relaxed into natural openness, you can use its easeful rhythm to wash your internal pressure back to sea like waves lapping up on a beach, inhaling and exhaling, inhaling and exhaling.

In every present moment, your angry energy arises in the openness of who you are. When recognized as such, anger is felt as an energetic ripple in an ocean of deep being. In the space of this openness, aggressive energy loses its "kinked" quality and moves as loving passion. Your sexual actions flow like relaxed thunderbolts of love-desire, ravishing your woman into openness. Your sexual play may continue to be rough and wild, but your actions originate from love and communicate care. Your woman feels your heart in every moment of sexual "struggle."

If you have spent years fantasizing about violent sex, it may be difficult to remember love in the midst of intense or angry sexual energy. First, you may need to practice the kind of energy-circulating breathing exercises described in *The Enlightened Sex Manual.*[*] While you remain present with the flow of angry energy during sex, practice moving it through your natural internal circuitry. Breathe the energy of anger down your front and up your spine as you feel through you and your partner from your heart, relaxing deeply as the openness of love.

By persistently practicing in the ways we have described, your sexual ruts are loosened, whatever your unique fantasies and habits happen to be. Your energy and attention grow free enough to practice recognizing, loving, and allowing your fantasies to uncoil and liberate themselves in the vast openness of being.

Eventually, you no longer approach your fantasies with guilt or lust but with skill and a very wide embrace. You no longer need to suppress or act on your fantasies but you let them arise in the ocean of your being, notice them rippling on the surface, and then, through a skillful combination of breathwork, active love, and sustained openness

---

[*] David Deida, 2004. *The Enlightened Sex Manual.* Boulder CO: Sounds True, Inc.

of feeling, they become metabolized in the light of your consciousness and reabsorbed in the ocean of your depth.

Your greatest gifts are often intertwined with your most perverted energies. Men and women who have given greatly to the world are often also given greatly to strange sexual desires and energies. Sexual energy is a reflection of your energy altogether. If you are really giving great gifts, then you are flowing with great energy. A tiny rivulet of flow can become magnified into a huge turbulence of force. That is, a mild sexual fantasy that every man might entertain for a moment can become amplified in a man who is gifting with great energy.

This is one reason why so many political leaders, entertainers, and spiritual teachers are involved in "sex scandals." These people conduct huge energy, so the common and murky dreams of the mediocre man become extraordinarily energized and enlarged into powerful actions that may be gloriously light *and* dark, virtuous *and* perverse.

As part of the process of spiritual growth, it is incumbent upon all of us to metabolize our sexual deviations in the humor of open love. As our energies grow in magnitude, so do our sexual desires and fantasies—our kinks speak as loudly as our gifts shine. As we give our gifts more fully, we become more aware of our sexual kinks. They become exaggeratedly energized.

If we hold back our energy to avoid feeling these kinks, then we also hold back our deepest gifts. Without being shy, we should allow our gifts to grow and our strange sexual desires to come to the surface. Then, with compassion, consciousness, and skill, we can undo these forces of habit-energy, which are often carved by a history beyond our control.

FOR HER

You are at a party and have had a few glasses of wine. Your intimate partner is not to be seen. One of your favorite songs comes on the stereo, and suddenly a man pulls you on to the dance floor. You don't know him too well, but you know he is a single doctor who has written a few books on spirituality and enjoys piloting his own jet to tropical islands in between taking care of his ranch and donating money to help feed the hungry. He is also quite good at dancing.

The wine has loosened you up and your body flows with the music. Your dance partner tunes into your rhythm and style, synchronizing his movements with yours. Then he begins to lead, teasing you with more complicated and humorous dance steps, drawing you into his happy energy. You pick up the ball and run with it, finding out if this guy can really keep up with you, if he can match your grace and joy. He can.

Without warning, he embraces you and dips you backward. You are startled but feel totally safe in the gentle strength of his arms. You feel yourself swooning, whether from the wine or the dance you're not sure.

He brings you toward him and looks into your eyes. Your body is open and full of energy. His gaze is playful, intense, knowing. You feel naked. He holds you more tightly against his powerful body as you breathe together suspended in timelessness.

The feminine is a miracle of surrender, a flower of force that either opens or closes. As a woman, you can use your masculine discrimination to decide which direction to move in, but when you are polarized into your feminine energy—by a man of great masculine presence, for instance—then you may lose access to your masculine directionality. In moments like these, you may find yourself able to open or close. That's it.

This is why the issue of sexual integrity is so important for men who are in positions of offering women their masculine guidance as teachers, therapists, or religious counselors: even a highly discriminative woman loses her sense of perspective in the moment of being polarized by a very present man into her extreme feminine. Just as a woman's radiance can attract a man into doing almost anything, a man's presence can open a woman into trust and vulnerable permeability; in a highly polarized moment, she might open and agree to have sex, whereas in a less polarized moment she might have chosen a different direction.

On the dance floor, swooned in the arms of a loving, strong, completely present man who desires you, your body opens along with your heart. Sure, you can resist. You can keep yourself closed enough so that you are not swept away by his magnetic presence. But if you're open enough to really dance freely, then you're probably also open enough to be more "available" to his masculine presence than you would otherwise be.

When you open physically, you open emotionally. If your actual intimate partner were to suddenly walk up and see you limp in the arms of a stranger, locked eye-to-eye in a swoon of surrender, he might wonder what was going on. And so would you.

It is totally natural to open in response to a man's strong presence, even if he is a stranger. And when you open, you will feel it physically and emotionally. The feminine thrives on surrender, finds bliss in surrender. However, whether you surrender to a man's desire, to your own desire, or to divine desire is a matter of your current level of love.

Love is love. You are either open as love, or to some degree you are closed. But what you open *to* is determined by your level of growth, by your maturity as a spiritual being. Suppose you are on the dance floor with the suave stranger who has swept you off your feet. You have opened totally. Your body is open. Your emotions are open. You are swooned in the bliss of surrender. But what are you surrendering *to?*

In your openness, you could give yourself to this man. You could surrender yourself to *his desire.* This is a rather low level of openness in which your direction becomes shaped by his desire. Again, this is a totally natural and inevitable way to open; once you are swooned, you really can't help it—until you have grown to the next level.

At the next level, you still open and surrender, but the force that moves you, the force to which you are truly surrendered, is larger than the man in front of you. Perhaps you are married, and your deepest surrender is to the force of your commitment in marriage. Even though your body and emotions may open wide in response to your dance partner, you are primarily guided not by your dance partner's desire but by your *own desire* to maintain your marriage, which is a deeper, more heart-true form of devotion than what you feel in a brief swoon with the man on the dance floor.

But what happens if you turn your head and see your husband on the dance floor near you, locking lips and grinding hips with a lively lady who can't seem to get enough of him? How full will your bliss remain? How open will your heart be? Devoting your heart to marriage is certainly much deeper than devoting it to a man who happens to swoon you on the dance floor. But there is a devotion that is even deeper, less fragile, and more true to your heart's deepest yearning.

It is very difficult to describe this devotion since it is not common in today's world and doesn't lend itself to our everyday use of words. It is a devotion to the force of love itself. It is a devotion of your whole body and entire heart to divine love, so that you are utterly filled by love, lived by love, and moved by love—rather than by a man's desire or your own desire. In the light of this love, your suave dance partner and your distracted husband are both whisker-covered twinkles, regardless of how sexy, present, or committed they might be.

The presence of a great dancer and the integrity of a man who is totally committed to you are both stepped-down versions of the depth and power of divine love. The presence of divine love fills you, invades you, really, like a passionate lover. The trustability of divine love is absolute—it is who you are, it lives as everything and everyone, you cannot ever be separate from it. The dancer's presence and your husband's commitment fill you with a kind of bliss and contentment because they are mini-versions of the deep love who you are, but for which you still seek, because of the heart-vacuum created by your unsurrender.

The bliss you feel with a graceful dancer or your loyal husband is real; no matter how open you are in divine love, you will still feel swooned by a great dancer's presence and opened in devotion by your husband's commitment. You will still feel let down if the dancer turns out to be a jerk or devastated if you find out about your husband's mistress. Devotion to divine love doesn't eliminate the pleasures and pains of relationships. You simply no longer *depend* on relationships to give you what you already are: blissful fullness surrendered as radiant love.

Until you breathe divine love throughout your body and surrender as the force of love itself, it seems you only have two options in relationship: dependence and independence. You can either give yourself to a man, or you can be your own woman, committed to your own desires. But your desires are as selfish and ultimately futile as any man's. You need only to look around to see that women who are devoted to themselves—"independent" women, perhaps committed to a social cause or to their own economic freedom—are not necessarily more blissful than women who are devoted to a man.

A woman experiences bliss whenever she opens in devotional love—to her man, to herself, to her art, or to her community—but her bliss deepens as she opens to deeper sources of devotion. Who can argue that devotion to a child is one of the deepest blisses a mother can experience? Only a woman who has surrendered open as radiant love, alive as the deep compassion of Mother Divine—only such a woman can feel the pinch of limiting her love and devotion to a handful of exclusive relationships.

Few women are willing to surrender as this depth of love-fullness, just as few men are willing to feel through their entire pursuit of success and rest as the depth who they are all along. Nevertheless, all women are pulled every day, swooned every day, by hints of divine love, on the dance floor, in their children's eyes, and in their lover's smile.

Eventually, you open as deep love-fullness, giving and receiving divine love through every breath, through every gesture of your body, in every relationship, including your family and friends. Until that time, you will settle for the occasional bliss of brief surrender wherever you can get it, as your yearning builds to utter devotional desire to live full as the love from which your unsurrender has divorced you.

16

USE DESIRE AS
TRANSMITTER OF GIFT

*She is standing at the sink in the kitchen, wearing nothing. Her
buttocks are perfectly formed, and her long legs draw my eyes like
pouring water. As she turns to me her breasts come into view, and
my desire continues to grow.*

*I can feel I want her. I want to touch her. I want to press
against her. I want to enter her so deeply we become melded and
desire is gone to light in the edgeless chasm of our loving.*

*I can feel various strands of my desire for her. Part of me wants
to possess her. Part of me wants to experience her, touch her, taste
her, smell her, and feel her feminine resplendence in every way.
Part of me wants to be released of my desire for her, spent, so as
not to feel this urgency anymore.*

*But when I feel my most essential need, it is to recognize the
absolute truth with every inch of my being. Love. The fundamental
openness of being that is love. I need to be this love, spread wide
and large, in harmony with all, beyond all, or I suffer. The tension
of ignoring this vast truth—aggrandizing the self-eddy while
pulling away from the ocean of being—is unbearable.*

*And so sex becomes a false solution. If I spend myself fully, I
think, I can empty myself of tension, at least for a while. But deep
down I know this to be fruitless, degrading, and weakening. So, to*

the best of my ability, I practice another way of sex.

If I allow myself to feel my deepest sexual desire—to be gone fully in an intensity of love-bliss so profound as to be unexceedable—then I fall through the hole of my yearning heart. I look at her beautiful body, I feel my desire for her, and I give myself through that desire. I allow desire to draw me to the deepest truth of being.

She represents all that I want—not as an object, but as an evocation. Everything I live for is summarized in her form and in the promise of our union. Everything crass and weak and stupid, as well as everything effortless, free, and profound.

And so I approach her. Not to spend myself. Not to possess her. But to actively digest my separation in the acid of untargeted desire. Without craving this or that, without narrowing need to a nipple or vagina, I proceed to consume myself in the hole of immense desire. We fall into this space, attracted by the seeming promise, cognizant of the endless want, surrendered as the power of original desire. We give ourselves fully, not just in the blissful disappearance of our self-tension, but in the ceaseless effulgence of love.

We give our gifts through the opening of desire. We give our human gifts of pleasure and care and affection, yes. But we also unfold as the moment, rippled from the corner of a smile so revealed as to remain invisible to our daily stare. Peeling back the familiar, we gaze as the light itself. What began as tits and ass lucifies as the radiant tremendum, fully dissolved and fully expressed, undifferent from this instant. Such is my desire for her form.

Allow your desire to draw you into the deepest giving of love as possible. When you yearn for your lover, don't resist the desire, but also don't attach it to something less than your deepest feeling-truth. No carnal embrace in itself equals eternal love. No anatomical perfection satisfies the emptiness of gifts ungiven. No genital friction adds up to the fire of the heart unbound.

Allow desire to be a doorway through which to give your gifts, rather than a needful urge through which to acquire something. Convert the course of sexual want from contentment to boundlessness. Give from your heart so fully you die into the light of love, risen up together with your partner by the flame of sexual combustion, all edges vaporized.

Receive the moment of desire as an urgent invitation to remember and actively animate your deepest longings and heart-gifts with your whole body. What you really want is also what you really want to give. Love. Without end. Deep down, you know it. Sex can be the present exposure of this eternal shine of knowing. Desire is a shard of this light. Go through the desire, through love's invitation, and emerge reawakened in the same brightness, now recognized, as you began.

FOR HIM

You can only offer your woman as much consciousness as you are. Men often fantasize about having a big penis because it gives them the sense of really being able to penetrate a women, to split her open, to "give her what she wants," to fulfill her deepest cravings. But the penis is merely a physical sign for consciousness, both in religious iconography and on your body.

Men conflate "big penis" with "big consciousness." They secretly want a woman to worship their penis as if they were God. Most men really, deeply, want this. What most men don't know is that they *are* divine consciousness, and they can totally "fuck" their woman with huge consciousness, regardless of the size of their penis. Men intuit their capacity to ravish a woman into total love, bliss, and surrender—they even feel it as a kind of duty—but then they look down at their little wanker and begin to doubt their ability to give her what she needs.

To give your woman "what she needs" means to bring her beyond the merely personal aspects of love and sex through the strength of your consciousness. Most men consider consciousness to be something associated with their head. This is a mistake. Consciousness is another word for love, the open space of existence, the cognizant radiance of being, in which all things shimmer, including your body. And the only way your woman is truly "fucked" by your consciousness is *through your body*.

Most men get what it means to grow spiritually through words, books, discussion, self-inquiry, and understanding. Most women do not (except for the approximately 10% of women who have a masculine sexual essence). Women can certainly understand anything men can, but a woman's *growth* is more often based on cultivating fullness of love-energy than clarity of understanding. Self-inquiry and "spiritual discussions" are sometimes useful to women, but rarely conclusive or revelatory in the way they can be for many men. Most women identify with light or energy rather than consciousness, and thus it is through light or energy that their growth is most directly served.

Because they identify with light and energy, most women want to be seen as beautiful and felt as love. Your woman probably wants to be worshipped, adored, and desired as the main attraction in your life, just as you probably want your woman to worship your penis and treat you like God. Women confuse their fullness in radiant love with their personal worth in intimacy, just as men confuse their fullness of consciousness with their sexual prowess (and success in the world altogether).

As every young Casanova knows, nothing hooks a woman more than telling her how much you love her and how special she is, exclaiming her true beauty, proclaiming that you will always be together, and treating her like a Lady. And as every seductress knows, nothing hooks a man more than revering his mastery, venerating his Awesome Tool, and treating him like a Lord.

These desires in men and women are strong precisely because they are minor revelations of our deepest truths. Full consciousness and full radiance *are* worthy of worship. A man intuits the fearless, boundless, unthreatenable force of open consciousness that pervades the world, and so he wants to feel these qualities in his life, financially, creatively, and sexually. He wants to feel that he can "fuck" or pervade the universe into surrender, that he can give all of himself and bloom the world and woman into grateful and blissful openness.

He is smitten when a woman treats him like the best lover in the world because he feels a resonance with the deep truth that divine consciousness—with which he most deeply identifies—*is* that which pervades the world, the "ultimate lover."

A woman intuits the abundance, glory, beauty, and radiance in her heart, and so she wants to feel her love valued and adored in relationship. She wants to feel desired by her man and the world so she can give of herself totally, bodily and emotionally, as a blessing of love, grace, and life—the divine flow of light who she truly *is*. She will even give up her own authority in the hope of gaining a man's desire for her selfless giving, which is a miniature version of the abundant love and devotion that flows naturally from her heart.

In sex, the trick is to use these desires for the sake of growth. Rather than avoid or denigrate them, enjoy them consciously, transforming them from obstructions into boons.

For instance, feel as if your penis were *huge*. Not just ten or twelve inches, but *really* huge. While making love with your woman, feel as if your penis extended through her entire body like a massive balloon of light and force, filling her vagina, her womb, her entire belly, chest, face, and head.

Feel as if your belly were the base of your penis. For several breaths, inhale energy down the front of your body and fill your belly with deep force. Lower your center of consciousness from your head to your belly. Penetrate your woman from your belly, as if it was the source of your sexual love-force. And all the while, open your awareness, feeling outward, into and through your woman, from your heart, as you continue to breathe force down into your belly.

The amount of consciousness with which you can ravish your woman—the size of your "spiritual penis," so to speak—is determined by how fully you have surrendered as openness and love. Practice resting as openness, as free being, as unbounded love, even as thoughts come and go, fears clench and pass, and desire ebbs and flow.

Feel through the delights of your woman's body as well as the fantasies that may arise in your mind. Don't hold back as some kind of observer who stands apart from the sexual swashing and buckling. Open *as* the entire moment, including the feelings, sensations, thoughts, and desires of both you and your partner.

Feel through it all, and thus bring your woman through it all with you. Bring her to a place of absolute freedom by *being* free and totally heart-open while penetrating her with strong and sensitive love-energy, transmitted through your whole body, especially from your belly and breath.

If your belly is full of enough force and your presence is strong and "ballooned" throughout your woman's entire body, then you will be able to "give her what she needs." First, she will be smithereened in the intensity of pleasure and energy wracking through her body. Then, she will be vanished into a love that is her most essential desire, as well as her most true nature.

This love is much larger and more real than her need to feel valued for how she gives of herself. And your fullness of consciousness is much more eternal than the penile worship for which you would sell your soul. But you can use these lesser desires to pave your path toward utter dissolution in the fullness of love with your woman.

FOR HER

Suppose your man criticizes you. Perhaps he points out a way you have been selfish. In response, you may feel hurt and then angry. You've done so much for him, given so much of yourself, how dare he call you selfish?

To grow spiritually means to gradually identify more and more with who you really are, which is love itself, rather than with your self-image that is so easily coddled by praise and prickled by criticism. But how can you be the deep love who you are when you feel so closed, contracted, angry, or upset in your body?

The feminine way is not so much about feeling through emotion, sensation, and thought into the openness or space of being. This is the masculine way; since the masculine is at home in emptiness, it is attracted easily into the openness or space of awareness. But the feminine is at home in energy or light, the "stuff" of life. The feminine doesn't *want* to feel through everything into the openness of being. The feminine wants to feel. Everything. Fully. And in doing so, the feminine relaxes as love, which *is* the openness of being.

When you are angry, be angry! Forget about trying to feel through it. Forget about trying to go beyond anger. Be anger entirely. Feel anger in your toes, legs, vagina, and buttocks. Let anger move through your belly, chest, head, face, arms, and hands.

Be a body of anger. Move with anger. Breathe with anger. Dance with anger. Know anger from the inside out, as a force, as an energy, as a feeling, as a motive. Live as anger.

You will notice that when you allow your *entire* body and breath to flow *freely* with the energy of anger, eventually—in minutes or hours—your heart opens with the rest of your body. The feminine grows spiritually by realizing its identity with fullness, with energy—not by trying to go beyond an emotion or a "block," but by *becoming* it, totally, with the entire body. When you allow your body and breath to fully be and express any particular energy, then you are also able to feel the energy's "essential texture," which is love.

Anger is sharp love. Sorrow is hurt love. Fear is contracted love. As a woman, you realize love not by trying to go through or beyond obstructions, but by embodying the so-called obstruction, and thus *being love* in that particular energetic texture.

Feminine spiritual growth requires your willingness to feel everything and anything—including the most painful emotions—with your entire body and breath. This takes great practice, courage, and a willingness to feel that you are worthless.

Most women have a strong sense of what it means to be a "good woman." Their sense of value and self-worth often becomes based on being nice, good, loving, self-giving, helpful, generous, or beautiful. A woman like this will resist incarnating any energy that doesn't fit her sense of being "good." She won't allow certain emotions to run wild and free through her body and breath. She won't allow herself to express certain feelings or feel them entirely.

She will refuse to live as the fullest incarnation of love, moving and breathing as all of love's textures, "ugly" as well as "nice." And thus parts of herself feel empty of love. She denies herself the fullest depth of love by denying her body the freedom to live as every shade of love: rage, fear, grief, hate, joy, lust, sorrow, need, vindictiveness, vulnerability—every texture in the entire range of emotional energy.

To grow spiritually as a woman means to be able to live, move, breathe, and act as all of love's energies, spontaneously, without inhibition, and with every inch of your body. As you do so, you will naturally relax as love. When you embody an emotion—even a so-called "block" or "obstruction"—with your entire body and breath, then you are open as what the energy feels like from the inside. The feeling of *everything*—the nature of everything, the essential light of all existence—is love, who you *are*.

Even the most painful emotions are only love, rippled in a texture of pain. Whereas a man is predisposed toward emptiness, and so will gladly feel through the pain into the openness of being, a woman is more predisposed toward fullness, and thus won't be very motivated to feel what lies beyond the pain. She would rather be filled with painful love-energy than feel empty of any love-energy at all.

However, most women stop short of allowing themselves to be *entirely* filled with painful love-energy, so that their body is a body of pain and their breath is a breath of pain. If a woman does not stop short, she will find herself alive as the essential love-energy of pain. And this love-energy flows as the same openness of being that a man discovers when he feels through his emotions and sensations. *The feminine desires the fullness of love and the masculine desires the freedom of emptiness, and so there are two sexual paths to one spiritual bliss.*

When your man criticizes you—perhaps he calls you selfish—and you find yourself enraged, don't try to go beyond the rage or be free of the rage. Instead, wear rage like a fancy coat. Drink rage like delicious juice. Breathe rage like your favorite fragrance. Move rage like a crazy dance. Be rage, from your heart to the tips of your fingers, toes, and tongue.

This doesn't mean to simply go wild with rage. There is a big difference between wildly "expressing yourself" and totally *incarnating* wild rage. Merely to express yourself, you don't need to breathe fully or open your heart as rage. But to completely incarnate rage, you allow yourself, through practice, to breathe and move as rage with an open heart. Then you can love rage. And when you love rage, then you are love, dancing as rage. This is very different from expressing rage freely but superficially, without softening your heart and body as love in the texture of rage.

As you open every part of you so you can breathe and move as rage, you are likely to uncover the emotion that lies under your rage, which is often a wound of hurt. When your man criticized you, you probably first felt hurt before becoming angry. By incarnating rage fully, you allow yourself to feel the emotion behind it, the primary emotion, the hurt. Practice, then, to incarnate this hurt.

Allow your body to open as one big hurt. You may cry, your body may tremble, you may collapse in a ball on the floor. While doing so, breathe. Breathe as hurt. Relax your body open so you can feel hurt in your knees and jaw, thighs and heart, every part of you. As you do this fully, love will emerge through your body, inevitably. But in the meantime, it requires great persistence to continue keeping your breath, heart, and body open so they can flow with the energy of your emotions.

As you feel the hurt, you will feel how deeply you want to be valued and loved. You may recognize how often you do things for your man in order to feel loved. Seeing this, you may react by doing things for your own sake, so you feel less dependent on a man for your sense of worth. Both of these feminine strategies—giving yourself to others and finding self-worth independently—must fail, because they are not expressions of your essential nature, which is abundant love alive as all energies.

Until you can be alive as all energies, you will feel something missing in your heart and body. You will feel this emptiness or "hole" as a lack of love and self-worth. You may seek to fill this hole with love by pleasing others, by being a "good woman," or by standing independently and filling yourself with affirmations. Because you reject certain "ugly" textures of your own feminine incarnation of energy, you want to be reassured by your man that he desires you, that he wants you, that he finds you beautiful—or you try to convince yourself that you are worthy, whether a man desires you or not.

This is all a natural outcome of our spiritual naïveté. Men want to feel successful at their mission because they are naturally oriented toward the freedom of consciousness; the relief of accomplishment (and ejaculation) is as close as most men get to relaxing as the spaciousness of open being. Women want to feel loved and desired because they are naturally identified with the light of love. But most women resist incarnating the totality of light—the entire spectrum of love-energy—and so they feel like something is missing in their heart and body.

As a woman, you may attempt to fill your emptiness with energies of all kinds—from the taste of chocolate to the heat of passion. You may give of yourself in all kinds of ways in the hopes of feeling a man's desire for you, so deep is your fear that you are not valued, and so fragile is your self-worth. But if you allow yourself to fully incarnate these feelings of fear, need, and emptiness—if you open as them, breathe as them, and allow your body to be moved as them—then you allow yourself to live as the full power of love. You allow your body to be filled by every possible energy, all of which are textures in the full spectrum of the love who you are.

Then, the fullness of your love can teach your man how to embrace life—and your energies—fearlessly. The openness of your man's deep being can teach you how to be free and full even as your body ages and all of life passes. You can teach him the bliss of fullness while he teaches you the bliss of emptiness. You can teach him how to commune while he teaches you how to let go. You can enjoy your intimate relationship without obliging it to fulfill you, and he can enjoy his projects without obliging them to give him a sense of relief. Already alive as love and openness, you and your man can stop demanding from each other the adoration that you secretly doubt you deserve.

17

NEVER BREAK THE
THREAD OF SEX

*We had been making love for almost an hour. A sweet and bright
cocoon of love surrounded us. And then, I hurt her.*

*I didn't mean to. My penis went in a little too far, at the
wrong angle. Or something. Whatever I did, I hurt her. She
flinched. For a fraction of a second I couldn't tell that her flinch
was from pain and not pleasure. So I continued moving within
her. And hurt her again.*

*Then, she really closed down. She pushed me away, held
her hands up over her face, and began crying. She seemed more
emotionally wounded than physically hurt.*

*My accidental movements couldn't have lasted more than a
second or two all together. It was as if her memory of the previous
hour of deep loving had been totally erased. She was acting like
I was an abusive man, rather than a man who loved her, who
had been loving her with real empathy and sensitivity, and who
accidentally hurt her for a moment.*

Consciousness and love must be transmitted through every
thrust, moan, and gaze. A single dissociated movement or
sound can break the heart-threads connecting you and your

lover, triggering an emotional collapse. The feminine partner, especially, is very sensitive to this thread. Even a moment of the masculine partner's drifting can collapse the love, energy, and connection that had been established up to that point.

Trust can evaporate in just a moment of emotional dissociation or heart disconnection, especially during times of deep sexual vulnerability. The deeper you and your lover have relaxed into love, the more sensitive your hearts are to disturbance by subtle disconnection. The wind blows, the window creaks, you remember an important paper you left in your car; your attention wanders or drifts, for a moment your movements are mechanical or automatic, and your lover feels your distraction, acutely. The flow of desire drops to zero.

Hopefully, such moments can be felt, understood, and laughed about. Everyone drifts occasionally. Everyone, man and woman alike, has moments of distraction, forgetfulness, and sexual automaticity. Yes, these moments may cause hurt. They may break the thread of exquisite loving that has developed over a long and heart-opening sexual occasion. The best thing to do is to recognize what has happened without blaming either partner. Find the humor in the bumbling. Return awareness fully to the present moment of breath and smile. And wash the residues of forgetfulness away in the remembrance of love.

FOR HIM

Sometimes you want to kick back and let your woman do you right. You don't want to be responsible for guiding the sexual occasion. You want her to initiate it. You want her to be lusty and wild, a whore, a nympho, hungry for your sex. If, instead, your woman always requires that you remain super-sensitive and aware of her subtle needs, then sex begins to feel like a burden.

Many men feel burdened by life. They don't feel at home in life. For them, life is something either to master or to escape. Rather than relaxing as a lover of life, most men attempt to "win" and be victorious in life or "retreat" and escape from its demands. To most men, life is something "out there," and it has to be dealt with. Especially women.

Women are raw life. They are life in your face. They give you life's sweetest fruits and most bitter fruits.

Very little in life is more delightful or burdensome to you than a woman. Most men can handle financial calamity, creative struggles, and natural catastrophes with greater aplomb than they can handle their woman's moods, needs, desires, and energy. Women are as good and bad as life gets, for most men.

Sometimes woman and life are good, sometimes not so good, but almost always you are waiting for more, that imaginary time in the future, "one day." You probably suffer from the masculine delusion that if you work hard enough now, *one day* things will be different. You may not be living your life exactly how you want to right now, but *one day* you will. Maybe even *one day* your woman won't be quite so bothersome.

The masculine error is to live life as if it is going somewhere fundamentally different from this very moment. It is not. Life in this moment is as deeply fulfilling, blissful, and free as you are willing to *be,* right now. And the same is true of every moment.

Your capacity to relax as the openness of the moment does change over time—and not always for the better—but the things that you *do* in your life never amount to a fundamental change in how fulfilled or free you *are* in any particular moment. And neither do changes in your woman.

No matter how much your life or woman changes, you will not be satisfied as long as you are *waiting* to be satisfied, waiting for things to be different. To not be fully relaxed as consciousness, coincident with the pleasures and struggles of this very moment, is to postpone that for which you are waiting. And this is why your woman reacts so strongly to your lack of presence—even for a moment—during sex.

She *is* life. She feels your lack of presence immediately. She wants your fullest surrender in love, your deepest relaxation in consciousness, *now*. The fact that for the previous three hours you have been very present with her makes no difference if *now* you are in your head, drifting into thoughts of what you have to do tomorrow. A moment's loss of presence with your woman—or while mountain climbing, car racing, or boxing—results in immediate feedback, regardless of how present you have been up to that point.

Most moments of life seem more lax. We can drift for a moment without serious suffering. Life seems to give us plenty of room to be unconscious, distracted, wandering in thought and reverie, without killing us in response to our lack of presence. When we feel up to it, we enjoy a good challenge. But most of us are pretty slack, even though we may keep ourselves busy. We may occupy our attention with things to do, but we rarely commit ourselves to relaxing as the total presence of deep being in the present moment. Therefore, in the midst of our projects and our sex, we remain somewhat shallow and dissatisfied.

Most men tolerate a sense of chronic dissatisfaction while they wait for *one day* when things will be different. This masculine laziness—postponing your full presence and the deepest giving of your gift for a future moment—is intolerable to the feminine.

Your woman suffers your postponement, even if in the meantime you are working hard to "get there." She intuitively knows there is no "there" to "get." If you are not present now, if you are reinforcing a lack of depth now, how will this enhance your capacity to be more deeply present in the future?

Even if there is work to be done—as there always is—true growth means cultivating the capacity to remain free and present in the midst of action, not only when it is done. Focus is fine; a rigid collapse of love—being an asshole until your work is completed—is not. Neither is postponing authentic bliss for the sake of drifting in the mediocrity of functional attention, trivializing the depth of your being for the sake of achieving shallow goals.

The burdens you make of life and woman never seem to end. Yet, there is no need to look forward to *one day* because, even now, your life's tasks and your woman's moods do not actually limit your freedom in any way. In this moment, you are as free, deep, and relaxed as open being as you allow yourself to be.

You have probably made a habit out of paying attention to "things" and "doings" *as opposed to* opening as the freedom of deep being. Habits are hard to break. It takes effort to relax as deep being even *while* you are doing things because you have established a strong momentum of superficial attention. It is this superficiality, this lack of deep presence, that disturbs your woman, not your need to work—or your need to kick back and rest without being bothered.

Everybody needs to rest. Everybody needs "time off." Restoration or rejuvenation is an essential part of life. But your woman is rather sensitive to your self-deception. She is probably more than happy to support your need for rest. But resting and being superficial are two different things. When you feel trapped, constrained, or burdened by life, you can be sure you are being superficial, attending merely to the unending tasks and decisions that arise as life. When you are not sourced in the depth of open being, then you begin to hate life.

Your woman can feel when you hate life. She feels it as a "hate" of her, even if you don't mean it that way. The feminine *is* life. When you've "had it up to here" with life, your woman suffers your masculine error rather than simply feeling your need to rest. She feels your lack of depth and awareness, your lack of love, and she cannot trust you.

In most relationships, this dynamic may be quite subtle. Most men are almost constantly postponing their depth of presence for the sake of accomplishing a task or project, and so a woman learns to acclimate to her man's shallowness and his associated moods of dissatisfaction: burden, frustration, unfulfillment, or anger. In response, she collapses her radiance by shutting her body down so as not to feel her own pain, disappointment, and the lack of trust in her heart. Her closure and lack of radiance make her man feel even more burdened. And so on. Without knowing exactly why, mutual resentment and subtle tension begin to pervade the relationship.

Your woman can't fully open sexually unless she trusts you fully. She can't trust you fully unless you are clear in your deep purpose, have aligned your life so you are able to give your gifts, and are always doing your best to relax as who you really are, as deep presence, even while you "do things." Your woman wants to open herself to your deep presence, not to a self-deluded man who doesn't even know his awareness is absorbed in a stream of duties that leads nowhere but to more duties until death.

This moment is divine bliss. This moment is as deep and free as you are willing to be. But even if you are willing, it takes practice, because you have spent so many moments attending to the ripples of events rather than the ocean of deep being in which they arise.

Losing the thread of awareness while having sex with your woman is a miniature version of what you do most of the day. You'd think it wouldn't be such a big deal to your woman. You may feel, "Hey, what's wrong? I just remembered something I had to do at work, and so I wasn't totally present with you for a few seconds. It's not a big deal." But to her, the initial moment of feeling hurt may cascade into a primary lack of trust.

Fortunately, she will forget your lack of presence—if it is an exception, rather than the rule—as quickly as she forgot the three hours of total presence that preceded your infraction. Just come back to presence as soon as you are able. Be open, honest, and humorous about your drifting, and deepen the both of you in love.

If you recognize that you are chronically absorbed in superficial doings, then have compassion for your woman and yourself. She has suffered untold days or years of your lack of depth and presence, as you have suffered them yourself. Lack of depth *is* suffering. *The masculine error is to believe that this suffering can come to an end through activities and accomplishment.* Your woman reminds you that depth—love—is now or never.

Depth is your nature. You are inherently open and loving. You *are* openness and love. Relax as who you are, which includes woman and world. You will never master them nor escape from them. They *are* you. The light of your consciousness appears as woman and world. The moment you drift into assumed separation, as if you could surmount or escape them, they will bite you—that's how the universe reminds itself who it is: consciousness appearing as its own radiance alive as love.

Even when you are fully present and alive as love, woman and world may *still* bite you—just for the heck of it. "Mommy" may *not* take care of you if you are good; "she" has her own momentum. In this world, your love is as likely to be met with crucifixion as exultation.

Your idea of where things are going has very little to do with where things are going. If you haven't noticed, woman and world are far beyond your control. *One day* it may *not* all work out. But in any moment of utter surrender as the depth of who you really are, everything doesn't have to work out in order for love to be true. Just as things are, you *are,* alive as love, open as consciousness, appearing to itself as all forms. Your actions and true gifts, your need for victory or escape, your woman and the entire world, bloom spontaneously from—and dissolve in—this blissful ocean of open being.

FOR HER

Without a woman's strong influence, men tend to become divorced from the flow of life. Men like to pursue "ultimates"—ultimate spiritual attainment, ultimate athletic victories, ultimate scientific theories. Men use their bodies as vehicles for achievement, pushing themselves to finish projects, eating whatever is in front of them, having sex to relieve tension so they can rest and get back to work.

For men devoid of feminine influence, the world becomes a problem to solve rather than a flow of living energy. They no longer feel plants and animals, but study them. They no longer respond to the moods of nature, but try to analyze weather in order to plan properly. Often, they are barely aware of the natural, sensual world, so caught up are they in offices, computers screens, books, magazines, newspapers, television, meditation, and projects.

Without strong feminine influence (from their inner feminine, a woman, or an external feminine source like nature), men lose touch with loving relationship, sensuality, pleasure, and the flow of life itself.

What happens when a woman lacks strong masculine influence (from her own inner masculine, a man, or another external source)? She becomes *embroiled* in relationship, sensuality, and the flows of nature. Her life becomes like the weather, moved mostly by forces of mood and relational circumstance.

She never quite seems able to accomplish what she plans to do when she plans to do it. The phone rings, and she talks to her friend for an hour instead of working on her taxes. Her mood swings, and she spends a few days tangled in shades of crimson, bereft of humor and perspective. Her disposition is colored by the way her body, emotion, and intimate relationship feel today, rather than by the bloom of love that always beats her heart.

Men, by themselves, tend to neglect the fullness of life and relationship for the sake of possible goals; women, by themselves, tend to neglect life's possible depth for the sake of their current emotions and relationships. Many women, for instance, find it difficult to leave a bad relationship for the sake of a possibly better one that has yet to appear.

Most people are born with either a significantly more masculine or more feminine sexual essence. About 80% of all women are born with a more *feminine* sexual essence, and so prefer flowing to going. While shopping, they would rather browse and take their time than dart in, get what they need, and dart out. While eating, they would rather enjoy flavors and textures than eat just what is necessary to accomplish their goals. While talking, they would rather enjoy the flow of energy than make a point, conclude the exchange, and get on to something "more important."

If you are in this majority of women, you probably feel a need for external masculine influence in order not to become chronically embedded in your flow of emotions and relationships (just as the majority of men need external feminine influence in order not to become heart-dissociated robots of achievement and ideas). These needs are natural. Your emotional and sexual health depend on taking these needs into account. Furthermore, to grow spiritually without creating gaps in development, everybody must understand their true emotional and sexual needs in relationship.

There is a big difference between being *needy* and having a simple, honest *need*. If you hide chocolates in your purse and secretly pig-out on ice cream—only to feel guilty and bloated later—then this behavior can be called *needy*. Everybody, however, has a healthy and honest *need* to eat sweets occasionally, without complication or excess. In the same way, most women need external masculine influence, usually in the form of an intimate partner. But having this need doesn't mean you have to be needy.

If your life is not going where you want it to go—if you are not even sure where you want it to go—then you need more masculine influence in your life. If you feel stuck in a relationship that doesn't feel right, or if you tend to be swamped in emotions of hurt, self-loathing, or "numbness," then you need more masculine influence in your life.

We have already discussed the feminine practice of fully incarnating an emotional energy in order to unveil the heart's depth of love. Now we are talking about the gifts of practice that can be given *between* partners.

Masculine influence creates spaciousness and perspective in your life. You feel the big picture rather than feeling stuck in today's moods, feelings, and flows of relationship. There is obviously nothing *wrong* with moods, feelings, and relationships—just as there is nothing wrong with pursuing ultimate attainment of perfection—but it is only one side of the whole. The feminine tends to reduce life to "Do you love me?" in its many forms, and the masculine tends to reduce life to "How can I be ultimately free or successful?"

Feminine and masculine—love and freedom, embrace and letting go, radiance and presence—are not separable. For instance, the more you are concerned with love, the more you will be attracted to—and attract to you—a partner concerned with freedom. Your desires and your partner's will tend to be of the same depth: If you want to be appreciated for your body, your partner will probably want to be appreciated for his money. If you want to be appreciated for a deeper form of your feminine radiance, your partner will probably want to be appreciated for a deeper form of his masculine presence.

Feminine and masculine attract each other, creating a whole. Furthermore, each relationship grows through different levels of feminine love and masculine freedom. At the lower levels, a relationship is rife with neediness. If you have a feminine essence, you are needy for constant reassurance that you are loved, desired, and attractive, and your masculine partner is needy for your admiration of his success and attainments.

The next step of growth often involves throwing out the baby of need along with the bathwater of neediness. You realize that you don't like to feel needy (which is a sign of growth), and you think that you can develop your own inner masculine enough so that you don't need a masculine partner.

Some women—the 10% born with a neutral sexual essence or those old enough to have already "rounded out" their born disposition—can achieve this self-contained wholeness. Many women cannot. Many women—including the 80% with a feminine sexual essence in early and middle age—need appropriate masculine influence, whether it comes from a lover, teacher, therapist, or friend. You might like the idea of being an "independent woman," but the fact is that all of us are linked interdependently, and our health is based on the appropriately balanced give and take of air, food, ideas, money, love, *and* sexual energy.

Without proper and sufficient masculine influence in your life, you become depressed. If you do not rectify this sexual imbalance, you become needy. You develop excessive cravings for Mr. Right. You hunger for a man who can somehow enter your life—emotionally or physically—and bloom you into happiness. You seek a savior in the form of a lover, teacher, therapist, movement, or even a career. Eventually, if you can't find a source of masculine influence that you trust enough, you may resign yourself to a life of aching empty-hearted but self-directed independence.

However, if you can honestly own your natural need for the masculine to enter your life, then you can get it without becoming needy and therefore playing the victim role. The sexual truth is uncomplicated: You need your moods opened by masculine humor, perspective, and spaciousness. Your man needs his rigid thoughts and doings softened in the body of your love and brightened by the radiance of your heart. For most women and men, it's as simple as that.

You needn't feel weak or guilty because you have these needs, any more than you feel weak or guilty because you need food. Truly healthy relationships are not based on neediness or fear of neediness, but on a deep understanding of the mutual gifts and blessings of the masculine and feminine sexual forces.

At times you may notice yourself making a demand of your man that you know is unreasonable. This demand may be in words, but you may also express it through your moods. This "unreasonable demand" may be a sign that you are not getting the masculine gifts you need, and so you have begun to develop needy cravings.

The need for masculine gifts grows through stages. In the early stages of growth, a woman might be satisfied with a man who provides her with affection, money, perhaps children, and commitment. In the middle stages of growth, a woman needs a deeper exchange of ideas, shared interests, life-improvement, and a sense that they are growing in comfort and enjoyment together—the "good life."

As growth continues to develop, a woman longs for a man whose deep presence fills her heart with the bliss of love-devotion and surrender. (Notice that this deepest exchange has nothing to do with the external accomplishments or personality of a man. A woman at this stage might choose to open as blissful fullness in devotional relationship with the deep presence of divine being, without any intimate partner. She may also, at this or any stage, prefer to receive the masculine gifts she needs from another woman.)

You will attract a lover who matches your depth, stage by stage. For instance, if a secure relationship is more important to you than deepening love (which may or may not require a relationship to continue in its current form), then you will attract a man who is more concerned with security than with risking everything for the sake of deep heart-openness.

Because you don't necessarily grow in one piece, you might feel confused or divided inside. A less spiritually mature part of you may crave security in relationship while another part of you may yearn for the bliss of surrender in unbounded heart-openness. If you have chosen a loyal man who is committed to you and your children, earns a good living, and shares interests with you—but whose deep presence is compromised by his needs for external accomplishment and security—then part of you will feel safe while another part of you begins craving more depth. You may eventually feel anger and resentment toward your man even though he is trying to do everything right for you and your family.

Have you resigned yourself to a sexual and emotional life far less full than you know you want? If you have, you will feel frustrated and angry with your man. You will find yourself attacking him energetically, testing him with energies you know he can't handle. And for what? If you chose him from the part of you that wants comfort, mutual interests, and emotional security, then you can't blame him for not taking you to deeper places. A man with the depth to consistently love you into blissful heart-surrender certainly won't give a damn about conventional emotional security—he will have left that neediness behind long ago.

The emotional neediness of your growing identity and the inherent needs of your deep heart-essence are two different things. At some point in your growth, you will be ready to practice opening as the love that you really are. You will be ready to meet the needs of your deepest heart, which often have little to do with comfortable security in relationships of emotional attachment. At this stage, a man whose needs meet yours will have grown beyond his neediness for financial security and a sense of accomplishment.

This doesn't mean you *reject* relational commitment or financial attainment as you grow. You may enjoy a fully committed relationship and great financial success, but these needs are contextualized by deeper needs. If your relationship must change form or your means of livelihood need to be rearranged in order to better cultivate your heart-fullness and gifts of deep love, so be it.

If you want to help your man learn to be fully present with you—not needily preoccupied with his thoughts, concerns, and projects—then be fully radiant with him—not preoccupied with your emotional neediness to feel desired or valued. If you have attracted a man who lacks full presence, who dissociates during sex and breaks the thread of your heart-connection, then you can be pretty sure that your love-radiance is likewise compromised. You have attracted each other to learn the necessary lessons for continued growth.

You grow by learning to gift each other with what you truly need without catering to neediness. He honestly admits that he sometimes needs your radiant love to help pull him down from his head into deeper heart-connection. You honestly confess—without guilt or feeling weak—that you sometimes need his presence, humor, and perspective to help free you from your emotional closure and confusion into open-hearted joy.

While misguidedly trying to "do it all yourself," you may fluctuate through cycles of boredom, emotional hysteria, confusion, and the staunch close-heartedness of a falsely independent woman. Before your unmet needs develop into needy cravings, find a way to receive the masculine influence that your feminine essence might require for its balanced health and continued growth. Although there are many ways to do it, intimate relationship is one of the best ways for the masculine and feminine to share their genuine gifts of freedom and love.

18

BE SEXUALLY
AVAILABLE TO LOVE

She walked up to me with that look in her eyes. Her hands held my waist as she brought her body slowly against mine, her breasts first touching me, and then her belly and legs. She moved one hand up my back to my neck and head, running her fingers through my hair while she continued looking into my eyes with longing.

I wasn't in the mood for sex. I wasn't even in the mood to love. I was tired, thinking about all the things I had to do. The last thing I wanted was a woman rubbing herself against me, wanting my attention.

However, I had come to know that my own closure was a habit. A bad habit. It's one thing to have business to attend to. It's quite another to imprint the body with a posture of self-enclosure and relational refusal. It's a childish stance. It's the epitome of unlove.

And so, rather than pulling away from her, I felt her call to love. I consented to relax into my body, be present with her loving, and loosen the hold on my energy, so that as we stood and embraced a warmth flowed between us, easing through our soft surfaces.

My body became more alive from her loving. She brought her hand to my crotch and gently squeezed. A few moments before, while I was still closed down, I would have gritted my teeth and pushed her away, not wanting to be distracted from my narrow do-mode. But, having opened, I received her gesture of love and inhaled deeply, becoming larger through the gush of her administration. As she revitalized my sexual root, energy and desire infused up through my trunk and every branch of my body.

Breathing deeply together, relaxed and enlivened, our bodies transferred love through their flesh entire. At that point, we could have had sex. My heart and body were as ready as hers. Or, we could have happily parted ways. I could have continued with my work, refreshed, grateful for her loving ministrations, which had made my energy far more powerful, whole-bodied, and grounded than it would have been had I not consented to her love. Whether we had sex or not, she had opened me by gifting me with her love and energy, reminding me to choose love rather than closure. By skillfully evoking the force of desire, she rounded out the flatness of my life.

I n a sexually polarized relationship between healthy lovers, sexual availability is often a sign of open-heartedness and energetic bodily fullness. Sexual closure, on the other hand, is often a sign of unlove, closed-heartedness, and dissociation from the body. Practice keeping your body relaxed, your heart open, and your energy flowing. In other words, practice the disposition of sexual availability to love, without necessarily having sex. Sexual availability simply means you have the capacity to respond to love with the energetic openness of your body.

Whether you are a man or woman, when you are stuck in your head, in your ideas, plans, and concerns, then your body is denied consciousness and energy. It is as if you exist only in the top few inches of your skull, the rest of you hanging there like a puppet attached to the stings of your mental intention.

When you deny yourself full and conscious embodiment, your body begins to wither and stiffen. When you unceasingly withdraw energy upward into the heady realms of strategy and future goals, sex dries up. If you have sex at all, it becomes a lurid quickness, an expeditious method to make contact with your partner, spasm in lust, and thunk into sleep. This kind of sex depletes the body of what little energy it retains, helping you to conk out so that the next day's work can begin when the alarm rings.

It is no wonder that many people are sexually unavailable to their lovers; they are stuck in their heads, drained of sexual energy, narrowed in their emotions, or simply disconnected from, and unaccustomed to, the full flow of love in their bodies.

If your lover comes to you in love, and you are simply too busy to respond sexually, fine. It is healthy and necessary to be able to focus on your work or your children and say "no" to your lover when appropriate. But if your "no" is accompanied by a limp body, a dry body, an empty body, a resistive body, an angry body, a fearful body, a body of shallow breath, rigid pelvis, and genital absence, then you are not *choosing* "no." You are a slave to the habit of unlove.

A readable sign of the degree of your bodily inhabitance is genital readiness. Man or woman, does energy flow through your body when your partner touches you lovingly? Or, are you so enclosed in your head that your body resists such ministrations? Again, there is a difference between choice and resistance. Choice is a loving, soft, intimate decision, "No, my love, not now." Resistance is a reflexively closed or simply numb non-response, an inability to receive or give love through the body.

If your body can't receive love and be moved by love, then you won't be able to give your true gifts through your work or to your family. All true gifts are gifts of love. Sexual availability, your capacity to flow with sexual energy, is a quick measure of your love capacity. If your body is unable to receive and give sexual energy—even for a moment, before you get back to work—then more than likely your life is suffering from lack of love.

If your energy is blocked, practice receiving and giving love with your whole body, through every inhale and exhale, even as you perform your necessary duties. Sexual availability is a matter of relaxing into the natural openness and power that you are, through breathing and feeling from your deep core fully and persistently. Then, your true depth of love and consciousness can freely express itself through your body as you engage in intercourse with the world, day and night.

FOR HIM

As your heart and penis become more connected—through circulating energy up your spine and down your front, breathing fully and deeply, and learning to love even during intense sexual stimulation (as detailed in *The Enlightened Sex Manual*)—you will find that your whole body awakens sexually. When you see a sexy woman, your toes splay, breath deepens, belly relaxes, and heart opens. At this point, promiscuity becomes obsolete and your commitment in intimacy can deepen. You aren't randomly moved to have sex with all the women who turn you on. Instead, you are inspired much more deeply, and your entire body shows it.

Your energy doesn't get stuck in your head or penis, resulting in hungry fantasy or genital urge. Instead, your energy circulates through every part of your body and emotions, refreshing and enlivening your spirit, bones, and heart. Beholding a sexy woman becomes an occasion of inspiration and blessing.

A sexy woman can inspire you. She can move you. But to what? At the animal level you are moved to penetrate her physically. At the conventional human level you are moved toward social intercourse: "Hello. You seem very interesting. Care to have a drink?" As you grow spiritually, you allow your attention to be pulled toward her—as it will in any case—and then you feel *through* her and rest as the timeless "orgasm" of infinite openness.

Who you really are—the openness of radiant consciousness—is who she really is. You need not *do* anything to experience the bliss of deep union with her sexy radiance. As you behold her and surrender your boundaries, bliss swells as the open radiance you are, aroused in consciousness by the tease of her appearance.

However, if you don't recognize her light as your light, then you will inevitably "want" her in some way. Her radiance is your very nature, but as a man you tend to identify with consciousness apart from light. You are "here" and she is "there" and by god you wish the two of you were intermeshed in bliss.

As long as you neglect to recognize the deep being who you are, you will think and perhaps act promiscuously. No matter how committed you are in intimacy, you will be pulled and distracted by the seeming promise of a sexy lady. Her body, lips, and eyes; the way she moves, smiles, and looks at you. She seems so alive and luscious. She seems to offer you a radiant cure for your dis-ease, a freshness to enliven your weary soul, a release from the desire that stresses you. You want to dive into her beauty and be relieved of all burdens in the bliss of love's union, if only for a few moments.

So, do it. But do it *totally*. Without touching her, without even moving toward her physically, do what you really want to do: combine yourself with her to the point of oneness. From a distance, feel her body as if it were yours. Breathe her breath and relax in her energy. Inhale her fresh radiance and circulate it through your body fully. Feel the desire in your heart to open *with* her and do it, now.

Worship her, sexually, with the fullness of your consciousness. Her radiance naturally evokes your presence, like a magnet. Allow your presence to be as deep as her radiance is bright. This evocation is her gift to you, her feminine blessing. She attracts you into worship, into open-hearted, open-bodied awe. She smacks you with the baptism that life is not only ideas, projects, and lofty goals. Life is *alive*. Life is *energy*. Life is *she*. And you do miss her so, especially when you have forgotten her, forsaken her, and ignored her in the missile pursuit of your mission.

To worship the feminine and receive her blessings is what it means to be sexually available, not only within your committed intimacy but also as you move in the world. Allow the feminine in all her forms to evoke your awe. From head to toe, submit to the inevitable pull of your *deepest* desire, allowing your presence to coincide in bliss with her radiance. Then, from your deepest purpose, direct the love-energy of your arousal for the sake of all beings.

Although women want to be honored for their natural radiance, they don't usually want to be hit on. Outside of your committed intimacy, it is important to receive a woman's energy without interfering in her life. If your heart-dissociated sexual want is projected toward her, her body will wince and close down to protect itself. In a world of psychic masculine projectiles, the feminine must guard her true heart. This diminution of radiance is everyone's loss. Allow a woman's sexiness to serve the purpose of unfolding your depth of presence into the world, for everybody's sake.

FOR HER

For the feminine, sexual availability means, among other things, to be available to humor. If you are too moody, serious, or tense to see the humor of a situation, you are unavailable to this important masculine gift.

Humor is different from enjoyment. Nature is full of pleasure (and pain), but there is no humor in nature. The trees, ocean, stars, and mountains are full of radiance, energy, and joy, but absolutely bereft of humor.

Humor comes from the ability to see a situation from the outside and have perspective on it. Everything comes and goes. Everyone who lives, dies. Everything that you feel is important—your body, your family, humankind, the earth, the solar system—passes.

Ultimately, every situation is transient and unnecessary, regardless of how serious or real it seems when you are in it. Cosmic humor is to see the unnecessary nature of everything. This utter freedom is a primary masculine gift.

The feminine laughs with pleasure and delight. The masculine laughs because ultimately nothing matters, everything is one big joke. The joy of life and the humor of its non-necessity are both part of full human realization. For a woman to be sexually available to the masculine means, in part, being able to receive the spacious freedom of humor.

Suppose you are in an agitated mood. Your man approaches you with humor, making light of the situation. In various ways, his message to you is "Why are you so upset? It's no big deal." But you can't let it go. You are momentarily unavailable to the vision of masculine humor.

There is nothing wrong with this. At times you *are* unavailable. In these moments of being stuck emotionally, practice embodying and breathing the emotional energy so you can dance as love in its texture. This is a primary feminine practice, as we have already described.

But spiritual growth also involves the mutual gifting of bliss. Your radiant energy can serve your man's relaxation into bliss just as his presence and humor can serve yours. Although, there will be times when he won't open to receive your radiance, just as there will be times when you won't open to receive his humor.

Being sexually available means that you are open to receive his humor. You welcome his freedom to infiltrate your mood-energy. Sometimes he could do the silliest thing—make a funny face, dance a ridiculous jig—and suddenly you are smiling. Don't cling to your mood as if it were your precious "right" to bitch and moan. Honor his humor as you would like him to honor your radiance. Open in response to his humor as you would like him to open in response to your love-energy. Receive his humor as a blessing. Humor can be very sexy.

A man's humor can wash away your heavy energy in an instant, opening you in freedom and happiness. His humor can liberate you from being caught in the swirl of relationships, emotions, and thoughts. The more you feel stuck, heavy, or confused, the more you have denied receiving true masculine humor in your life.

Life is very full. Relationships do matter. Your feelings are important. Do not deny the reality of your physical and emotional life. But also do not deny the masculine gift, which would liberate you in laughter. Ultimately, nothing matters but love. You are either living as love or you have forgotten love in the confusion of up and down, left and right, him and her. To be "fucked" open in this freedom of love depends, in part, on your availability to the masculine gift of liberating humor.

19

USE YOUR
DARK SIDE TO
INCREASE ENERGY

We are making love, and it is feeling a little plain. The love is full, in a medium kind of way, but our motions are pallid. Our affection for one another is real, though our coupling is somewhat glib.

I'm trying to feel as deeply into my heart and hers as possible, but I feel stuck. Our energy feels muted and shallow.

So I go into my darker depths. I find the animal parts of myself, the untamed, wild, and aggressive parts of myself. I begin pinching her, grabbing her flesh and squeezing with my claws, biting her, licking her with my sloppy tongue.

She joins me, hitting my chest, scratching my back with her nails, wrestling me with all of her wicked strength.

I go darker. I become a nightmare man, a demon, a murderer. I am thrusting into her, forcing into her from my darkest energy.

She loves it. She goes really wild. She becomes the destructress, strangling me with her hands, biting me really hard, pulling my hair, thrusting against me with huge power.

We look into each other's eyes and smile. In the midst of dark discord, our hearts and bodies frolic. Our energy has been liberated from niceness.

After a few minutes of dark, heaving, murderous ravishment, we lie together, loving with a force beyond everyday smiles and

kisses. Even as we lay motionless, in deep embrace, gazing deeply
into one another's eyes, no timid affection lessens our heart
    Through every bite, growl, and silent merger, the energy of our
love has been expanded.

One source of great sexual energy is your dark side. Here lies your animal past, your heritage of blood and boil. You can't ravish your partner in sexual love if you have the emotional disposition of tea and toast. It takes bent knees and slinky pelvis to do the wild thang. You need the tongue of a snake and the tail of a tiger to wind taut the wicked line of sex, hoisting vulva and penis up through the heart and all beyond. Without the dark side, sex is flat, quiet, a genital peck.

Most people are dissociated from their dark side. They fear their own passion, which includes the energies of anger, aggression, and hunger. Passion sometimes pounces, sometimes crushes, sometimes devours. Passion is dangerous. Without love, passion is destructive. But without passion, love is wimpy.

Passion and love intertwine in the fabric of sex. Together, they rile and provoke, soothe and calm. But with too little love, passion becomes abuse. With too little passion, love becomes lukewarm. The way to give more love is through opening your heart, trusting, and giving from your deepest core. One way to generate more passion is by giving love from your dark side. The darker the expression, the greater the passion.

By accessing your dark side, you can increase and move energy when it is low. A little dark breathing, like a lion or whore, or even some slapping, clawing, or fanging, can suddenly enlarge desire and move energy. Whether you want to move stagnant energy or magnify what is already moving, a short burst of sincerely felt dark energy, circulated with love, synchronized with breath and movement, is one of the best ways to do it.

FOR HIM

If you have a masculine sexual essence, a part of you is probably fascinated by violence and death, at least in entertainment. You may enjoy action movies involving war, cops, martial arts, or political intrigue. Or, perhaps you prefer more ritualized competition-to-the-death in the form of sports, poker, or even chess. Any kind of man-to-man "combat," from business deals to political debate, can arouse a man's masculine essence.

Some of this is pure biology, a by-product of testosterone-drenched male nervous systems programmed through years of evolution to "fight," "fuck," or "flee." Some of it reflects the masculine spiritual preference for emptiness, the timeless and deathlike cessation of desire and thought that "peak" moments of combat and competition often provide. Some of it derives from enjoying the masculine game of putting yourself in a constrained situation or trap (in sports, gambling, philosophy, martial arts, crossword puzzles, or meditation), and then fighting/figuring your way out it: for most men, there is no greater pleasure than finding their way to freedom and achieving their goal, whether in an end zone or in pure transcendental being.

This masculine trip can serve to defile or purify you. If you take yourself and the game too seriously, you will debase yourself, losing touch with the essence of who you are as you identify with how the game is going. However, if you can remain aware of your deepest being—and more importantly, if you can live *as* the expression of this open depth and loving presence—then playing out the masculine game can actually help dissolve the tendencies that trap your attention and create suffering.

Imagine you are at the movies with your lover. On the screen you see a violent scene: In the woods, a naked lady is tied spread-eagle to the ground. The bad guys are sexually teasing her, and they are about to have their nasty way with her. Just in the nick of time, the hero appears on the scene and barely escapes death himself. But in the end, he manages to use his courage and superhuman skills to kill the bad guys. His shirtless, muscular body is covered in grime and blood as he unties the grateful woman who embraces him, pressing her vulnerable and smooth body against his sweaty chest.

You come home with your woman and get in bed. The movie really got you going. Your adrenaline is pumping. You are filled with images of bound women and close calls with death. Even your lover seems a little excited. You start having sex more aggressively than usual. She bites your shoulder, scratches your back, and pounds your chest with her fists. You go wild, really thrusting hard and deep. Is this kind of sex good for your spiritual growth or is it a corruption of love?

The movie has probably elicited certain engrams or patterns of action that have been conditioned into you biologically, psychologically, culturally, and spiritually. How you choose to approach the "problem" of your aggression will depend on where you think your aggression is rooted. However, after you have grown sufficiently and cultivated relatively free and deep awareness, it becomes largely (although not entirely) irrelevant whether your sexual aggression is rooted in your animal heritage, too much violence on TV, or your warrior's heart. What matters in terms of further growth is this: are you lost in the pleasure of aggression or are you alive as love in the texture of aggression?

This difference can be illustrated by an example. Suppose you are a father. When you and your two sons play ball together, their whole world can become reduced to the game, whereas you know you are *playing* the game. Your sons might become pissed off for hours depending on the game's outcome, but for you the game is just a way to share love with them; it doesn't matter who wins.

In the midst of the game, your awareness is much more spacious than theirs. You keep track of the hands on your watch, keep an eye on your daughter who is playing in the yard with her friends, and really enjoy the love and "quality time" with your sons. It is natural and pleasurable to spend this time playing ball with them, but the transmission of love might just as well occur while you are camping, eating at a restaurant, or reading a bedtime story.

One of the beautiful aspects of intimacy is that it gives you a chance to love in the texture of all energies—to play "ball" gentle or rough and everything in between. In doing so, all energies become an expression of love.

Without the spaciousness of love, aggressive sexual energy is simply an expression of its causes. Maybe your sudden passion is testosterone speaking, or perhaps it is the uncorking of long suppressed emotions created when your parents beat you. It may feel good to "let it out." It may feel good to "express your dark side." But the real difference is made when you can let it out and express it with the same love with which you would play ball with your son. Otherwise, you are reinforcing, rather than transforming, the energy of aggression.

Aggression by itself can be destructive. Because all habits are reinforced by use, simply acting out your aggression is a good way to continue being aggressive. It might feel good to do, and it might be healthy for you to release pent-up tension, but nothing is truly transformed. You might help to heal an old wound, but you don't grow.

Growth—as we are using the term—involves a shift of emphasis from getting lost in the game to playing the game as a transmission of love. Having rough sex with your woman might be enjoyable and even healing if you have suppressed the aggression within you. But growth involves being love, breathing love, feeling the love in your woman's heart, and allowing yourself to open so the force of love can live *as* you—while also enjoying aggressive sexual play.

Over time, you learn not only to express the whole of your energies, dark and light, but also to transform "defiled" emotions into expressions of love. No matter how aware you become, there are probably still some corners of your psyche that remain hidden. Often these corners are concealed in sexual shadows. Although you can encourage and support the growth of your awareness, you can't always "make" yourself more aware of these areas. These dark corners emerge into view at their own pace. And when they do, it is important that you can recognize and work with them.

Maybe you go to a movie that riles some sleeping snakes from the corners of your sexual psyche. Afterward, at home in bed, you find yourself more sexually aggressive than usual with your lover. This can be a healing moment, one that can express your oft-hidden dark side. Beyond that, however, you can consciously embrace the dark energies, practice to relax into the depths of your open being, and allow love to live in their form. Then, rather than reinforcing the energy of aggression, you reinforce your capacity to live as love—in whatever form is spontaneously called forth.

When you notice your attention getting lost in rough sex—like your child lost in a ball game—remember love. Relocate the love in your heart and in your woman's heart, the love that is living as the dance of this moment. Breathe love, receiving love as you inhale and giving love as you exhale. Established in love, notice the specific experiences of this moment, including your lover's teeth sinking in the flesh of your shoulder and the aggressive pressure urging you to ejaculate. Feel the "who" that is aware of these experiences. Practice relaxing as this spacious, open "who" of awareness as love flows in aggressive sexual play. *Be* cognizant openness, alive as the energy of aggressive love.

It takes practice and requires real growth to transform your aggression. You can tell your son, "Hey, it's only a ball game, and what really matters is that we love each other." He might agree for a moment, but he'll probably get lost in the game again and again, until his awareness grows enough so that love is his priority and the game is just one more way of living love. The same goes for transforming emotional and sexual "defilements" into expressions of love, depth, and open being. You will only grow beyond the fixation of your games when you are ready.

You can't predict when a hidden part of you will pop up. Some of your obsessions with violence, death, and competition have been buried under years of strategic denial that have long ago become subconscious. When these parts do come to the surface, you may be lost in aggression in one form or another for a long time before you realize that you are ambitiously trying to win some game rather than living as love in the form of the game.

Most men spend the majority of their lifetime trapped in the seriousness of a game—trying to win financially, sexually, emotionally, or spiritually—rather than relaxing as open being, living as the spontaneous flow of love, blessing all others with the gift of their deepest presence. It is important for each of us to approach our self-created suffering with great humor and compassion. We have created our opposition in order to express love in the form of a struggle to be free, which is the great masculine pleasure. But once we realize that our suffering is due to being lost in the game, we can relax open as the freedom of deep being. We can learn to enjoy the game and play it impeccably, not as an aggressive compulsion but as our chosen expression of love.

FOR HER

You may find that certain clothing not only expresses your mood, but adorns it, magnifies it, and resonates with it in an almost archetypal way. One day you enjoy wearing a fluffy summer dress. The next day you skulk around the house in a black slip and four-inch heels. Far from frivolous, a woman's relationship to energy—via clothing, jewelry, and make-up—can be an important domain of spiritual practice, if understood fully.

Just as no man is satisfied until he feels absolutely free, no woman is satisfied until she feels the fullness of love. The feminine seeks love via bodily fullness. Besides food and drink, this fullness can be sought through pregnancy, sex, pain, and pleasure. Anything that fills the body with sensation (chocolate, bathing, massage) or emotion (love stories, gossip, music) is preferable to emptiness.

This fullness can be sought in many ways. A group of women can gather for a "tea party" of sorts, eating and drinking, but mostly exchanging energy—chatting, laughing, saying nothing of "importance"—and yet feeling fulfilled and refreshed by the love transmitted between friends. The feminine doesn't need competition or conclusions—as the masculine often does—in order to clarify its consciousness. The feminine is more often served by the full flow of love-energy than by intellectual clarification.

As we've discussed, an important aspect of feminine growth is the capacity to embody the full spectrum of energy in all of love's forms. Clothing, make-up, and jewelry are an integral part of this practice of energy incarnation. Our culture has become so masculine-oriented that men and women often consider these things petty or superficial, but they are not. Neither are their associated feminine pleasures such as shopping, checking out what other women are wearing, looking at images of well-dressed models in magazines and on TV, or talking about accoutrements and accessories with friends.

Such interest and discussion is the equivalent of men talking about sports scores or the ultimate nature of reality. Sports, business, philosophy, and science are masculine endeavors to achieve freedom, whereas dance, food, dress, intimacy, and communion-via-chat are feminine endeavors to enjoy the fullness of love-energy. Every man and woman engages to some degree in both masculine and feminine endeavors.

Although at first glance some might be tempted to say that the masculine endeavors are more important, this prejudice is due largely to today's masculine bias. Which is more important for human happiness, philosophy or dance? Scientific analysis or bodily healing? Obviously, both are necessary and equally important. Obsession with clothing—which is only a form of energetic proficiency, a feminine mastery of the subtle forces of bodily energy—is no different than obsession with sports, which resonates more with the masculine desire to break through constraint into freedom.

Obviously, there is nothing wrong with science or sports. But human growth involves more than fascination with technology and playoffs. The masculine in all of us must grow to embrace the *depth* of freedom—true relaxation as the openness of deep being—in order for its enjoyments to be contextualized in love, defusing them from purely achievement-driven motives.

Likewise, the feminine must grow to intuit and embrace the fullest depth of love through relaxed surrender as effulgent radiance. Then, conversation, dress, and make-up are no longer ways to *seek* love-energy, but are ways to energetically adorn, express, and commune with love-energy. Knowing how to dress becomes a feminine art—a means of energetic healing and balancing, magnifying the flow of joy in the world and yourself—rather than a hope to *get* more love and attention.

Lingerie can have as much meaning for a person with a feminine essence as Heidegger does for a person with a masculine essence. The artful use of dress or philosophy can lead to greater realizations of love-energy or freedom. Of course, in actuality, most purchasers of lingerie are as superficial in their love as most readers of philosophy are superficial in their awareness. Dress (or whatever energetic art you enjoy) and philosophy must both be practiced in the context of real depth in order for them to reach their fullest potential.

Any nerd can fervently read philosophy and think they are getting it, yet fail to relax as the open freedom of deep being. Any floozy can shop for lingerie and yet limit the bliss of love to admiring her butt in the mirror or feeling desired by men. The arts of intellectual challenge and bodily adornment resonate with divine freedom and divine love *if* they are done with depth. Otherwise, they are simply ways that people recycle their endless desires.

Suppose you and your women friends get together for an evening of feminine growth and enjoyment. What might that look like? One of the many possibilities is a dress-up party. Everybody brings all kinds of clothing—lingerie, furs, leather, bikinis, elegant gowns, high heels, slippers, etc.—as well as an assortment of jewelry and make-up, from black nail polish to silver glitter.

Then you dress and adorn each other. Use your intuition to feel what would most heal or open each woman into a deeper incarnation of love-energy than they usually allow themselves. You might decide that one of your friends needs to wear a fur boa, black fishnet stockings, red lipstick, white pearls, and nothing else. You suggest it, and she says, "I wouldn't be caught dead dressed like that." Notice if she becomes tense, distant, nervous, or closed down. If she does, then you probably picked just the right thing to help heal her.

The practice is to learn to relax in full love-communion with your friends while incarnating the entire range of energy, especially the aspects you resist (in yourself and others). One of your friends might be totally comfortable in a see-through teddy, but absolutely refuse to dress like her mother. Another friend might never have thought of wearing a steel-studded leather dominatrix outfit; she doesn't resist it when you put it on her, but it certainly brings out an aspect of her "bitch" energy that she has kept hidden under a "nice" woman persona, especially when she holds a whip in her velvet-gloved hand. Perhaps you dress an ardent business-woman in a gauzy gown of soft, sensual, and ethereal splendor, and she breaks out in tears as she allows everyone to appreciate her beauty.

Once everyone is dressed in ways to serve their incarnation of energy, then the "party" proceeds to oblige deeper love. Play your favorite and least favorite music, dancing to the entire spectrum from classical to disco, from religious choirs to hard rock.

It can be easy for women to deny depth for the sake of fun, laughing, dancing, and enjoying their time together, but without devoting their energy to open-hearted surrender. Be careful to persist through any woman's tendency to remain superficial. Through your dance with her and the way you touch her, oblige her to open more fully and surrender in love-communion with you more deeply. Trust your deepest intuition and you will spontaneously know what to do to serve your friends' openness moment by moment.

Continue coaxing each other into opening more fully. Open your hearts and bodies through a wide range of dance, dressing and undressing, laughter, massage, and perhaps some wine enjoyed with strawberries dipped in chocolate. Praise each other's beauty, open-ness, and courage. Celebrate in sensual delight without reservation, but more importantly, practice to open yourself into ever deeper love-communion with your friends.

While dressed in the clothing you are most afraid (but secretly yearn) to be seen in, while dancing the aspects of your energy you keep most hidden, open yourself as love without closure. Practice incarnating full energy into the parts of your body and heart that feel empty, and practice communing in love no matter how silly, nervous, uptight, or closed down you feel. This kind of party is not merely about "expressing your dark side" or "being free." It is about deepening your capacity for sustained love-communion.

If you are practicing fully, you will probably have tears of both pain and laughter. Moments of disgust and desire. And when you all get so tired that you can barely go on, continue practicing to stay open with great intention. There really is no excuse to close down and stop loving. Your body may be weary, but that doesn't mean your heart must cease communing with your friends in love.

Most women (and men, of course) have their personal justification for not living wide open as love-bliss: they're too tired, they're not loved, they can't trust their friends, they have to keep their guard up for social or financial reasons. Although these may seem like facts of life, with practice love can be lived even while lying on the couch in exhaustion, dealing with a misguided friend, or earning money.

In part, feminine spiritual practice involves repeatedly drenching your body in the fullest love-energy possible, saturating your heart with the urge to open, in spite of your tendencies to remain closed. Men often benefit most by calling each other on their shortcomings, pointing out their tendencies to remain held back by fear, and lovingly challenging each other to "go for it," to take the leap into the unknown. Most women, however, don't grow so much by having their limitations pointed out verbally. When a woman's personal tendency to close down is described to her, she is more likely to feel devalued than inspired. The feminine grows more through the non-verbal coaxing of love than through verbal challenge.

Through dance, dress, touch, and sensual enjoyment, the feminine in each of us is given the same opportunity to open beyond fear as the masculine is through honest criticism and challenge. Most men—or anybody identified with their masculine aspects—thrive on looking at their limits. They love to be challenged. They often need to have something to "fix"—even their own limitation—in order to feel like they know what to do to continue growing.

But most women—or anyone identified with their feminine aspects—thrive on praise. They grow more through resonating with love than through hearing about their limitations. For a woman, the bodily "demand" to open in love, communicated by her friends through ecstatic dance, sensual delight, and heart fullness, helps a woman through her characteristic love-refusal more than any amount of discussion usually does.

Dress, dance, and the "demands" of bodily delight offer the feminine the same context to grow as the masculine is given by a challenging consideration with close friends. In both cases, care must be taken so the gathering doesn't remain superficial; the intention must be to go deeper than mere fun or intellectual competition. The feminine desire for love, and the arts that serve love's embodiment, deserve as much honor and cultivation as the masculine desire for freedom and its arts. Sacred dance and sacred philosophy are revelations of the same openness of being. True equality is based on the validation and embrace of both the feminine and masculine ways.

20

USE DOMINATION AND SUBMISSION TO MAGNIFY DESIRE AND POLARITY

Sexually speaking, the masculine is the force of direction and the feminine is the force of energy. That is, the masculine provides the form in which the feminine can freely flow, like the structure of the riverbank guides the energetic flow of water. Less obvious is the fact that the force of the river's water carves the shape of the riverbank that guides it.

Neither masculine nor feminine is superior or inferior. Both are part of the same process whereby men and women learn to recognize their oneness and love their twoness. Masculine and feminine are both necessary for the fully polarized sexual dynamic. Whether homosexual, heterosexual, or bisexual, in any given moment, one partner must be more like the water and one partner more like the riverbank or else the flow of sexual energy will become shallow or dry up.

For instance, if neither partner is willing to take the masculine lead and direct the moment, then the immense feminine power of sexual energy will go all over the place, never stabilizing in the deepest gorges of love. Sex may be fun, intensely pleasurable, and wild, but it will tend toward the superficial, repeating the same pleasurable patterns over and over without growth in depth.

On the other hand, if both partners insist on taking the lead, there will be no flow of water, no force of sexual energy, no abundant liquid ecstasy in which to dive and commune. The rigid stance of control will predominate if both partners are willing to be the riverbank, but neither is willing to let go and flow freely in the pleasure of love.

Every man and every woman should be able to enjoy both aspects of sexuality, masculine and feminine, deepening the sex as well as widening the energy of ecstasy, directing the flow as well as creating the energy of the flow. Although both aspects of sexuality can be accessed and enjoyed by every man and woman, each individual will have a preference dictated by his or her sexual essence.

Every man and woman, heterosexual or homosexual, will find their sexual complement in a partner who most enjoys playing the opposite sexual force to theirs, masculine or feminine. Therefore, it is important that every person understand and be willing to embrace the fullness of both masculine and feminine forces without denigrating or shying away from either.

Sexually, the masculine can be felt as the force of directive penetration and the feminine as the force of energetic reception. Both partners should be able to sensitively penetrate the other partner's moods and resistances and bloom him or her into love from the inside out. And both partners should be able to receive the love of the other, opening in pleasure, trust, and surrender, thus actively evoking greater energy and love. Penetration and reception are both active roles. Neither is passive. And neither can function without the other.

At the physical level, both man and woman should be able to play the active feminine force by opening to receive the penetrative love of their partner (orally, anally, or genitally, via tongue, finger, penis, or sex toy). Everyone has their preference for various forms of sex, and nothing should be forced on anyone. But to continue growing, it is important to discriminate between healthy preference and deleterious fear.

It is fine, of course, if you simply don't enjoy a finger entering your anus in a gentle and loving way; but if you automatically and totally shut down emotionally and physically to your partner's penetrative love, then you probably have a resistance to opening in other ways to receive masculine love, sexually or spiritually. Perhaps as a child you were abused by penetrative masculine force, emotionally or sexually, and thus developed a resistance to opening to the masculine aspects of your lover even as an adult. Or, perhaps for other reasons, you simply don't trust relaxing, surrendering, and opening your heart and body so thoroughly that you allow yourself to be ravished by masculine spiritual force, which invades your being and opens your depths to the absolute one of love.

The deep love that is your very nature embraces both masculine and feminine, in yourself as well as in every man and woman. Therefore, you will limit your capacity to rest as the depth of your natural openness if you resist embracing the masculine force of spiritual penetration or the feminine power of spiritual surrender, whether you are a man or woman.

Another way to characterize these sexual forces of spirit is that the masculine is the force of pervading presence and the feminine is the force of attractive radiance. Sexually, the masculine partner practices allowing himself or herself to be attracted beyond separation into the radiant love and abounding energy of the feminine partner. The feminine partner practices allowing every cell to be pervaded and opened by the masculine partner's strength of presence. Strong masculine presence and powerful feminine radiance make for a sexual polarity full of consciousness and love.

If you are playing the masculine sexual pole (whether you are a man or woman), one of your gifts is to be able to sweep your lover off his or her feet, to ravish your lover, and to obliterate your lover in love, so that all layers of resistance are pervaded by your presence of consciousness and dissolved in deep love. Both partners should have the capacity to do this at times, though the partner with the more masculine sexual essence will enjoy "taking" or "ravishing" his or her lover into a total surrender in love more often.

If you are playing the feminine sexual pole (whether you are a man or woman), one of your gifts is to be so radiantly alive, allowing so much love and pleasure to flow through your open body, that you become irresistibly attractive, drawing your lover's attention into the realm of overwhelming feminine pleasure, so your lover can no longer hold back but must yield bodily into the oneness of love. Both partners should have the capacity to do this, but the partner with the more feminine sexual essence will more often enjoy incarnating this power of attractive radiance and "enchanting" or "seducing" his or her partner into a total surrender in love.

If you do not have the opportunity to enjoy this deep play of ravishment and pleasure, then the need to do so will go underground in your psyche. You will begin to develop "kinked" versions of this healthy masculine and feminine play. The healthy masculine desire to penetrate your lover's emotional resistance and open him or her into love will become rape fantasies, or fantasies of controlling and dominating a sexual partner. The healthy feminine desire to uninhibitedly flow with the power of attractive ecstasy and be surrendered as the water of love in your partner's trustable riverbanks will become a fantasy to be controlled, raped, bound, restrained, and forced to give and receive pleasure.

These twin desires to dominate and be dominated, to command submission and be submitted, are simply expressions of the irrepressible human need to play the full range of masculine and feminine sexual force. These universal forces are in each of us, man or woman, though they are most apparent in those individuals with more extreme masculine or feminine essences. However, each of us can learn to express these forces in love with our chosen intimate partner. If we suppress these natural forces within us, then our internal circuitry becomes kinked. Our bodies develop symptoms of tension and closure. Eventually, due to the pressure building up behind the kinks, we may find ourselves desiring extreme versions of these same forces.

If we are too ashamed to live our actual desires with our lover, then we may try to experience them from a safe distance without personal involvement. We may want to read about domination and submission in romance novels and porno stories, or see them lived out in movies, on TV shows, or in adult magazine pictorials. If we are unwilling to embrace and metabolize our own secret desires, then our fascination with forced sex and pleasure will eventually manifest in the culture at large, being lived out by people less suppressed than ourselves.

The entire answer to the widespread depiction in the media of abuse, self-abuse, violence, victimization, and rape, as well as the actual perpetration of these behaviors, is not simply to make such conduct illegal. This is a necessary first step. But these desires and behaviors will continue to manifest themselves in our culture until, in addition to healing our past wounds, our deep spiritual masculine and feminine desires are acknowledged and acted upon.

Ultimately, a necessary part of the solution is to learn to live our natural desires in love, with a trusting and trustable partner (before our desires become pathological, manifesting as internal symptoms or external projections). Then, the deep and healthy spiritual desire behind the need for sexual domination and submission makes itself known: it is the heart's deepest desire to navigate to truth (masculine) and surrender in love (feminine) beyond all fear and resistance into the open trust of unbounded being.

The following exercises can be done by both men and women, in homosexual as well as heterosexual relationships. Since most readers of this book will be heterosexual men with a masculine sexual essence and heterosexual women with a feminine essence, I will use this more common sexual orientation in the examples to simplify the descriptions. However, these exercises can be effectively practiced by anyone, man or woman, heterosexual or homosexual, in accordance with the principles outlined here.

If you are a man (or playing the more masculine partner), try to get in touch with your masculine sexual desire to guide, penetrate, and ravish your lover so deeply that she is gone in love. If you have become weakened in your ability to do this, a good way to get in touch with this part of yourself is by exaggerating it. For some specific period of time, play master to your lover, while she plays your slave. Command her toward greater pleasure, her own as well as yours. Train her to open and receive more and more love. Punish her for disobeying. Reward her for submitting to your direction. Tie her up and force her to experience so much pleasure that she can only surrender, since she has no other choice.

Of course, this is as much of a test for her as it is for you. Does she really trust you? Does she trust that you will lead her to greater pleasure and love? If she doesn't, what is the basis of your relationship? Are you worthy of her trust? Have you navigated to your own deep truth, so you have the capacity to guide her heart to its depth? Are you attentive to her needs when she is at your mercy? Can you feel her emotional and sexual flow, and thus guide her to deep love and ecstasy, or are you an unfeeling klutz, a master unable to serve your slave?

Perhaps she doesn't trust you because she shouldn't. Perhaps you have never taken the lead with love and integrity, guiding her into more love and openness than she has ever experienced before. Now is the time to learn how to do so.

When you are both ready, then reverse this play, so the woman is the master to the man who is her slave. This time, the man is commanded toward greater pleasure and openness, disciplined, punished, and rewarded, with the woman taking full responsibility to navigate their play to the deepest possible ecstasy and love.

Whether man or woman, playing the slave is not simply a matter of passively submitting to the whims of the master. Rather, the slave is the active force of pleasure and attraction. The slave's moans, writhes, and vulnerable expressions of trust attract the master into deeper love and service. The point of the exercise is the magnification and deepening of love, trust, and pleasure—vulnerable obedience is just one way to elicit this openness. If you are the slave, allow your body to freely exhibit the signs of your pleasure, moving in unconstrained ecstasy. Allow your trust to be so complete, and your love so total, that you would literally do anything your lover wanted.

In many ways, it is the slave who has the sovereignty in this kind of sexual play. It is the slave's ongoing choice to transfer his or her power of command that creates the master. This choice is a choice of trust and love that grows over time.

As master or slave, when you test your limits by exaggerating your natural play, you will discover the little nooks and crannies of your distrust and unlove. It is easy to hide your resistance to giving and receiving pleasure and love during a normal day, but in the midst of exaggerated play these limits will become glaringly obvious. What don't you trust about your partner? What pleasures are you afraid of experiencing or expressing? Are there parts of yourself or your partner that you don't really love? Do you trust your own capacity to bring your partner into the very depths of open and unfettered being?

With practice, you can work through your limits and doubts. Consciously encountering your resistances, you can learn to breathe love through them. Then, you and your partner will be able to freely express love, trust, and pleasure as both master and slave. Fear will not limit the openness and humor of your play. At this point, when you are both freely loving, the practice of domination and submission no longer serves your growth. However, it may still be useful to play this way on occasion to reinvigorate the energy of your partnership if old roles and sexual styles become too set and mediocre. Such play may also arise spontaneously as a delightful expression of the extreme masculine and feminine dynamic in any moment of sexual enjoyment.

However, be aware of this kind of play becoming fetishistic or obsessive, whether you are a man or woman. For example, some men become obsessed with the feeling of a woman sexually dominating them. If their intimate partner is not available for this kind of play, these men will pay a lot of money to be bound, whipped, and forced to serve a sexually dominant woman. This is an exaggerated version of a man's healthy desire to contact his own feminine energy, to learn to open and trust the pleasurable guidance of another, to freely let go into ecstasy without having to be in charge, to be bound by a woman's desire, to be the water freely flowing within the banks set down by the masculine command of a dominating woman.

There may be many reasons for his need to submit to domination: He may be acting on a spiritual desire to contact a higher feminine archetype to which he can devote himself. He may be healing—or wallowing in— the wounds of childhood abuse. He may simply want to shift from being stuck one-sidedly in his masculine at the corporate office all day.

But whatever the reason, he has developed a strong need to relax and open, guided by another's command. He wants to feel controlled, restrained, and taken by a partner he can trust. He wants to feel forced to submit to pleasure. He wants to enjoy obeying a force of love more masculine than himself, relax his own volition, surrender in ecstasy, and flow where he is guided. If he is homosexual, he will play this with another man. If he is heterosexual, he will want to surrender to the command of a dominant woman.

This play can be natural and good and healthy—if it is occasional and filled with humor, trust, and love. But if a man (or woman) becomes addicted to this play, if he depends on it for sexual arousal, then he must face the kinks that perpetuate his exaggerated desire. Perhaps he has a true feminine essence and this is the only way he will allow himself to express it. Perhaps he is afraid of his own strong masculine, and so must project it outward and receive it from another. Perhaps he's tired of being responsible for making the decisions all the time and now he wants to enjoy following someone else's lead for a change. In any case, there is a big difference between addictive obsession and rejuvenative play.

The play of domination and submission is only truly restorative when it leads both participants to love beyond their present limits. With practice, the dominator learns to take total responsibility for guiding both participants into devotional surrender—to one another, and then through one another into open love. The dominator learns to navigate the sexual play toward divine surrender, not simply toward egoic pleasurization. The desire to trustfully guide a lover toward heart surrender in whole-body ecstasy is one thing; the self-aggrandizing need to control someone in order to feel strong is quite another.

Just as the dominator may have loving or selfish motives, so may the submittor. Individuals who simply degrade themselves are not exercising the deepest responsibilities of the submittor. To submit in total love and trust can be a gesture of fearless and empowered communion, rather than an expression of self-loathing or self-abnegation.

The power is in the river, even while it submits to following the banks. As a conscious slave, your ongoing choice to transfer command to your partner creates the dynamic of the play. Your willingness to be totally unprotected deepens the trust between you. Your display of vulnerable pleasure attracts your partner into greater responsibility and sensitivity. To play the slave in a healthy and heartfelt way is to create a dynamic of deep love, not to feel inferior to the master. Yes, in the sexual play you obey a master whom you trust—but as an act of powerful love, not as an act of weakness. To play the submittor is to be the river whose power of openness and flow of love shapes the riverbank even as the river conforms to the riverbank's shape.

A weak person is afraid to lose love, and so will obey a partner in the hope of garnering security in the relationship. A weak person obeys in the hope of being loved. But a strong person realizes that the highest form of existence on earth is as a servant. We are here to serve each other. We are here to serve our lover, which means to heal our lover with pleasure and enlighten our lover with love. Such a servant is a slave to divine love, and will do anything to draw a partner into the relaxed openness of total love-abandon and communion in divine fullness. This is true submission: communion in divine love and surrender to the openness of being itself.

The unhealthy play of master and slave reduces each partner to a narrow role in the hope of satisfying their egoic self-image while securing a partner who is hooked to them by selfish need. Alternatively, the healthy play of domination and submission always increases the recognition of each partner's divine nature and expands their capacity to commit themselves to the total communication—sexually and otherwise—of love, respect, compassion, pleasure, and trust.

The process of sexual deepening is served by anything that heightens the *conscious* play of masculine and feminine, penetration and reception, ravishment and surrender, the command of love and the obedience to love. Anything that allows you and your lover to navigate toward a greater depth of being, to surrender more fully, to bypass your social sense of self-control, and devotionally yield into the throes of unguarded communion and openness in love—anything that allows this deepening will serve the both of you.

Why defend yourself when all you want to do is give and receive love? Why hold back when all you want to do is be free to ravish and be ravished in love? With your committed intimate partner, in humor and tenderness, use the practice of domination and submission to explore your areas of fear and to expand your depth of conscious passion in the play of masculine and feminine love-gifting.

21

EMBRACE YOUR
DARKEST DESIRES
IN LOVE

Whatever aspects of your "dark" energies you don't embrace in yourself, you will tend to project into the world. You will continually be faced with the energies you most fear, in yourself or in others, until you learn to love in the midst of them. Therefore, learn to lovingly embrace your full spectrum of human energy, dark and light, aggressive and gentle. In this way, you quench your excessive need to experience the more aggressive or wrathful aspects of the human energy spectrum—in others and in entertainment—because you have drunk deeply and fully metabolized your own dark energies in love.

When you can be open in love with your partner in the sexual play of pseudo-violent situations, you will no longer find violence so fascinating when you see it in books, in movies, or on the news. By playing with these kinds of experiences in love with your partner, you no longer oblige entertainment or other people—so-called "bad people"—to carry the energies that you are afraid to embody and own in yourself.

By enjoying the consciously wrathful and lovingly aggressive aspects of ourselves, we reduce our desire to watch exploitive TV shows about needless human suffering and aggression, serial murders, and violent tragedies in order to satisfy our need to experience the full range of human energies. Then, TV and other forms of entertainment are free to inspire our deepest truths and creativity, rather than merely function as disowned extensions of our nervous system, projecting back to us, at arm's length, the more "aggressive" and "victimized" parts of ourselves that we are unwilling to embrace and metabolize in our own conscious heart.

Our fascination for, and resistance to, dark, violent stories of victims and abusers evaporate when we can lovingly play both the victim and abuser roles in the humor of love. When a sudden desire to be "taken" or to "take" arises within us, a few moments of playful tussle in bed satisfies our natural yearning to experience these darker, more frightening and intriguing aspects of natural human energy.

The tragedies of abuser and abused, of aggressor and victim, are stepped-down versions of our spiritual desire to let go into openness or surrender into love. Tragic "entertainment" is usually a dark play on our most essential desire and our most essential terror: death, which feels like letting go or surrendering.

You can recognize your dark desires as occasional and extreme expressions of your deep desire for ego death or spiritual surrender, which is practiced in two ways, masculine and feminine.

In the masculine way, you practice ego-death by letting go of everything you hold onto, persisting in simply witnessing your desires for consolation and comfort as you relax and die into the unknown, into the free-fall of unsupported open being, moment by moment. In the feminine way, you practice this voluntary surrender beyond fear by relaxing as an uninhibited willingness to be permeated by love, invaded by love, ravished by love, *in* love and *as* love, so any sense of self other than love is obliterated in love's fullness.

Ego death or spiritual surrender can be terrifying. It requires that we realize to our core that every moment of life is a fleeting mirage of security. Everything we hold onto—from our precious independence to our beautiful family—is in the process of change and will sooner or later disappear forever. Everything and everyone dies, though we fight against this fact. We live in stress because even though we fight against death, we also know it awaits us, tempts us, and threatens us in every moment. Dissolution is our overt physical terror and secret spiritual hope.

In fact, if we are really sensitive, we can feel that, as in a dream, our experience right now feels rather spacious or transparent, simultaneously real and inconsequential, altogether unnecessary, even as it continues; in a sense, it is as if we were already dead. This total openness without any thing or body on which to ultimately depend is the way it is. It is also what we fear most.

Most people intuit their life's temporariness and the ultimate futility of trying to hold onto anything, including life itself. They may try to avoid thinking about it, but deep down they know that, in the end, nothing matters but love. Love is the open nature of this very moment. It is the spacious fullness that abides as every person's essential being. Most people intuit their spiritual need to surrender everything into this love, to "die" in order to be "reborn" as this fullness of conscious and open being. If people don't live their everyday life on the basis of this need to surrender, relaxing into this "death" directly and consciously in their spiritual life, then their natural need for surrender or "death" gets expressed in sexual fantasy.

One of the most common feminine sexual fantasies is to be "forced" to surrender into pleasure and love, hopefully by a sensitive and committed lover. One of the most common masculine sexual fantasies is to feel a lover surrender and *want* to surrender to the demand to open into pleasure and love.

Furthermore, the masculine in all of us is obsessed with "death" in the form of violent or life-risking situations, whether at the movies or in sports. Our deepest masculine desire is to yield the separate-self sense into blissful openness and freedom. This is the "death" the masculine truly desires. It wants to "break through" all limits into the freedom of the limitless.

But since most of us are unaccustomed to the bliss of direct spiritual surrender, we settle for substitute breakthroughs. Instead of breaking through our fear and "dying" into our natural stress-free being, we get all excited about breaking through a defensive line and "killing" an opposing football team. We may spend years directing our lives toward the post-climactic freedom of making a financial "killing" or a philosophical "breakthrough." Probably, the most common realm into which the masculine misplaces its desire for breaking through resistance, releasing stress, and dying into bliss-ful openness is sex.

Violent challenge and the possibility of death often tease the mas-culine in us sexually, rather than reminding us of our inevitable need for spiritual surrender into open being. Without spiritual support, this need often gets played out in bed: the masculine in us either wants to break through our own tension and surrender into the death-like release of orgasm or break through our partner's tension and feel him or her surrender sexually. Or, if possible, both.

The feminine in each of us wants to be disappeared or "murdered" into love, too, but by means of fullness rather than breakthrough and release. The feminine in us wants to lose itself in the fullness of over-whelming love. But if we don't surrender directly and open as the deep fullness of love that is the nature of our very being, our feminine might try to fill us "to death" with "love" in the form of chocolate, shopping, conversation, and children.

Chocolate is delicious. Football is exciting. Family and friends are wonderful. But if we use them as *substitutes* for the fulfillment that only occurs when we relax as the true openness of our very being, then we never quite get it. Something always feels missing. We do not feel filled with absolute love. We do not feel released in absolute freedom. Unfulfilled and tense, we begin to look for darker, more stepped-down versions of love and freedom, of fullness and release.

Sex and death are potent reminders of the central spiritual need in men and women to let go of all holding and be, simply, unbounded and unprotected in deep love, free in the natural openness of this moment. The need for love and freedom—to be love, totally free and open—drives all of us. The *feminine* in each of us wants to be filled with love to the point of blissful surrender, and the *masculine* in each of us wants to be released in freedom to the point of blissful dissolution.

Whether we use chocolate or sports, shopping or gambling, sacred dance, meditation, or orgasm, we seek to surrender ourselves and open to the blissful fullness of love or break through limits and lose ourselves in the freedom of limitless openness, empty of stress. Through feminine or masculine means, we seek to experience obliteration in fullness or dissolution in emptiness. And sex is where we most often allow this pleasurable "death"—or else we fear doing it ourselves, and therefore try to satisfy our craving by requiring it in stepped-down and sometimes twisted versions on TV, in movies, and in books.

What can you do to learn to be free as love in the midst of dark energies? How can you experience the depth of sexual fullness or release you really want? As a sexual practice, with a partner whom you trust, play with your various dark energies. Talk vile filth with each other. Dress in leather and chains. Rip off each other's clothing. Take turns and playfully pretend to strangle one another. But do all this in the flow of love.

While playing with these dark energies, breathe fully (circulating energy up your spine and down your front, as described in *The*

*Enlightened Sex Manual)** while giving and receiving love from the depths of your being. Remember to be careful. You are not trying to hurt each other; you are learning to give and receive love and remain open to the core of your deepest being while consciously enjoying the dark, aggressive, or deathly aspects of human energy that you might otherwise tend to disown.

While remaining sensitive to your partner's needs and chosen boundaries, practice by pretending and playing with your darkest sexual energies. Pretend to be the "rapist" and the one "raped." Pretend to be the "abuser" and the "abused." Pretend to be the "perpetrator" and the "victim." Act out these dark energies with love, humor, and playfulness. The mood should be passionate and wild, but also exquisitely sensitive and caring.

As you express these dark energies, always remember to breathe through any tensions that arise, emotional or physical. Keep your belly and chest soft, open, and full of energy. Stay emotionally connected with your partner, always practicing to feel him or her from your heart. From the depth of your being, offer your deepest love to your partner's deep being, and receive your partner's love, while also playing with these dark energies sexually.

Over time, you will find that by learning to remain open, loving, and full while playfully expressing these dark energies during sex, your capacity to access the fullness of your power throughout the day increases. Rather than cutting yourself off from your own dark energies, you learn to embrace them, be empowered by them, and use them for the benefit of everyone. After all, these dark energies are often what we socially refuse but secretly desire or are fascinated by. So why not learn to wield them with love, for the sake of magnifying love?

* David Deida, 2004. *The Enlightened Sex Manual.* Boulder CO: Sounds True, Inc.

By learning to stay open while we express our internal energies, we also learn to stay open when the darker energies of life meet us from the outside. We can directly enter into life with strength and humor, without hiding from the violent and aggressive energies that characterize many aspects of our present world. These dark energies are not truly separate from us. They are part of all of us. And we must learn to give and receive love in their midst—otherwise darkness reigns *without* love.

When our heart's desire to lovingly ravish our partner becomes unconscious and dissociated from love, it becomes a rape fantasy or a need to be "entertained" by violence toward the feminine. When our heart's desire to be lovingly pinned down and ravished by our partner becomes repressed and separated from love, it becomes a self-sabotaging and often subconscious desire to be victimized or hurt by masculine force.

When we don't allow ourselves to lovingly cuff and be cuffed by our lover like playful tigers scuffling in bed, then, over time, our aggression builds up. No longer connected to our heart, our aggression can fester into loveless rage, expressed outwardly (the masculine way) as the abuse of others, or expressed inwardly (the feminine way) as self-abuse.

Rather than disconnecting from aspects of our heart's deepest desire, it is better to embrace and express the whole spectrum of human energy, dark and light, with great respect and tremendous love. We must learn to stand strong as love, to give and receive love from the depths of our being, even in the midst of dark energies. Then, abuse and self-abuse cease. Estranged versions of our true desires relax in the "welcome home" of love: blind aggression relaxes as tender passion; victimhood relaxes as fearless love-surrender; and titillation with death relaxes as the worship of free consciousness.

PART IV
REMEMBRANCES

22

HONOR FEMININE
INSPIRATION

*When I look at her, I am awed. Her beauty, her lusciousness, her
smile, her eyes full of love; she makes my life worth living.*

*When I look at her, I am repulsed. Her ugliness, her resistance,
her anger, her need; she makes my life an unending burden.*

*She drives me crazy. I would do anything for her, give my life
for her. At other times, I want to be away from her, without her
constant emotional twists and turns.*

*Altogether, nothing inspires me more than her. Her
attractiveness pulls my heart, body, and mind toward her. I want
to take her, make love with her, and enter her deeply, until we are
both turned inside out in love.*

*When I see a radiant woman on the street, suddenly, the
bright light of the world shows itself, and my drudge is instantly
combusted in delight. Her attractiveness fills me with life and
energy, awakening my happiness.*

*And yet, it is not enough. She is the most delicious fruit,
woman. But, so what? And thus it is her insufficiency, too, that
draws me through appearance. Her lips, her legs, her apparition,
are not enough. Her mind, her laughter, her embrace, are not
enough. Finally, her love is not enough. I am not satisfied.*

First drawn to her in every way—sex, conversation, laughter,

*love—then finding myself disappointed in the trap. I want to
leave, find a juicier fruit, but I don't. She is ugly now, dangerous
with poison hate, and I have been tricked, loved into the jaw.*

*It goes nowhere, this woman thing. And so, splayed between desire
and dissatisfaction, I am forced to yield my hope directly through the
surface of this moment. There is no in or out; only recognition born of
absolute frustration, in place, exactly now and here.*

*No motion actually ever moves me closer or farther from her,
though in my stupidity I dream of approaching the bosom of her
love, and she also snarls in my nightmares. She is everything, the
world, every possible world, every reward and punishment. She is
everything I want and everything I want to avoid.*

*Woman. She moves my mind and body and heart. She fills
my fantasies. She makes me cry. She evokes poetry from me.
She gives me perfect moments. Horrible moments. And I'm still
thinking of her.*

*I realize I cannot get enough of her to not want more. Nor can
I get away from her and be done. Nothing I do, no movement I
make closer or farther, changes anything fundamental. I cannot get
her or escape her because—so suddenly obvious—she is me.*

*I try to be other than her so I can have a reason to live, some
pleasure to look forward to, some fear to conquer. But she has
cornered me in the sound of my own effort. Every attempt I make
rings only of hope and fear, but nothing changes. She laughs
at me, loving me, hating me, indifferent to me. Nothing means
anything to her. Meaning is the flavor of my own search. And,
usually, she is the meaning.*

*She is the carrot I am reaching for while holding the other
end of the stick. The closer I get, the farther she goes. When I
think I have her, I want more, I want different, and again, she is*

just out of my reach. When I don't want her, she is everywhere,
unavoidable. I can't get away. There is no option. It is endless.
And so, in place, I stop reaching for her. I stop running toward or
away. My game, meaning nothing or everything, is over.

Suddenly, her pull and push vanish. She stands here,
motionless, as my experience, every stitch of dread and secret want
unwrinkled into smooth. I feel into her, putting on her body like a
skin. Her emptiness is my home. I offer myself through her form.

The feminine in all her forms is the ultimate inspiration. Earth, beauty, ocean, music, light, your best friend's girlfriend. She is muse. She evokes desire, fear, and effort. Sexually and creatively, she is the motive power of life. Women and men are attracted to her equally. Poems are written, wars fought, monuments built, marriages begun and ended, for her. But she somehow eludes our grasp.

The feminine form is incomparable beauty, to man and woman alike. All of nature is summarized in her body, her moods, her energy. We must honor the feminine in all her glory, dark and light, without getting lost in her. She is ultimately attractive, all motion and color, and ultimately nothing, a Cheshire smile without the cat.

We can bow to her, knowing this secret. We can enjoy her and make love with her and through her. Her smile can continue to inspire us, and fill us with happiness. However, if we don't understand who she really is, we will only fear and desire her. We will hurt her, negate her, exploit her, run from her. All men and women are either lusting for her or turning from her, in every moment, unless they are at one in love, feeling through and as her shimmering, magnificent, endless, and empty form. And sex is the epitome of this practice.

23

COMBINE SEXUAL
ENERGY WITH
CONSCIOUSNESS

As I stand in the living room, she jumps onto me and wraps her legs around my waist. She kisses me with a wet open mouth, her tongue searching for mine, as her hands grab my ass and pull me closer between her legs. She is grunting through the kisses, wanting me, begging with her groan and hungry body.

For a moment I am lost in her energy. She is so beautiful, and her desire makes me hot for her. Her wild energy gets me going, and momentarily I become her partner in lust, grinding against her, shoving my tongue through her teeth into her mouth, wanting to plunge myself more deeply into her.

But it is not enough. It feels empty. Shallow. Pure lust without depth is fun, but ultimately boring. I want her, no doubt about it. But I want her horny and deep, not just horny. And I want the same of myself. So I align my desire with consciousness.

I feel through her wet lips, my hardening erection, her silky moan. I feel through the heat of need, the wild energy that moves us both against each other. My breath deepens. My face relaxes. My belly expands with power, and she feels it, as if my body has become one big phallus of consciousness from toes to head. She continues bucking against me as I become more rooted in open awareness.

Her energy begins to become aligned by my consciousness. She can feel that I am not lost in the energy, but stand full, free, and in love. I am not suppressing her energy or mine. I am still fully alive. Even more alive than before. More forceful in my sexual presence. But I am not swirled into her frenzy. Rather, her frenzy is penetrated by my consciousness. She seems to love it.

After a few minutes, I begin concentrating on my breath. I draw the inhale down my front, filling my belly, sinking my feet into the earth, and then exhale the force up our spines, so we both hover above in the space of wide light.

However, she begins to sense that I have become too mechanical. Instead of being lost in her energy, I have become lost in my technique. So she moves her body against mine, bites my ear, and makes the most erotic sounds imaginable.

Her amplified expression of delight awakens me from technical ardor. I realize that I have indeed become ensconced in my narrowness of purpose. I have disembodied into the realm of goal and practice. I have forgotten love and pleasure. But now she has reminded me: consciousness without energy is boring to her. Dry. Rigid.

So, I relax my effortful technique and inhabit every cell of my body and hers. I feel into her. I submit to the openness of her love and embrace the energy of her pleasure. I breathe the force of consciousness into her and through her. In doing so, my heart is opened by the force of her sensually loving embodiment, and her heart is opened by the invasion of my unrelenting awareness.

Consciousness and energy must always love together, or else we become lost in either dry practice or wet frenzy. The basic rule is this: Align energy with consciousness and transmit consciousness via energy.

Without consciousness, energy tends to rule, and sex is reduced to mere sensuality and pleasure without the recognition of selfless love and deep truth. Without energy, conscious sex becomes a heady, rigid, technical exercise of awareness, almost clinical. Rather than make these typically feminine and masculine mistakes, always align energy with consciousness and transmit consciousness through energy.

In general, the masculine in each of us tends to get lost in thoughts and fantasies during sex. The feminine in each of us tends to get lost in bodily sensations and emotions. To grow as a lover, practice keeping your heart wide open, relaxing in the effortless consciousness of deep being, and allowing energy to flow fully, throughout the sexual occasion. If your partner gets carried away by either clinical technique or sensual frenzy, then help him or her back to fullness by offering your deep energy or deep consciousness.

Unite consciousness with energy, without limiting either. Instead, magnify both beyond all limits. As rigid as your partner's technique, be that energetic in the bodily expression of ecstasy. As wild as your partner's pleasure, pervade him or her that strongly with vast consciousness. In this way, the fruits of love bloom fully without rotting into a sweet mess of sensual chaos or drying up in the waterless sun of distant awareness.

24

EARN THE
FEMININE'S TRUST

*It was morning. She was still lying in bed. I was exercising on the
floor near the foot of the bed, sweating, concentrating, and working
hard. I felt her watching me, and I looked over at her. She was
gazing at me as I worked out, her eyes smiling with desire.*

*I continued stretching and going through my exercise routine. I
could feel her looking my way, and the next time I looked up she
had peeled down the covers. Her naked body was fully exposed,
and she was running her hands up and down her thighs, slowly,
while thrusting her open pelvis slightly into the air.*

*She was very beautiful, very sexy, but I wanted to finish my
routine. She began masturbating herself, calling me to her, telling
me she wanted me to take her, now. I smiled, but otherwise didn't
respond to her begging.*

*She got out of bed and came to me. I was sitting on the
floor now, going through a set of breathing exercises. She stood
three inches away from my face, using her hands to spread her
crotch, showing me the juices running down her legs, rubbing the
glistening liquid into the skin of her thighs.*

*I smiled at her taunt. I knew I wanted to finish exercising,
and that was that. She pouted and ended up walking away,
humorously exasperated. Getting back into bed, she continued*

touching herself, watching me, and making little mewling sounds.

Eventually, after finishing my workout, I joined her in bed and we began making love. About ten minutes into it, she began grinding against me in the way she does when she wants me to have an orgasm. But I didn't want to have an orgasm yet. So, as she rammed her vagina up and down my penis, as she tried milking me with her hungry muscles and begs, I circulated my internal energy. I opened my attention and felt through her. I took her as hard as she wanted to be taken, but I remained in love and demanded her love through my touch, movement, and gaze. I didn't allow her to get lost in lust without also staying present in love.

Then, she suddenly slowed down, as if trying to lose me to the exaggerated momentum of our previous sexing. I practiced being right there with her, matching her modulations, movement by movement, breath by breath. I pressed into her body and heart, leading her into deeper loving, beyond her pleasure, tricks, and play. And she received me fully, dropping more deeply in the profound of love, and pulling me in with her.

Then, unexpectedly, she revved up, testing me again. Her devilish eyes narrowed. Her sharp teeth took my neck and shoulder. Her vagina gulped me deeper. Our sexing became more and more intense, her urgent maw and spittled pleads squarking beyond control. I practiced as best as I could. Luckily, my love and awareness did not waver.

Nor did I pull away. I was feeling through her, pervading her, riding the waves of energy with her. She did not shake me, though she enjoyed trying. I stayed present with her, suffusing her with love no matter how frenzied or coy were her bucks and wobbles. Feeling this, she let loose. Went kazonkers. Her eyes became unrecognizable, alternating between fiendish and slavish, her

tongue stabbing the air, her lips sucking some unseen need. Her
spine convulsed and breasts bounced brownian as she screamed my
name and came, and came, and came.

Finally, as the end rounded near, she wrapped me with legs
and arms and tears. Her body trembled beneath me as she softened
into an open pool of love. Into that pool I also dissolved, our
hearts ever wide, our faces wet, all defense and tryst rested, opened
out, and yielded in love.

A man's (or a masculine partner's) stability in consciousness is one of the greatest turn-ons for a woman (or a feminine partner). His ability to stay present and open in love—no matter how extreme her physical or emotional expressions—is a huge gift to her.

Many men err on one side or the other: They remain rigidly self-controlled, as if they were feelingless robots of purpose. Or they get lost in their woman's energy, spewing their seed—or simply losing their conscious presence—moments after she begins to get really sexually wild. Most men either hold themselves back or get absorbed into the sexual swirl.

A man can learn to participate fully in sexual play without holding back, while also remaining centered, present, and rooted in consciousness rather than becoming lost in energy. Feeling his constancy of love and awareness, knowing that he won't get lost and carried away, a woman can trust him fully and yield herself in full emotional and sexual expression.

But if she feels he is holding himself back in order to maintain control, then she can't trust him. Where is his love, spontaneity, and passion, his ability to meet her and dance with her? What turns on a woman most is not simply a man's consciousness, held back and separate. Rather, it is his consciousness, strong and full of feeling, pervading her through and through, even while his body and emotions meld freely with hers.

She is turned on by his fearless loving, his unshakable purpose, his humor and spontaneity, his sudden surprises. She is turned on by feeling his consciousness so strong it invades her, body and soul, coaxing her to yield into a deeper love and wider ecstasy. She is turned on by being able to trust him completely, because he is so present and sensitive with her, but also because he will stop at nothing to bring her to an ever new place of love.

Then, she can go wild. Then, she can even go wild in ways she knows will test him and challenge his capacity to remain conscious and loving. By doing so, she can once again enjoy the erotic moment of feeling that she can't derail him, or slurp him over the horizon of his consciousness, or make him pull back in order to steel himself against her attractive power. She can't make him have an unwanted orgasm, she can't distract his awareness from feeling through all experience, and she can't frighten him with her sexual ferocity. His loving continues no matter what. He remains present.

She can trust him. She can be free in her own expression, without concern that she will lose or offend her man. In fact, having tested his stability in conscious sensitivity during the whole range of vicious and cuddled sexual play, she can simply open herself and receive him. She can open her most hidden heart chambers, allowing him in, relaxing her guard. She can invite him to take her, absolutely.

Ravished thusly, pervaded to her absolute depths by his unchanging, trustable consciousness, she can give herself utterly in love. Feeling her total surrender, he is drawn in so deep that he is moved beyond his masculine fears. He gives himself entirely, without any self-holding. Now, both gone in love, yet alive as man and woman, they love as the cosmos loves: One loving itself as an other, yet remembering itself as One.

25

WORSHIP THE DIVINE THROUGH THE FORM OF YOUR PARTNER

*We are trying to make love, but she doesn't really seem to be into it.
What's her problem? Why can't she just relax? I'm frustrated. I look at
her face and she seems uglier than usual. The lines in her face seem to
have grown more noticeable, her breath rotten, her smell thick.*

*I am disgusted. I am withdrawing, emotionally and sexually. I
don't want to have sex with this horrid woman.*

*I can also feel how weak I am being. What am I afraid to
embrace?*

*Now aware of my resistance, I practice feeling through my desire
to separate from her. I practice embracing her, relaxing into her, feeling
her completely, without pulling away. When my heart has relaxed
open somewhat, I practice feeling her as an aspect of the divine.
An ugly aspect in this moment to me, perhaps, but of divine nature
nevertheless. I continue to practice relaxing into and as the love that
pervades us both.*

*Then I notice I am pulling away again. And so I practice through
my resistance, giving more love while consciously recognizing the
same love within her, the love that resides in all. I am breathing this
love through her, with her; gazing deep into her eyes and feeling her
openness, her very nature; letting every pore of my body open into love
with her, commingling as one.*

Her face changes. The color of her skin shifts hues. Her eyes become soft and dark, and behind them her openness is infinite, only love, and endless. Her mouth opens slightly. Her vagina seems to become the universe, and she receives me without limit. She has become a divine form, a goddess, the eternal beloved. All measure has been absorbed in the open of love.

Practice worshipping and relaxing in communion with the divine through the physical form of your lover. Actually feel your lover's form to be the form of the divine. How would you make love with the most holy of beings? How would you kiss a perfect sage? How would you touch the breasts of the wild woman who eats the stars for breakfast?

Even if your lover seems anything but the divine incarnate, practice to feel him or her as a god or goddess. If you treat your lover as a closed or unhappy person, he or she will remain so. But if you treat your lover's form as divine, as a sacred incarnation of infinite spirit, then your sexing will serve to liberate him or her from anything less. Your lover will be free to be of spirit, devoted to spirit, just as he or she is, without having to fit the peon mold of your need.

26

Do Sex to
Serve Others

*I don't really want to have sex. I'm a little tired. I'm not
particularly horny. But my lover seems to need it. We both need it.*

*She's not particularly horny, either. But I can feel her need.
Her body is tense, like she's not quite sunk into it completely.
Her mind is chaotic. Her emotions are agitated, ungrounded in
anything real. She has lost touch with profundity, and so have I.*

*The events of her day have dispersed her attention, so she is
spread thin. She needs to be penetrated into deep feeling. I know
that if I relax as my own deep being and enter her core with love,
all of our superficial thoughts, energies, and emotions will resolve
themselves in the singularity of deep heart.*

*And so, I make love with her. Often, it is during these times—
when, ostensibly, I am making love for her sake—that I myself
sink into a deeper realization of love. It is when I go beyond
myself, giving myself fully, expecting nothing in return, that I am
most dissolved in the giving. This dissolution-in-action reawakens
both of us to the true form of our loving—the true form of our life.*

You should do sex like a saint serves others; like you are doing God's work. Give of yourself totally, as a service to your lover. Alleviate your lover's suffering. Open your lover's heart more fully. Bring the divine into your lover's life through your sexing. Do sex to give, rather than to get. Sexing in this way is far more blissful than sex done in expectation of your own satisfaction. Satisfaction comes and goes. Giving love—to the point of recognizing existence as love—is the purpose of your life.

27

DO SEX TO
ENLIGHTEN THE WORLD

Embracing her in my arms, she is the world. I feel her breasts
against my chest, and they are the soft flesh of everyone. Her
breath on my neck is of the same wind breathed by a dying Swede
or a swimming Polynesian. Her skin is made of atoms recycled
from beetle, stone, and rose. Her love is the same love residing
in the hearts of children in ancient Egypt and grandfathers in
modern Tokyo. Holding her, I feel everyone, all beings. I am loving
the world through her.

As I enter her, I am entering the world, giving love to the
world. Her body becomes all bodies, even the earth itself. Soil,
water, men, and women, I feel them all through her, and pervade
them all through her. With each thrust, kiss, and press, I offer all I
have, give all I have to give, practice loving with every ounce of my
being, through her, to all.

As you grow spiritually, sex becomes service to others. In the
midst of sex, you may occasionally choose to feel and visu-
alize someone to whom you want to send love and healing.
Eventually, through practice, you feel all beings through your lover.
You love through your lover, as a portal to all beings. Rather than

having sex for your own pleasure only, you have sex for the sake of giving love to all beings.

If your lover is emotionally upset, breathe his or her dark energy into yourself, and breathe out only love to your lover. Over time, with practice, feel that you are inhaling the pain of all beings and giving them love. Receive their suffering, their fear, their lack, and give them your love. Feel sex as a blissful ritual of sacrifice, in which your body and mind are surrendered totally for the sake of all beings, to receive their pain and bring them love.

This doesn't mean to create some kind of righteous ceremony wherein you feel special for being so kind and spiritual. It is simply the case that, eventually, you realize sex is no great shakes. It is what it is. At the personal level, it can be very pleasurable, but so what? Sex becomes a means to give love to all beings, through your partner. This total giving in the midst of active embrace is the true form of life, as well as sex. To live simply for your own sake is to generate constant fear and tension.

Living your life in the truth of full giving is bliss itself. You are always dissolving. Every moment you are dying to all that has been. Consciously participating in this death without resistance is love. It requires practice to love this fully, to receive others this fully, to let go this fully, and to give yourself entirely—especially in the midst of sex or suffering.

No amount of skin friction can equal the pleasure of coinciding with the deepest purpose of your life, which is to be love. And no sex can exceed love itself, expressed as the body, embraced as all beings, and given through the form of your lover, until there is no other. Only love.

28

MAKE LOVE
AS IF DEATH
WERE IMMINENT

The true consideration of death cracks the heart open. Everything you know will soon be gone. All you ever had or will have, all experiences, and all relationships, will be gone forever. Everyone you love and struggle with so dearly will disappear and be forgotten, over time, as if they never existed.

In your death, you won't be able to experience your thoughts, your body, or your self as you know it. Death evaporates all experience during life to nothing.

The contemplation of death strips you of all false pursuits. All hopes and dreams are over. No children, no family. No work tomorrow. Nothing to look forward to. No future to wear. You are naked in this moment, feeling fully, with no veil of time to hide your vulnerability. In the true contemplation of death, your heart stands bare in the present moment.

With no excuse but to be present, your heart gathers strength. No longer dispersed in dreams of future fear or hope, your heart's force becomes coherent. Without a shell of waiting, without the buffer of tomorrow, unclothed of expectation or fear, no longer waiting for things to be different, you can fully be the love you are, right now.

To deepen sex, feel this moment in the immensity of what comes before and after your individual birth, and make love.

While having sex, feel your precious partner. Feel your pleasurized body. Feel the love you can magnify through your sexing. Feel all of this while remembering your death. Actually imagine your heart stopping right now, in the midst of sex. Give the gift that would be your last gift of love, the giving that would leave you complete in death, nothing left ungiven.

As you make love, feel this moment as your last. No future. What pleasure can distract you from this depth? Feel your sexual organs engorged with blood, and feel death. See your lover's beauty, and feel death. Allow desire to move your body, and feel death. Continually remind yourself that this moment could be your last. Maybe there will be no orgasm five minutes from now. Maybe this will be your last kiss, ever. Make love now, as if death were imminent. Give yourself completely in love.

DAVID DEIDA
RESOURCES

BOOKS

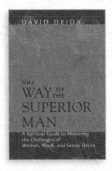

The Way of the Superior Man

A Spiritual Guide to Mastering the Challenges of Women, Work, and Sexual Desire

David Deida explores the most important issues in men's lives—from career and family to women and intimacy to love and sex—to offer the ultimate spiritual guide for men living a life of integrity, authenticity, and freedom.

ISBN: 978-1-59179-257-4 / U.S. $17.95

Dear Lover

A Woman's Guide to Men, Sex, and Love's Deepest Bliss

How do you attract and keep a man capable of meeting what you most passionately yearn for? To answer this question, David Deida explores every aspect of the feminine practice of spiritual intimacy, from sexuality and lovemaking to family and career to emotions, trust, and commitment.

ISBN: 978-1-59179-260-4 / U.S. $16.95

Blue Truth

A Spiritual Guide to Life & Death and Love & Sex

David Deida presents a treasury of skills and insights for uncovering and offering your true heart of purpose, passion, and unquenchable love.

ISBN: 978-1-59179-259-8 / U.S. $16.95

Wild Nights

Conversations with Mykonos about Passionate Love, Extraordinary Sex, and How to Open to God

Meet Mykonos—scurrilous madman, and speaker of truth. A recollection of a unique relationship between a student and an extraordinary spiritual teacher.

ISBN: 978-1-59179-233-8 / U.S. $15.95

Instant Enlightenment

Fast, Deep, and Sexy

David Deida offers a wealth of priceless exercises and insights to bring "instant enlightenment" to the areas we need it most.

ISBN: 978-1-59179-560-5 / U.S. $12.95

The Enlightened Sex Manual

Sexual Skills for the Superior Lover

The secret to enlightenment and great sex is revealed
to be one and the same in this groundbreaking
manual for adventurous lovers. The ultimate
collection of skills for opening to the physical,
emotional, and spiritual rewards of intimate embrace.

ISBN: 978-1-59179-585-8 / U.S. $15.95

ALSO AVAILABLE

Intimate Communion

Awakening Your Sexual Essence

David Deida's first book lays the foundation for
his teaching on the integration of intimacy and
authentic spiritual practice.

It's a Guy Thing

An Owner's Manual for Women

David Deida answers over 150 of women's most
asked questions about men and intimacy.

AUDIO

Enlightened Sex
Finding Freedom & Fullness through Sexual Union

A complete six-CD program to learn the secrets to transforming lovemaking into a spiritual gift to yourself, your lover, and the world.

ISBN: 978-1-59179-083-9 / U.S. $69.95

The Teaching Sessions:
The Way of the Superior Man
Revolutionary Tools and Essential Exercises for Mastering the Challenges of Women, Work, and Sexual Desire

A spiritual guide for today's man in search of the secrets to success in career, purpose, and sexual intimacy—now available on four CDs in this original author expansion of and companion to the bestselling book.

ISBN: 978-1-59179-343-4 / U.S. $29.95

For information about all of David Deida's books and audio, visit **www.deida.info**.

To place an order or to receive a free catalog of wisdom teachings for the inner life, visit **www.soundstrue.com**, call toll-free **800-333-9185**, or write: The Sounds True Catalog, PO Box 8010, Boulder CO 80306.

About the Author

Acknowledged as one of the world's most insightful and provocative teachers of our time, bestselling author David Deida continues to revolutionize the way that men and women grow spiritually and sexually. His teaching and writing on a radically practical spirituality for our time have been hailed as among the most original and authentic contributions to personal and spiritual growth currently available.

Known internationally for his unique workshops on spiritual growth and sacred intimacy, Deida has designed and developed a remarkably effective program of transformative practices that fully addresses spiritual awakening in mind, body, and heart. He is a founding associate of Integral Institute and has taught and conducted research at the University of California's Medical School in San Diego, University of California–Santa Cruz, San Jose State University, Lexington Institute in Boston, and Ecole Polytechnique in Paris, France.

Deida is known worldwide as the author of hundreds of essays, audios, books, videos, and articles that bring to light a fully integral approach to spirituality. His books are published in more than twenty-five languages worldwide and are required reading in university, church, and spiritual-center courses. They're also used as source texts in men's and women's groups around the world and are considered among the deepest resources for real spiritual transformation available. His recent books include *Blue Truth, The Enlightened Sex Manual,* and *Instant Enlightenment.*

For more information about David Deida's books, audios, videos, and teaching schedule, please visit **www.deida.info.**

Sounds True was founded in 1985 with a clear vision: to disseminate spiritual wisdom. Located in Boulder, Colorado, Sounds True publishes teaching programs that are designed to educate, uplift, and inspire. With more than 600 titles available, we work with many of the leading spiritual teachers, thinkers, healers, and visionary artists of our time.

For a free catalog, or for more information on books and audio programs by David Deida, please contact Sounds True via the World Wide Web at www.soundstrue.com, call us toll free at 800-333-9185, or write

The Sounds True Catalog
PO Box 8010
Boulder CO 80306